Praise for Hooman Majd's

THE AYATOLLAH BEGS TO DIFFER

"Part memoir, part travelogue, part cultural criticism, *The Ayatollah Begs to Differ* captures like no book in recent memory the ethos of the country, in elegant and precise prose." —*Los Angeles Times*

"This book is a vital antidote to both the wishful thinking of exiles who declare the Islamic Revolution's inevitable doom and to the exaggerated alarm of those who see it as an existential threat to the world order. It also provides some very American clues to understanding the Iranian experience." —*The New York Review of Books*

"A refreshing and mind-opening book, a nuanced and informed portrait of one of our most misunderstood global neighbors." —*National Geographic Traveler*

"Essential reading for anyone wanting to understand the paradox that is Iran (as well as America) in the post-Bush world. . . . Imagine if Alexis de Tocqueville had returned from America to France and then, with the gimlet eye of a native son who'd spent years abroad, explained his oft-misperceived country to the world. That's what the ever wise and witty Hooman Majd has accomplished in his captivating new book." —*GQ*

"Majd is well placed to provide a privileged glimpse into Iran and Iranians. . . . He conveys brilliantly the weird mix of breast-beating and vulnerability, the superiority and inferiority complexes that inform popular and political culture [there]." —*Financial Times*

"Majd has written perhaps the best book on contemporary Iranian culture and all of its complexities and contradictions. Don't go to Tehran without it." —Reza Aslan, *The Washington Monthly*

"Majd's subtle central point is that 'the lack of meaningful relations between Iran and the United States . . . has brought little advantage to either nation.' With a new U.S. president who may be willing to talk, and Iranian leaders who have tentatively welcomed that proposition, Majd's timing is as impeccable as both his Farsi and his English."

—*Newsweek International*

"In this delightful book, Hooman Majd, a gifted storyteller, takes us on a tour of his own private Persia, which is also the Iran of Mahmoud Ahmadinejad. The results are illuminating, humorous, sobering, and ultimately reassuring." —Jon Lee Anderson, author of
Che Guevara: A Revolutionary Life
and *The Fall of Baghdad*

"For anyone trying to get a deeper perspective on Iranian society and the future of the relationship between Iran and America, this book is an excellent place to begin. . . . *The Ayatollah Begs to Differ* demonstrates that America and Iran have, however improbably, a great deal more in common than one might expect." —*Asia Times*

"A witty, timely perspective on the nation posing the greatest challenge to our [current] president. Travel writing often makes for easy reading at the expense of relevant information, which gets lost in the details. Not so with *The Ayatollah Begs to Differ*." —Bill White, Mayor of Houston
and U.S. Secretary of Energy
under President Clinton

"Majd is a stylish and engaging guide through the by-ways of Iranian life. Leading us from seminary to opium den to the presidential compound, his wry sense of humor makes this book a pleasure to read."
—Gary Sick, Ph.D., Senior Research Scholar
at Columbia University and member of
the National Security Council staff under
Presidents Ford, Carter, and Reagan

Hooman Majd
THE AYATOLLAH BEGS TO DIFFER

Hooman Majd was born in Tehran, Iran, in 1957, and raised and educated in the West. He has written about Iran for *GQ*, *The New York Times*, *The New Yorker*, *The New York Observer*, *Salon*, *The Huffington Post*, and *The Daily Beast*, published short fiction, and has also held senior positions in the entertainment industry. A contributing editor at *Interview* magazine, he lives in New York City.

www.hoomanmajd.com

THE AYATOLLAH BEGS TO DIFFER

THE AYATOLLAH
BEGS TO DIFFER

The Paradox of Modern Iran

Hooman Majd

ANCHOR BOOKS

A Division of Random House, Inc.

New York

FIRST ANCHOR BOOKS EDITION, SEPTEMBER 2009

Copyright © 2008, 2009 by Hooman Majd

All rights reserved. Published in the United States by Anchor Books, a division
of Random House, Inc., New York, and in Canada by Random House of
Canada Limited, Toronto. Originally published in hardcover in slightly different
form in the United States by Doubleday, a division of Random House, Inc.,
New York, in 2008.

Anchor Books and colophon are registered trademarks of Random House, Inc.

All photographs not otherwise credited are copyright © 2008 by Hooman Majd.

The Library of Congress has cataloged the Doubleday edition as follows:
Majd, Hooman.
The ayatollah begs to differ / Hooman Majd.—1st ed.
p.   cm.
Includes bibliographical references and index.
1. Iran—Politics and government—1997–   2. Majd, Hooman—Travel—
Iran.   3. Iran—Description and travel.   4. Iranian Americans—Biography.
I. Title.
DS318.9.M35 2008
955.06'1—dc22
2008004648

Anchor ISBN: 978-0-7679-2801-4

Author photograph © Ken Browar

www.anchorbooks.com

Printed in the United States of America
10   9   8   7   6   5   4   3   2   1

For Nasser and Badri

Contents

Acknowledgments

I have based this book mostly on personal experience. In 2004 and 2005 I spent several weeks in Iran as a journalist, and in 2007 I spent almost two months living in Tehran, working on what was to become the manuscript. Both in Iran and in the United States, I have relied on my family, friends, and contacts as sources (as well as many other ordinary Iranians I have spoken to in Iran), some of whom I acknowledge in the text and others whose identities I have disguised for their own safety or who wish to remain anonymous. I have also served on a few occasions as an unpaid adviser to the Islamic Republic, bringing me into close contact with Presidents Khatami and Ahmadinejad and numerous members of their staffs, who have all contributed to my knowledge.

I am particularly grateful to President Mohammad Khatami, who took time out of his schedule, both during his presidency and afterward, to engage in long discussions with me and to answer my many questions, and to his brother (and chief of staff) Seyyed Ali Khatami, who spent even more time with me and who introduced me to many other influential Iranians, most of whom I continue to speak with on a regular basis. I learned more about the intricacies of the politics (and the history) of the Islamic Republic from Ali Khatami than I could have from reading dozens of books, and he gave me invaluable lessons on the personalities of the characters who make up the ruling elite of Iran.

I am deeply indebted to the former UN ambassador Mohammad Javad Zarif for his keen insights (and his patience with me) and to the ambassadors Hossein Fereidoun, Sadeq Kharrazi, and Mehdi Danesh-Yazdi, all of whom contributed to my understanding of the politics of the Islamic Republic. I'm also grateful to Foreign Minister Manouchehr Mottaki for the time he set aside to meet with me on his visits to New York.

In addition to those who are already named as characters in various chapters, I would like to thank the following persons in Iran, in no particular order, for their assistance and their contributions to my knowledge: Ali Ziaie, Mohammad Ziaie, Amir Khosro Etemadi, Seyyed Hossein Khatami, Maryam Majd, Mohammad Mir Ali Mohammadi, and Mehrdad Khajenouri.

Finally, I'd like to thank my editor, Kristine Puopolo, and my agent, Lindsay Edgecombe, and her colleague James Levine for their hard work in making this a readable book. And, of course, thanks to my father, Nasser Majd, and my mother, Mansoureh Assar, for what they've taught me; and to Karri Jinkins, Davitt Sigerson, Michael Zilkha, Selim Zilkha, Simon Van Booy, Daniel Feder, Eddie Stern, Michael Halsband, Paul Werner, Suzy Hansen, Roger Trilling, Glenn O'Brien, and Ken Browar.

Preface to the Anchor Books Edition

On June 12, 2009, Iran held a presidential election, one that was to be a referendum on four years of President Ahmadinejad's rule. The results stunned most observers, as they almost always do in Iranian elections, but importantly, this time they stunned Iranians, too, leading to street protests, a brutal crackdown by the government, and the deaths of ordinary Iranians who were not protesting their system of government, but the way in which they believed the election had been stolen. I was once again in Iran in the weeks before the elections, and my observations of Iran's Islamic democracy, one which I partly describe in this book as leading to the surprise but fair election of Mahmoud Ahmadinejad in 2005, reinforced my belief that changes, social and political, are under way in Iran. But it is important to understand that those changes, and they are uniquely Iranian changes, not imposed or borrowed Western ones, will not fundamentally alter the character of either the state or the people, both of which I describe in the chapters to follow.

On May 23, 2009, I was at Tehran's Azadi Indoor Stadium, twenty days before the fateful presidential election. I, and the NBC News team I was with, had difficulty getting in the gates; "all full," the guards kept telling us. And full it was, overflowing in fact, for the kick-off rally of the Mir Hossein Mousavi campaign. Mousavi, a onetime prime minister and part of the old guard of revolutionaries, who had transformed himself into a reformer, wasn't even going to be there; he was in Esfahan, "breaking the ice" in that city, they said. The rally featured former President Khatami and Mousavi's wife, Zahra Rahnavard, and the eager crowd—young, old, and in between—numbered over twenty thousand. I couldn't make my way to the VIP section, let alone the V-VIP section, and I didn't want to. I was happy to be crushed among the thousands of cheering, ecstatic even, Iranians who gave birth to the "green wave," the support the campaign was counting on to wrest the presidency away from Mahmoud Ahmadinejad.

It was not supposed to end the way it did. After all, what ensued is why Mohammad Khatami, the only early favorite to defeat Ahmadinejad at the polls on June 12, dropped out of the presidential race. That's what Iranians all assumed, all of those who were in Iran in the weeks and days leading up to the earthquake that was Iran's elections. Khatami would never be allowed to win, they seemed to understand. *Kayhan*, Iran's conservative daily and the Supreme Leader's mouthpiece, said as much, even threatening him in a thinly veiled editorial with assassination. Iran was theirs now, they were saying, and Khatami posed the biggest threat to their ownership. That's Iran for you—Islamic democracy, in all of its glorious contradictions.

Mir Hossein Mousavi, Iranians thought, posed no such threat to the conservatives—the landlords, let's call them—but his chances of winning weren't exactly good, even as recently as six weeks before the election. "If the turnout is in the twenty-five million range, we will be guests of Mr. Ahmadinejad's for another four years." That was Sadeq Kharrazi, former Iranian ambassador to Paris, deputy foreign minister, member of the nuclear negotiating team under Khatami, and one of the more influential reformists who also has close ties to the Supreme Leader, speaking at the end of April. It was another late-night salon at his house, like the other salons I describe, filled with photos of himself with Ayatollah Khamenei. "Ahmadinejad has ten to twelve million votes," he said, a number echoed by virtually everyone I spoke to in Tehran then; in Yazd, Esfahan, and Qom, too, "and he'll win if the turnout is low." He wasn't being pessimistic—just realistic.

The Mousavi campaign's early strategy, one of getting out the vote to counter Ahmadinejad's solid base, raised no eyebrows, but it began to pay dividends, and a fever for the democratic process started to afflict many up-till-then apathetic Iranians. "If the majority doesn't vote, the minority rules," proclaimed one billboard, rather more poetically in Persian, that I saw all over Tehran at the end of May. Ayatollah Rafsanjani, known as the second most powerful man in Iran, had paid for that one, his image next to the words. If the fever held, there would be enough votes to force a second-round runoff. Mousavi was going to win any runoff, and win big. Ahmadinejad might have his ten to twelve million, but he couldn't possibly defeat Mousavi if Mehdi Karroubi's and Mohsen Rezai's supporters (the other two opposition candidates in the race) coalesced around him, too. It wasn't as if Ahmadinejad's campaign didn't know this. Their strategy from the start had been to win outright in the first round (and *Kahyan*, curiously prescient, predicted his margin of victory to within a point or two), but his campaign was anemic compared to Mousavi's, which grew stronger by the rally, with the ever-popular Khatami front and center much of the time. I almost went with Khatami to Ahvaz, on May 30, when the plane he was to have caught back to Tehran was discovered to have a bomb aboard. The landlords weren't whispering anymore. This was shaping up to be an epic battle between them and the reformers, one they had never really seriously fought before; between those who believed Iran should finally move into its post-revolutionary phase and those who insisted it remain forever a revolutionary state. "If it's over thirty million," we win, Khatami had said to me in mid-May, announcing what the turnout had to be, but still hesitant to declare that the battle would be won. "Are you staying for the election?" he asked me, right before the Ahvaz jaunt. "No, but I'll come back for the second round,"

I told him. "There won't be a second round; we will win outright on June 12." Strong words coming from a cautious man two weeks before the election, a man who didn't believe he himself was going to win his landslide in 1997 until days before the vote.

And based on what I had seen in Iran over the last month, maybe Khatami was right, I thought. I had tried to find where Ahmadinejad's support was going to come from if he was going to add to his base to defeat three challengers who were all gaining popularity. Outside of Tehran? No, whether on the road, in truck stops, cafés, or in other cities, I saw more enthusiasm for the opposition than for the president, which surprised me. Even in South Tehran, his supposed base in the capital, I found Ahmadinejad detractors, four years after the district had come out for him in big numbers. Not that Ahmadinejad didn't have supporters everywhere; it was just that they seemed to be the apathetic ones this time. Perhaps that's the lot of an incumbent candidate steering the ship of a discontented nation. And maybe that's why the twenty-four million or so mythical Iranians, who braved long lines, thunderstorms, and 113-degree temperatures to vote for Mahmoud Ahmadinejad, didn't celebrate on the streets when their man won his landslide. Nor did some of the ten to twelve million who probably *did* vote for him come out to cheer, not until they were asked to, two days later. And even then, the photos of his victory rally were clumsily photoshopped by Ahmadinejad's experts, probably the same ones who gave us four rather than three missiles in an earlier propaganda show, to illustrate a sea of Iranians-for-Ahmadinejad where there was only a pond.

Over forty million voted in Iran's presidential election, 63 percent for the sitting president, according to his own Interior Ministry. It took a day or so, but that's when it struck dismayed Iranians: of course, they never were going to let *anyone* but Ahmadinejad win. That's why his campaign was anemic, that's why he didn't seem to care that his challengers were gaining on him, and that's why he was so arrogant in the aftermath. This had never happened before. Iranian elections had been generally fair up until 2009. You can't, as the Supreme Leader said at Friday prayers a week later, still endorsing his man, forge eleven million votes. One hundred thousand, maybe half a million, maybe a million, but not *eleven* million ballots! (With his admission of a million, the Supreme Leader sounded more pessimistic about Iran's democracy than even Khatami, who had once told me that the most an election could be cheated by was between three hundred thousand and five hundred thousand stray votes.) But what Ayatollah Ali Khamenei failed to concede at his sermon was that the only way to cheat by eleven million votes was to never count them in the first place, or to just make up the numbers regardless of what they really were. Could that have happened? Perhaps, but we'll never know.

Thirty years have passed since the revolution, exactly thirty years, and Iranians weren't mad that Ahmadinejad won reelection on June 12. They were and are still mad that the one thing, the one true element of democracy they had—their vote—had seemingly become meaningless. Stop looking at Tehran, the government kept saying to all, you're misreading the country. You in the West don't understand Iran, it pleaded; you don't know that Ahmadinejad really *did* have all the support of the country. It's only the Tehran Westernized elite who are unhappy, and the West and Zionists (always the Zionists) are stirring things up. I write about these Westernized elites, and about how distant they are from the vast majority of Iranians in the pages that follow. But this time there was Shiraz, Esfahan, Mashhad, Tabriz, and all the other places we know people didn't believe their government, where people *died* because they didn't believe the government's vote count. Many of them were ordinary Iranians, the kinds of Iranians who have no issue with their system of government, no, they're *happy* with their system of government, the kinds of Iranians that are portrayed throughout this book. These Iranians didn't start by protesting the regime, the "nezam" as the Supreme Leader called it; they weren't protesting anything but their right to their vote, a right that has always been sacred in the Islamic Republic. And Mir Hossein Mousavi wasn't waging a campaign to bring down the *nezam*. He only wanted to be a better president than Ahmadinejad, to ensure the progress of the Islamic Republic, and that wasn't and isn't a crime in the Islamic Republic, as he was quick to point out.

What started out as an outpouring of anger has turned into a battle royal for the soul of a nation. Or a battle to allow the nation a soul. It is a delicious irony that Ayatollah Hashemi Rafsanjani, a founder of the *nezam*, a man Iranians couldn't bring themselves to vote for the last time, would be on the protestors' side, that he would be instrumental in the push to allow Iranians their rights. And who would have thought that Ali Larijani, Speaker of Parliament, obedient son of the revolution, and close confidant of the Supreme Leader, would suggest, in contradiction of his mentor, that the Guardian Council, those who are supposed to be checking the vote, had erred? Iran's leadership cracked in June 2009, but didn't break. These leaders surface throughout my book, and their characters are today as they were when I first described them.

It's impossible to predict the outcome of the Iranian crisis at the time of writing. The protests may be quashed, life in Iran may return to something resembling normal. (Indeed, it is fairly normal in most places, even in many parts of Tehran.) The faction that supports the Supreme Leader and Mahmoud Ahmadinejad still has a large portion of the population behind it, the ten to twelve million, maybe more, plus all the guns. (If the West, or Iranians in opposition movements abroad, try to hijack the protests for their own causes, they'll have more, much, much, more.) And Mousavi, the unlikely hero of Iran's reform movement, may or may not continue the fight, but Iranians will, in their own quiet way. Khatami, Rafsanjani, and the other clerics who believe in reform and an Islamic democracy will also fight, whether overtly and publicly or from within the system, a system they are all a part of, after all. At a press conference before the elections, one Mousavi campaign manager was asked about the brutality of *his nezam*, way back, when he was prime minister in the eighties, a post since abolished. The staffer answered, "We were all Ahmadinejads then." He was right, as this book highlights. The question still remains whether Iranians want to all be Mousavis, Khatamis, or Rafsanjanis now.

Hooman Majd,
June 2009

THE AYATOLLAH BEGS TO DIFFER

INTRODUCTION

"Yeki-bood; yeki-nabood." That's how all Iranian stories, at least in the oral tradition, have begun, since as long as anyone remembers. "There was one; there wasn't one," as in "There was a person (once upon a time); but on the other hand, no, there was no one." Often, the saying continues with *"Gheir az Khoda, heech-kee nabood,"* or "Other than God, there was no One," a uniquely Persian obfuscation of the Muslim Arabic *"La'illa ha il'allah"* (There is no God but Allah), and which one might think makes much less sense than the original, but is in a way perfectly reasonable. Introduce a young mind to the paradoxes of life with a paradox, you see, which is what most of the Iranian folk stories are about in the first place. As a child, I heard those stories alongside English equivalents (which of course began with the seemingly far more sensible "Once upon a time"), but it never occurred to me then that the simple *"Yeki-bood; yeki-nabood"* said so much about the inherited culture that so deeply penetrated my otherwise Western life.

"Yeki-bood; yeki-nabood." Yes, we are about to hear a fantasy, but wait—is it a fantasy? While most Iranian stories that begin so are indeed fantasies, the fantastic Shia stories of early Islam are thought to be true history by the legions of believers in the faith, and if evoked, *"Yeki-bood"*

wraps itself in religious significance as well as the Persian art of the epic. On one of my trips to Iran, to Qom to be precise, I picked up some CDs of *noheh*, Shia religious incantations, usually sung to huge crowds on religious holidays, that tell the stories of Shia saints and their martyrdom. One CD contained a rather mellifluous version of the story of Fatimeh Zahra and Ali (the daughter and son-in-law of the Prophet) that began with *"Yeki-bood; yeki-nabood"* and continued with *"zeer-e gonbad'e kabood,"* or "under the bruised [or dark] dome [or sky]," alluding not just to the Islamic roots of "There was one, there wasn't one" but also to the Shia sense of the world as a dark and oppressive place. The singer claimed the tale to be one of "estrangement and woe," central themes in Shiism. There is no God but God, there was one and there wasn't one, other than God there was no One, and the world is under a perpetual dark cloud. Welcome to Shia Iran.

———

Iran is better known today by the outside world than at almost any time in its history, certainly since the fall of the Persian Empire, mostly because of the Islamic Revolution, which to many ushered in an era of successful but much-feared Islamic fundamentalism. As a child, I had to patiently explain to new friends in school where and exactly what Iran was, if they even bothered to inquire about my strange name; today I suspect that young Iranians have no such problems. When I look back now, both in my childhood and even as a young adult, I couldn't have imagined my country as anything more than a second-rate Third World nation subservient to Western powers: had someone seriously suggested to me, or any other Iranian for that matter, that the United States would one day be proposing to build a missile defense system in Europe to guard against an attack by *Iran* (as the United States has, to the great consternation of the Russians), with *Iranian*-made missiles, I would have instantly labeled that person as stark raving mad. Despite the negative connotations of a perceptibly hostile Iran, Iranians of a certain age can be forgiven for feeling a tinge of pride in their nation's rapid ascent to a position of being taken seriously by the world's greatest superpower, and all in just a little over a quarter of a century. One might argue whether Iran and Iranians would have been better off without the Islamic Revolution of 1979, but it is indisputable that had it not happened, Iran today would likely not have much of a say in global affairs.

Rightly or wrongly, the revolution and the path the nation took after its success have led to Iran's prominence and repute, but of course at the time Iranians could hardly have known that their revolt would have such far-reaching consequences and effects. For two or three hundred years Iran had been, in all but name, a proxy of Western powers—specifically Britain and then the United States when it took over the mantle of empire after World War II. Iranians overthrew a twenty-five-hundred-year monarchy in 1979 to liberate themselves from an autocratic dictator as much as to liberate themselves from foreign domination (a factor that most in the West did not understand at the time and that was also partly the motivation for the takeover of the U.S. Embassy), and for almost thirty years now, whatever can be said about Iran, it cannot be said that it is subservient to any greater power.

———

In the early summer of 1979, only a few months after the Islamic Revolution had liberated me from having to explain to geographically and politically challenged fellow students where I was from, I found myself at Speakers' Corner in London's Hyde Park, shouting until I was hoarse. I had recently finished my college studies and was visiting friends and family in London, and as I stood on the lawn surrounded by a very emotional crowd of recent Iranian exiles—many of whom had been forced, at least so they thought, to flee in recent months—I vehemently defended the Islamic Republic. I surprised myself: as a secular and thoroughly Westernized Iranian (or *gharb-zadeh*—"West-toxified" in the revolutionary lexicon), the nascent Islamic Republic should hardly have been my cup of tea, but I didn't find it hard, nor did I see any contradiction in it, to celebrate an Iran that, after years of subjugation to outside powers, finally had a political system it could call its own. That was certainly good enough for me. As a twenty-two-year-old who until recently had had very little idea of Iran's place in the world, I'll admit that my newfound political awareness of the country of my birth was heavily tinged with youthful idealism, mixed with a good measure of latent Persian pride. The English who looked on curiously at the screaming wogs (as I, along with anyone darker than ruddy, used to be called at my English public school, a school that boasted Milton as an alumnus) seemed bemused; a few shook their heads in disapproval. At least, I thought, now they know where Iran is, a country where *they* will no longer have a say.

I tell this anecdote because I often see Westerners react to Iran with a sense of bafflement. But that moment at Speakers' Corner and the seeming absurdity of my brief defense of Khomeini's Islamic Republic bring to light a paradox about Iran that is still conspicuous today. Many of my Iranian friends have had these moments, and perhaps the most surprising comes from my Jewish-Iranian friend Fuad. A few years after the revolution, in Los Angeles, I had dinner with Fuad and his wife, Nasreen, where he told me a story that called to mind my Speakers' Corner experience of 1979. He had recently arrived in L.A. from Tel Aviv, where he first sought asylum after leaving Iran, and he was recounting the days preceding the revolution in Tehran. He told me that on one of the nights when millions of Tehran residents protested the Shah's government by taking to rooftops on Khomeini's instruction and shouting, *"Allah-hu-Akbar!"* Fuad and his family found themselves up on their rooftop shouting the same words as forcefully as their Muslim compatriots. Even after leaving his homeland, after settling first in its archenemy Israel and then moving to Los Angeles, even while we were getting drunk on scotch and savoring Nasreen's kosher cooking, neither he nor I saw any contradiction in either his initial sanguine view of an Islamic Revolution or his chanting, at the time, the most Islamic of Muslim sayings.

Fuad's parents had fled Baghdad in the 1930s during a wave of pogroms and institutionalized anti-Semitism, when many Iraqi Jews made their way to neighboring Iran, settling in a country that had boasted a large and vibrant Persian Jewish community for millennia. But Fuad didn't feel in the least Iraqi, and despite his extended stays in Israel (where he also attended college before the revolution and where he learned his fluent Hebrew), he didn't feel Israeli; he felt *Iranian*. And as an Iranian, he was with his countrymen when they rose up against the Shah. Islam, particularly Shia Islam, was as familiar to him as it was to his many Muslim friends; he understood that it formed their character as much as anything else did, and although he didn't participate in the rites of Shiism, he and his family were comfortable with the culture that surrounded them, a culture that, although steeped in the Shia tradition (which has borrowed from Iran's pre-Islamic culture), was as much theirs as their fellow Iranians'.

In order to understand Iran and Iranians today, one needs to understand what it meant to shout *"Allah-hu-Akbar!"* in 1979. The expression has become known as a sort of Muslim fundamentalist battle cry, uttered in every Hollywood movie featuring terrorists and notorious as the famous last words of the 9/11 hijackers. But the "God is Great!" that Iranians shouted in 1979 predated the concepts we have of fundamentalism—there was no Hezbollah, Hamas, or Islamic Jihad then, nor an Al Qaeda or a Taliban (and the PLO, the Middle East's most prominent terrorists, was still famously secular, and very few in the West had even heard of the Muslim Brotherhood, let alone knew what it stood for)—and to the Shia people the words signified their fearlessness in confronting an unjust ruler.

When the revolution came, I greeted it with fascination. Only a few years earlier, I had believed that the Shah was all-powerful, and now he was improbably on his way out. I disagreed with other Iranian students in the United States, both monarchists and revolutionaries, who thought that Jimmy Carter was pulling all the strings in Iran; my American side liked Carter, who seemed to me a truly decent man in the White House, and I believed that he was caught unawares by the Khomeini-led movement, mainly because I believed in his naïveté. But Iranians hated him: the few remaining monarchists, because they felt the United States had intentionally abandoned the Shah; the revolutionaries, communists, Islamists, and everyone else, because he had not forcefully spoken out against the Shah (and had even toasted him at a New Year's party in 1978 in Iran) and was perhaps even conspiring to reinstall him, much as Eisenhower had done in 1953.

When I, along with countless Iranians at home and abroad, voted in the yes-or-no ballot following the Shah's downfall, we overwhelmingly chose an Islamic Republic. Islam had won the revolution; even the traditional and secular left-wing opponents of the Shah's regime had recognized that without Islam, without *"Allah-hu-Akbar!,"* the revolution would not have been possible. Iranians still very much believed that to the victor go the spoils, and the mosques (and Khomeini in particular) were the victors in a battle that almost all Iranians were involved in. Iran was an Islamic country, a *Shia* country, and now, because the very concept of the Islamic Republic was a purely Iranian and Shia one, for the first time in hundreds, if not thousands, of years, Iranians were defining their own political system and, more important, their own destiny.

———

This memory rang in my head when I was in Tehran in the days after Ahmadinejad's election in 2005 and as I tried to understand how he had become president. *Everyone* openly talked about politics, and I understood from the many unlikely people who had voted for him, along with the millions that make up Iran's underclass, that he had successfully expressed the hope, a hope that had withered over the years, that the revolution was for *Iran*, for all Iranians, and its glittering promise still held. Ahmadinejad has also always understood that his message, a message of independence from East and West, plays well not only to his Iranian audience, who overwhelmingly support his uncompromising stance on the nuclear issue (if not his style), but to a wider audience across the Third World that sees in the Islamic Republic a successful example of throwing off the yoke of colonialism and imperialism.

I spoke to Fuad almost two years into Ahmadinejad's presidency, and he again surprised me with his comments. Despite Ahmadinejad's anti-Semitic remarks, which like many Iranian Jews he just didn't take as seriously as we did—or as he probably should have—Fuad understood him and, yes, in some ways even admired him. *Admired?* It was simple for Fuad: he told me that if Ahmadinejad was sincere in what he desired for Iran, and until then there had been no reason for Fuad to disbelieve him, then as a patriotic Iranian he found it hard to argue with many of his ideas and policies. I've heard the very same thing from other Iranians in exile, even among intellectuals, and it brought to mind early opinion on Khomeini.

———————

I have spent the decades before and since the Islamic Revolution living in America. The son of an Iranian diplomat, I grew up in different parts of the world, attending kindergarten in London and San Francisco and grade schools at American schools, populated by the children of American diplomats, expatriates, and businessmen, in various other countries. As a teenager, I was deposited in boarding school in England, where I finished my secondary education before rushing back to America for college. I had, needless to say, a somewhat confused identity as a child and teenager who more often than not thought of himself as more American than anything else, although by the time I reached drinking age (which was eighteen at the time), I had made the decision to live and work in Iran. The revolution that arrived unexpectedly a few years later nixed my plans, mostly because I felt that with my father's background (he had been an ambassador of the Shah's regime) I would be rather unwelcome in Tehran, but also because I felt, with both regret and a little admiration, that Iran no longer had much use for my very American worldview.

But in the early days of the Islamic Republic, it was hardly clear that the new political system would survive very long, and Iranian exiles, like the Parisian Russians of the 1920s, promoted the notion that their stay abroad was a temporary one. I watched events unfold in Iran from afar, uncertain of what might happen in the nascent republic and whether I would ever be able to go back, and then the hostage crisis happened—hardly a time for a Westernized Iranian who was already in the West, watching fellow Iranians stream out of Iran by the thousands, to think about setting up shop in the old country. The hostage crisis played out long enough, with Iran's revolutionaries seemingly not only victorious in humiliating the great superpower but also determined to disengage from the West and Western ideas, that many exiles somberly calculated that they would not outlive the Islamic Republic (though some, particularly those who show up, Chalabi-like, on Capitol Hill from time to time, still cling to the hope). I had by this time started to settle down to an adult life in the United States, and as the years passed, any fantasy ideas of starting from scratch in Iran, an Iran that by the end of the 1980s had suffered a horrific eight-year war and that I, as an able-bodied young man and unlike my patriotic contemporaries, had played no part in, were inconceivable.

A friend once told me that I was the only person he knew who was both 100 percent American and 100 percent Iranian. Oxymoronic as that sounds, I knew what he meant. I was raised and educated completely in the West, but am the grandson of a well-respected *Alemeh* (learned) and

Ayatollah; my first language is English, but I am also fluent in Farsi and am told that I speak it without an identifying accent. But more important, my Western outlook on life doesn't interfere with my complete ease in the company of even the most radical of Iranian political or religious figures (and often theirs with me), and in my travels to Iran I have often thought that there must be a toggle switch somewhere along the electrical system in my brain that is magically triggered to "East" when my plane crosses into Iranian airspace. I live in New York—where the switch is unconsciously set to "West"—and in 2006, in front of my apartment building in lower Manhattan across from City Hall Park and one block from the World Trade Center site, an Egyptian food cart vendor of kebabs had been selling halal (unbeknownst to the majority of his customers) grilled meat for lunch for quite some time. I would often say hello to him on my way out, and one day I stopped and asked where he was from, and he asked where I was from. When I said Iran, his first response was *"A-salaam-u-aleikum!"* and then he proceeded to tell me that for the last three or four months he "had started to really love Iran." Why? I wondered. And why only in the last three or four months? Because, he told me, "Iran is the only country standing up for Muslims."

This immigrant is no radical: from my conversations with him I discovered that he believes in America, at least the America of his dreams; it's an America he'll one day make enough money in to bring his family to and an America where he, and his children, will have opportunities denied them in his native Egypt. An America where he can say what he wants, and do what he wants, even though he believes his religion (and he's deeply religious) is under attack in some quarters. "I really like that man," he told me that same day, referring to President Ahmadinejad, enemy of America in the day's newspapers, and if our government was to be believed. But Ahmadinejad spoke to him in a language he understood—a simple language stripped of any elitism—and his message reverberated around the Islamic world, even if that world was in Queens, New York, where the vendor retired every night to a small shared apartment. It was a message of hope for many Muslims from the Third World, hope that they could guide their own destiny wherever they were. The Holocaust, incidentally, has always held little meaning to most of these Muslims who grew up with neither the benefit of a history lesson on it nor a sense of collective guilt. But of course Israel, to them the product of a war among Christians, *does* hold great meaning. And men like Ahmadinejad know it. But what Ahmadinejad knew better from the start of his presidency than many other Middle Eastern politicians was that the promise of his beloved Islamic Revolution, in the wake of war, corrupt leadership in the region, and declining American prestige, could hold sway even over men like the Sunni Egyptian kebab vendor in lower Manhattan.

In late August 2006, a week after the cease-fire in Lebanon, and a week after President Bush simply declared Israel's victory over Hezbollah without a hint of irony, I happened to mention Sheikh Hassan Nasrallah during a brief conversation with the vendor, who had asked me a probing question about Shiism (presuming that I, to him a good Muslim—a notion I did not disabuse him of—would know). It was probably the first time in his life he had wondered about a sect that some Sunnis consider heretical, and when I mentioned Nasrallah, he held his hand up, signaling me to stop. I paused as he brought his hand to his chest. "When you mention his name," he said, "I get emotional, I feel tears coming; I'm sorry." I looked at him, somewhat surprised to see that his eyes were already moist. He then turned to sell a Snapple to a woman with a worried, no, nervous, look on her face, and then turned back to me and wiped his eyes with his fingers. "He is *something!*" he said. A Sunni man in tears of love and joy over a Shia cleric, a cleric whose power is a product of Iranian nurturing, had been, I thought, an impossibility until that day.

If we cannot understand the depth of feeling in the Muslim world toward Iran, Hezbollah, Hamas, the Muslim Brotherhood, and Islam as a political force, then we will be doomed to failure in every encounter we have with that world. True, the secular and intellectual classes we most come into contact with from that world are much like us, and often they would like us to believe that their countrymen would like to be too, but they make up a small percentage of the Muslim population on the planet and spend as little time with those who are in the majority of their countries as we do. But Iran and its Islamic society (or even Islamic democracy) are the adversarial powers we have to face in the coming years, and to understand Iran, we have to understand Iranians. Who are the Iranians? What is the Iranian mind-set, and, perhaps more important, what moves it? And what happened to Iranians like Fuad, including some thirty thousand other Iranian Jews who, unlike him, stayed in Iran and now make up its middle and intellectual classes?

Whether in exile abroad or inside Iran, Iranians rarely seem to behave the way we expect them to, and Iranian diplomacy and foreign policy have in recent years run circles around their Western counterparts. Iran is at the center of the United States', if not the world's, attention today, partly because of its nuclear program and the Bush administration's labeling of it as an enemy (and part of the "axis of evil") and partly because Iran's power and influence, in the wake of the wars in Afghanistan, Iraq, and Lebanon, have grown exponentially just as U.S. power and influence seem to be on the wane. It is important to understand Iran and Iranians, because American and Western conflict with Iran, armed or otherwise, is unlikely to abate in the next few years, and Iran will have the ability, as it surely does now, to directly affect all Americans through its vast oil reserves as well as its ability to stall, as it has now, American vital interests in a strategically vital region.

———————

Iran today, despite what many Westerners think, bears very little resemblance to the Iran of the Khomeini years. And yet the Iran that

Khomeini made famous, to many an Iran that had taken one giant leap backward, was always there, and probably always will be. Other than what we hear of Ahmadinejad, fundamentalist Islam, and Iran's nuclear ambitions, what seems to be the most popular picture of Iran, one that appears in the media and on book jackets, is women in chadors, or at least in some form of mandatory hijab. It is understandable that Westerners should focus so often on Islamic dress as a symbol of oppression in countries such as Iran, Saudi Arabia, or the Afghanistan of the Taliban, whether it be for reasons of feminist outrage or the more subtle (and perhaps subconscious) colonialist notion of "white men saving brown women from brown men," to borrow Professor Gayatri Chakravorty Spivak's expression (in her description of the much earlier British abolition of the sati in India, the Hindu practice of a woman immolating herself on her husband's funeral pyre).

But let me tell you a story about hijab. The last Shah's father, Reza Shah, made the chador for women and the turban for men illegal in the mid-1930s: he wanted, fascist that he was (and he was a quite proud fascist—an open admirer of the Third Reich), to emulate Turkey's Kemal Atatürk, who not only had banned the fez and the veil but had even changed the Turkish script from Arabic to Latin, rendering the vast majority of Turks illiterate overnight, to force his people into a modern, which he saw as European, world. As we've often heard, during the early days of the Islamic Revolution women were harassed and sometimes beaten and imprisoned for *not* wearing proper hijab, but the exact same thing, for opposite reasons, occurred on the streets of Tehran less than fifty years earlier. In the 1930s, women had their chadors forcibly removed from their heads if they dared wear them, and were sometimes beaten as well if they resisted. Of course, back then the vast majority of women in Iran could not imagine leaving the house without the chador, so the effect was perhaps even more dramatic than Khomeini's subsequent *enforcement* of the hijab.

My grandfather Kazem Assar was a professor (who also happened to be an Ayatollah) who taught Islamic philosophy at the University of

Tehran and was one of the foremost scholars of the great twelfth-century Sufi philosopher Sohravardi and the "School of Illumination." He decided immediately that he preferred not to leave the house rather than to appear in public without his turban, so his students, some of whom would go on to become Ayatollahs themselves, simply moved their classroom to his house and he continued teaching as if nothing had changed. (This act of civil disobedience did not go unnoticed by the Shah, who sent emissaries to my grandfather's door to try to persuade him, unsuccessfully as it happened, to return to the university campus.) My grandmother, meanwhile, was in despair. A very religious woman who spent almost every waking minute of the last years of her life reading the Koran or praying, but who nonetheless led a very social life, she couldn't imagine venturing outdoors without her veil, especially as she was the wife of an Ayatollah. She sought her husband's counsel, and he told her to go about her life: dress modestly, but obey the law, even if it meant wearing not the full veil but a simple scarf or even a hat instead that might attract less attention.

Neither of my grandparents was in any way political, but many other women and almost all of the religious establishment were vociferously against the Shah on this matter, and in the face of heavy resistance he eventually relented, instructing the government to cease enforcement of the law, even though it wasn't officially changed until his forced abdication (by the Allies) in favor of his son in 1941. The nonenforcement was a sort of acknowledgment that his people would not give up their beliefs on his command, and my grandfather once again ventured outdoors, and my grandmother resumed her chador-wearing or heavy-scarf-and-full-overcoat-wearing habit.

Years later, in the late 1960s, I was staying at my grandfather's house one summer on a family visit back home. My mother, who had by this time spent years in the West, had a particular routine when she wanted to go out. If it was for a quick errand around the corner or in the immediate neighborhood, she would pull a chador over her head and go about her business. Not only was the neighborhood a religious one where the chador was common, but the idea of the Ayatollah's daughter prancing about the streets bareheaded was anathema to both her family and herself. However, if my mother was going well outside the neighborhood, by taxi or by private car, she would go without the chador or even a scarf. One very hot day I remember my mother saying goodbye to me in the garden and telling me she would be back in a few hours. She was wearing a short-sleeved dress that I'm sure I had seen before. I went into the house, and a few minutes later I saw my mother, who I thought had already left, in tears. Alarmed, I asked her what was wrong. "My father thought I should change before I go out."

"Why?" I asked, my preteen mind truly puzzled, since I knew that my mother worshipped her father and thought him the most intelligent, wonderful man in the world.

"He says the sleeves are too short!" My mother dutifully changed into a long-sleeved outfit and went out, bareheaded of course, and I realized for the first time how different Iranian culture was from what I had presumed was mine. My mother's tears, even my young mind understood, were not because she objected to her father's expressing displeasure at her outfit; she could, after all, ignore him, as her siblings seemed to do with impunity. No, they were tears of shame: she had, after all these years away from her country, embarrassed her father, her hero, by presuming that the Western culture that she had outwardly adopted could cause no offense in her house or in her country. Had she momentarily forgotten who she was or, more important, what the culture she was a product of was? The Shah certainly had, as he discovered with a rude surprise some ten years later.

Today, the chador or full hijab (completely covering every wisp of hair and skin except for the hands and face) is still worn in poorer neighborhoods and almost all the provinces (and by my mother in London every time she prays), even though it is effectively no longer mandatory.

Although hijab is indeed a statute of the Islamic Republic, the definition of hijab, again, as with many Iranian concepts, is murkier and less
absolute than ever before.

Every spring as the weather warms, the police crack down on what
appear to be looser and looser interpretations as to what constitutes hijab, and therefore modesty, but the efforts often seem almost half-
hearted (and are mostly forgotten within weeks, or by the middle of the
summer). As a public relations scheme to appease the religious right, as
well as the simply religious, though, it has its juicy moments. In the
2007 crackdown, an unusually severe one and highly publicized in the
papers (and one that led to an unprecedented number of arrests), one
M.P., Mohammad Taghi Rahbar, suggested that the crackdown was important because "the current situation is shameful for an Islamic government. A man who sees these models [women with minimal hijab] on
the streets will pay no attention to his wife at home, destroying the
foundation of the family." Indeed. He must've wondered how on earth
anyone in New York or Paris could ever stay married. But despite the
occasional indignant calls by government officials to preserve the sanc-
tity of Iranian marriage, in the chicer parts of Tehran (where the chador
long ago gave way to the scarf and shapeless overcoat called the manteau) the women, many quite happily married, now wear hip-length
mock-manteaus (that could have, for all intents and purposes, been
sprayed on) along with a sheer piece of cloth casually draped over some
very small percentage of their expensive hairdos. They would undoubtedly be thrilled if the last vestiges of enforced female modesty are one
day removed, as many feel they must and will be. But then they may remember, if they ever bother to venture well outside their neighborhoods, what the culture they are a product of still is.

———————

There have been many books and articles on Iran, on Iranians, and on
the subject of Islam, particularly since 9/11 and Iran's inclusion in

the "axis of evil." Some offer a critique and judgment of the nation's politics or social mores. Some are travelogues, and yet others are memoirs that give a little bit of insight into Iranian life, usually a life in the immediate aftermath of the revolution. Iran under the mullahs is sometimes portrayed in the West as one-dimensional, usually because of the constraints of "news" reporting, and many American reporters who travel there for the first time say, some even with surprise, that it is not anything like what they expected. There are also, naturally, numerous newspaper articles and books on the subject of human rights and human rights abuses (whether recent or, in the case of books and memoirs, in the past), and they are important in bringing attention to the sad failures of the Iranian revolution. I refer to some of those failures, whether they be the imprisonment of student protesters or feminist activists or a crackdown on civil liberties, but this book is not about the injustices of Iran's political system or, more important, the sometimes outrageous abuses in that system which many courageous Iranians, such as lawyers, journalists, and activists living in Iran, fight against every day. Rather, my hope is that this book, through a combination of stories, history, and personal reflection, will provide the reader a glimpse of Iran and Iranians, often secretive and suspicious of revealing themselves, that he or she may not ordinarily have the opportunity to see.

Iran is a nation of some seventy million people, the vast majority (90 percent) Shia Muslim but with Sunni, Jewish, Christian, Zoroastrian, and Baha'i minorities (though the Baha'is, officially unrecognized and often persecuted by the state as heretics, tend to keep their identities secret). Ethnically, it is made up of Persians, Turks, Turkmen, Arabs, Kurds, and a slew of other races, often intermingled to the point where it is impossible to say with any certainty what one Iranian's heritage is, particularly since birth records and birth certificates (and even proper surnames) were only instituted in the 1930s. It is impossible to paint a picture of *all* Iranians, just as it is impossible to rep-

resent every aspect of Iranian culture or society, in any one book. There
are, of course, Iranians in every socioeconomic class, and then there are
the Iranians whom we most come into contact with, the ones who live
in the West, many of whom have adopted Western culture while maintaining, to one degree or another, their own in the privacy of their
homes, but who are not a relevant part of this story. The Iranians one
encounters in this book come from all walks of life inside Iran (although I have chosen to feature stories that reveal something about the
character of the Iranian people today without concern for their background), and I try to show how even the senior political and religious
figures we meet are representative—perhaps far more so than in countries that have had a longer time to establish an entrenched political
elite—of who the Iranian people are.

While American (and some European) politicians may often
come from ordinary backgrounds, their lifestyles usually change dramatically when they are in office, and by the time they have reached
the pinnacle of power, they are long removed from their more humble roots. Iranian leaders in the Islamic Republic, however, clerical or
lay, continue to live their lives almost exactly as they always have, living in modest houses in their own neighborhoods surrounded by
their social peers, driving nondescript cars, and maintaining their
social networks. There is no presidential palace, no equivalent of the
White House, in Tehran, and despite the wealth of the Islamic
Republic, no fleet of limousines, or even the level of security one
would assume, for Iran's leadership. The presidential automobile is a
Peugeot (albeit armored), and President Ahmadinejad lives in the
same house he always has in a lower-middle-class neighborhood,
while his predecessor, Mohammad Khatami, lives in a small villa,
nice but not especially so, in North Tehran. It was Khatami who remarked to me, on a trip to the United States after his presidency,
with genuine surprise and not a little admiration, that the security
offered him by the State Department (as well as the limousines and

SUVs) as an ex–head of state was far more comprehensive (and luxurious) than anything he had had as president in Iran. He also remarked how very much it resulted in his trip occurring inside a "bubble."

Iranians are known to have a public face and a private face, a public life and a private life. For millennia Iranians have built tall walls around their houses to keep the private and public separate; one reason for the endurance of the Islamic system of government, despite its restrictions on public behavior, is that it has understood that the walls, literal and figurative, and even movable, as they often are, mustn't be breached. The Shah by contrast, with his insistence on peering over the walls, was doomed to fall.

Sure, we may have heard of bacchanalian parties, of alcohol and drug consumption, even of expressions of extreme dissatisfaction with the regime behind those walls, wherever their borders may extend to, but how do we peer inside the Iranian soul? What is it about Iran that gave us Omar Khayyám and Rumi centuries ago, and gives us Ahmadinejad and the mullahs (but also Kiarostami, the celebrated filmmaker) today? One constant throughout most of Iran's history, certainly in Islamic times, is that Iranians, the mullahs included, are great lovers of poetry: it is the literary expression best suited to the Shia martyr complex and the very Persian allegorical way of looking at an unexplainable world. It is said that Ayatollah Rafsanjani, a former president and still very powerful figure, once said to a foreign visitor, "If you want to know us, become a Shia first." While Rafsanjani made a very good point, almost poetically so, he could have just as well told his visitor to read and understand Persian poetry, but of course the two, Shiism and Persian poetry, are not mutually exclusive. Virtually everyone in Iran, from the lowliest person (and even the semiliterate)

to the high and mighty to all the Ayatollahs, can and will at every op
portunity quote a favorite quatrain or *ghazal* (sonnet) from dozens of
poets, including Khayyám and Rumi, to either make a point or explain
life "under the bruised dome."

Indulge me for one moment (for I am not entirely immune to my
countrymen's predilection for verse) while I offer the reader a clue as to
what encapsulates the purpose of this book (and happens to also reflect what is, despite Western conceptions, very much part of the Iranian mind-set):

> Out beyond ideas of wrongdoing and rightdoing,
> there is a field. I'll meet you there.[1]

See you in the chapters that follow.

PERSIAN CATS

The cat, a sinewy black creature with dirty white paws, darted from the alley and jumped across the *joob*, the narrow ditch by the curb, onto the sidewalk on Safi Alishah. It took one look at me, and then fled down the road toward the Sufi mosque. "That's the neighborhood *laat!*" exclaimed my friend Khosro, a longtime resident of the no-longer-chic downtown Tehran street. "He's the local tough, and he beats up all the other cats. Every time my mother's cat goes out he gets a thorough thrashing and comes back bruised and bloodied."

"Why?" I asked.

"He just beats the crap out of any cat he doesn't like, which is most cats, I guess."

"And no one does anything about it?" I asked naively.

"No. What's there to do? Every neighborhood has a laat."

Iranians are not known to keep indoor pets. Dogs are, of course, unclean in Islam, and as such are not welcome in most homes (although not a few Westernized upper-class Tehranis do keep dogs, but generally away from public view). Cats, Islamic-correct, are far more common, although unlike their Western counterparts Iranians don't so much own their cats as merely provide a home for them and feed them scraps from the table. That is, when the cats want a home. Persian cats, and I mean Persian as in nationality, are (to use a favored expression in Washington) freedom-loving animals, and they wander outdoors, particularly in neighborhoods where there are houses rather than apartments. They do so as often as they like, which seems to be quite often, and they get pregnant, they have fights, and they even change their domicile if they happen to stumble across a better garden or, as is usually the case, a more generous feeding hand. Such as Khosro's mother's cat, who appeared at her house one day and took a fancy to her.

Persians, despite having been best known in the West for really only two things, prior to their fame for Islamic fundamentalism, that is, cats and carpets, spend an awful lot of time pondering carpets and virtually no time thinking about cats. The Persian cats we know in the West, the ones with the impossibly flat faces and gorgeous silky hair, are not as common in Iran as one might think, or hope, and there is a national obsession neither about them nor about their less sophisticated cousins, the cats one sees on every street, in every alley, and in the doorways, kitchens, and gardens of many homes. And some of those cats are just by nature, well, laat.

Laat, like many other Persian words, can be translated in different ways, and some dictionaries use the English "hooligan" as the definition, although it is in fact wildly inaccurate. The laat holds a special place in Iranian culture: a place that at times can be compared to the popular position of a mafioso in American culture, albeit without the extreme violence associated with him, and at other times a place of respect and admiration for the working-class code he lives by. Hooligans are anarchic; laats fight only when necessary and to establish their authority.

Iran's cultural history of the twentieth century prominently featured the laat and with perhaps more affection the *jahel*, the onetime laat who had elevated himself to a grand position of authority and respect in a given urban neighborhood. The jahel, a sort of street "boss," occupied himself with many different illegal and quasi-legal activities but, unlike gang leaders in America, rarely found himself the target of police investigations, partly because the police were often from his social class, partly because the police were doled out many favors by him, and partly because the governments under the Shah were loath to disrupt or antagonize a class of society that could be relied upon for support should it become necessary to buy it.

The last Shah, Mohammad Reza Pahlavi, when forced to flee the country in 1953 (in the face of a popular uprising in favor of Prime Minister Mossadeq), found great use in the jahels and laats of South Tehran when the coup organizers intent on restoring him to power (financed and organized by the CIA) hired a prominent and formerly pro-Mossadeq laat, Shaban Jafari, better known as Shaban Bimokh (Shaban the "Brainless"), to successfully lead a counter-uprising in the streets of Tehran and mercilessly beat any anti-Shah demonstrators they came across. Using street-savvy toughs rather than the military (which was anyway unreliable and caught between the authority of the democratically elected prime minister and that of the Shah) gave the Shah the cover of populist sentiment in his favor, not to mention the convenience of violent reprisal perpetrated in his name, rather than directly by him or his forces.

The laats and jahels came from the lower and therefore deeply religious strata of Iranian society and were strong believers in Islam themselves, but they were notorious drinkers and womanizers, not to mention involved in prostitution and drugs. The jahel code, at least they themselves believed, was one of ethics and justice, Shia ethics, and the occasional sin would be repented for later, as is possible in Shia Islam. The code extended to their dress: black suits, white tieless shirts, and narrow-brimmed black fedoras perched at an angle high on their heads. A cotton handkerchief was usually to be found in their hands as a sort of fetish, and the famous jahel dance in the cafés of working-class Tehran involved slow, spinning movements with the handkerchief prominently waved in the air.

The jahel, and the laat to a lesser degree, represented the ultimate in Iranian machismo, Iranian *mardanegi*, or "manliness," in a supremely macho culture. Upper-class youths affected their speech, much as upper-class white youths in America affect the speech of inner-city blacks. There was, and still is, a perverse male and sometimes female fascination with the culture of the laat that invades even the upper-most echelons of Tehran society. At a dinner party in early 2007, in the very chic and expensive North Tehran Elahieh district at the home of an actor who has lived in America, a young man who serves as a guide and translator for foreign journalists (some of whom were in the room) peppered his speech with vulgar curse words that would ordinarily have been out of bounds in mixed company, or at least unfamiliar mixed company. "You probably don't like me," he said as he pulled up a chair next to my seat, having noticed my occasional winces in the preceding minutes. He helped himself to a large spoonful of bootleg caviar on the coffee table in front of him. "Because I swear so much," he mumbled with his mouth full. "But I'm a laat, what can I do?" I hesitated, wanting to point out that a laat would hardly be eating caviar in a grand North Tehran apartment, nor would he ever employ the language I'd heard in front of women, not unless he was getting ready for a fight.

"No," I replied instead. "I have no problems with swearing."

"I'm a laat," he repeated, as if it were a badge of honor. "I'm just a laat." His wife, seated on my other side, giggled nervously, glancing at the other women around the table whose smiles gave tacit approval to his macho posturing. What would a real South Tehran laat make of this scene? I wondered.

———————

Despite their seemingly secular ways, at least in terms of drinking, partying, and involvement with prostitutes, the working-class laats and jahels had been ardent supporters of the Islamic Revolution of 1979, and even though some royalists had suggested they be bought again, as they were in 1953, the Shah seemed to realize that times had changed and Khomeini's pull, which unlike Mossadeq's encompassed virtually all of Iran's opposition, was too strong to be countered with cash. Islam's promise of a classless society, along with the promise of far more equitable economic opportunities in a post-monarchy nation, was appealing enough in working-class neighborhoods, but what's more, unlike the intellectuals and aristocrats who surrounded Mossadeq, those fomenting *this* revolution were, after all, from the 'hood. As such, the street toughs and their jahel bosses, the über-laats if you will, had assumed that an Islamic state would not necessarily infringe on their territory, but the clerics who brought about the revolution weren't going to let a bunch of thugs (in their minds) have the kind of authority that they considered exclusively reserved for themselves. The jahel neighborhood authority, along with its flamboyance of style and dress, also quickly went out of favor, replaced by cleric-sanctioned and much-feared paramilitary committees known as *komiteh* (the Persian pronunciation of the word), which undoubtedly numbered among their ranks many former laats.

In the few years of its existence the komiteh, often reporting directly to a cleric, involved itself in almost all aspects of life in each neighborhood where it was set up, and apart from enforcing strict Islamic behavior on the streets, it functioned as a sort of quasi-court where all manner of complaints were investigated. Among those com-

plaints in the early days of the revolution were charges of corruption
lodged against businessmen or the merely wealthy, usually by former
employees but sometimes by jealous rivals, that resulted in further investigations by real courts and sometimes the confiscation of assets, a
satisfying result for the early communist and left-wing supporters of
the Islamic Republic who numbered among them the now-archenemy
Paris- and Iraq-based Mujahedin, as they're known to most Iranians
(but referred to as *monafeghin*, "hypocrites," by the government), or the
MEK (for Mujahedin-e-Khalq), as they're known in the West.[1] (The
political left had also been undoubtedly pleased to watch as the new
government nationalized many of the larger private enterprises in Iran,
a program that has been in various stages of undoing since Khomeini's
death in 1989 and whose undoing continues today, even under an administration more ideological than the pragmatist and reformist governments that preceded it.)

The laats who joined a komiteh or even the Revolutionary Guards in
the dramatic aftermath of the revolution may have thought of themselves as finally empowered politically, but they quickly learned that in
an Islamic government, all real authority would rest with the clergy. In
one of the first acts of the post-revolution government, ostensibly for
Islamic reasons but also as a show of just who was in charge, Tehran's infamous red-light district, Shahr-e-No, or "New City," the stomping
ground of many a jahel and laat, was shut down and razed. Today, the
old district is bordered by a broad avenue lined with shops selling sur-
plus military wear, including, as I saw myself, U.S. Desert Storm boots
in mint condition and an assortment of other U.S. military clothes and
footwear newly liberated from Iraq. On the day I was there, and as I was
examining the various articles for sale in a storefront, an old man shuffled by slowly, wearing a dirty black suit and loafers with the heels
pushed down. "See him?" asked the friend who had brought me, a child

of South Tehran who spent many a day of his youth in the Shahr e No neighborhood. "He used to walk up and down this street, just like he is now, in the old days. But he was a big guy then."

Today, while laats still abound in urban areas, the jahel is but a fragment of memory for most Iranians, to be seen in the occasional old Iranian movie or to be talked about nostalgically. Once in a while, one can bump into one (or someone who at least affects the look) on the streets of downtown Tehran or farther south, as I did on Ferdowsi Avenue, just off Manouchehri, a street lined with antiques dealers, on a few occasions in the past few years. Among the Jewish shop owners and other stall vendors, one heavyset older man works out of an impossibly narrow shop carved into the side of a building.[2] His dusty window displays an array of old rings, bracelets, and other jewelry, the odd off-brand man's watch here and there, and he himself sits on an old stool just outside on the pavement. He wears a black suit, a slightly discolored white shirt, and a narrow-brimmed black fedora one size too small on the top of his obviously balding head. His thick black mustache, from which years ago he may have dramatically plucked a hair with his fingers to show good faith in a deal, is dyed, the reddish tint of the henna showing on the outermost hairs. His only concession to the Islamic state of affairs is the day-old growth of beard surrounding the mustache: snowy white growth that betrays the dyed mustache even more startlingly than the henna hue. I don't know if he was ever a jahel, but it seems likely that he was. He sits there on Ferdowsi, keeping his own hours, like a toothless old cat, a reminder for those who might care that the neighborhood's top laat is not what he used to be.

The Javadieh neighborhood of South Tehran was once the city's roughest; to the young male residents it was known as "Texas," presumably because of the association in Iranian minds of that state with the law-less Wild West. A rough neighborhood, though, meant poor and run-down but not necessarily dangerous in the way we might think in the West. Upper-class Iranians would never have ventured into Javadieh; they still don't, but not out of fear, rather because of the strict Iranian delineation between the classes. Some upper-class wealthy young males may want to affect the macho posturing of the lower-class laat, but they would never sit down with one and have a chat over a cup of tea. Nor would they know how to deal with a *chaghoo-kesh*—"knife-puller" literally, but someone who lives by his knife. Guns have never been pop-ular among Iranian toughs, mainly because they kill more often than maim, but also because guns in Iran have been associated with armed struggle or revolution rather than self-defense or criminal activity. As such, governments, whether under the Shahs or in the Islamic Repub-lic, have zero tolerance for guns, which they have viewed as threats to their power, but have had a wide tolerance for knives and other fight-ing equipment.

Knife fights, common enough even today, rarely end with serious injury, although on occasion death does occur, as it did recently on the street where I was staying when a fight broke out between two young men over the affections of a local girl, with whom neither had relations but whom each felt was his. The thrust of a knife, a little too hard and a little too close to the heart, probably unintentional, resulted in death, and the onetime chaghoo-kesh was transformed from street thug to murderer in an instant. But usually a knifing is meant to cut rather than kill, and in the old street tradition a knife fight begins with one or both of the men cutting themselves on the chest, to draw blood and to demonstrate the fearlessness of the fighter. That disregard for one's own well-being extended easily into the practice of fearless suicide mis-sions performed by the all-volunteer Basij forces during the Iran-Iraq war.[3]

The Basij ("mobilization" force), who come under the authority of the Revolutionary Guards, are recruited from lower-class neighbor-

hoods where laats once flourished, and they serve as paramilitary pro-
tectors of the Islamic Revolution. In the past they have been mobilized
to enforce Islamic behavior on the streets and even in homes; they can
be counted on to break up demonstrations and show up in force at
pro-government rallies, and of course they will be in the forefront of
any military conflict that involves action in Iranian territory. The local
mosque serves as their base, but loyalties that were once localized to a
gang or just a neighborhood have been transferred to Islam and the
velayat-e-faqih, the "rule of the jurisprudent," which is the very basis of
the Islamic Republic.[4] Upper-class Iranians have a particular disdain
for the Basij; it's as if the lower-class laats have been given the authority to rule over their lives, or, to use a Western expression, the lunatics
have taken over the asylum. The laats and jahels that the Shah once relied upon to support his rule had very little opportunity for advancement in a strictly class-based society with few institutions of higher
education, and as such formed an underclass that contented itself with
functioning within its own boundaries, venturing afar only to commit
the occasional burglary or car theft. The Islamic Republic, however,
now with hundreds of colleges and universities that are happy to recruit Basij onto their campuses, has given the underclass a significant
role in society, and one that they won't easily give up.

President Ahmadinejad, the son of a blacksmith and often derisively
referred to as such, may come from the underclass and take pride in the
fact, but he long ago elevated himself above what would have been his
social status in the Iran of yesteryear. He indeed grew up in a lower-
middle-class neighborhood and still lives in one, but his intelligence
and hard work secured him a place at university during the Shah's time,
a time when the nationwide university entrance exams filtered out all
but the brightest students in Iran. Wealthier Iranian students who
couldn't pass muster went abroad for their studies, usually to the

United States, where getting into a college, any college, was no great feat, but for ordinary working-class high school students (and assuming they even bothered to finish high school) the twelfth grade was the end of the line.

Ahmadinejad, by virtue of his university degree (and Iranians at the time understood very well that a Tehran university degree said a whole lot more about the student than a degree from a U.S. college, unless that college was Ivy League), was destined to break out into at least the working middle class, but he understood early that the Islamic Revolution was as much a social revolution as it was political, and he cultivated his working-class image along with his piety to good effect as he slowly worked his way up through the ranks of the Islamic government. His style, the bad suits, the cheap Windbreaker, the shoddy shoes, and the unstylish haircut, a style he proudly maintains well into his presidency, is a signal to the working class that he is still one of them. Many Iranians may aspire to wear European designers, and often do, but Ahmadinejad, president of the republic, knows his clothes send a message directly to those neighborhoods he most counts on for support—neighborhoods where the Basij are recruited, neighborhoods where there still are knife fights and the laats roam the streets if they're not persuaded to join the Basij, and neighborhoods where you can still buy your suit, if you really need one, from the *kot-shalvary*.

The kot-shalvary was a common enough presence in working-class neighborhoods when I was a child: I remember at my grandfather's house in Abbasabad-e-Einedoleh, a house he bought in the 1920s in a neighborhood that had by the 1960s already become unfashionably working-class, hearing the cries of *"Kot-shalvary-e!"*—"It's the suit man!"—on Fridays, the Muslim weekend. A vendor with a slow donkey-drawn cart would make the rounds of a particular neighborhood or two and announce his presence and the availability of men's suits with a staccato rhythm, a rhythm my brother and I would glee-fully imitate throughout the day to the annoyance of anyone within earshot. Growing up in the West with only occasional summer visits to Tehran, we found it amusing that our compatriots might actually buy their clothes from someone with a donkey cart, and as the years passed, I assumed that the kot-shalvary had gone the way of the camel caravans.

The nasal twang of the kot-shalvary of Abbasabad-e-Einedoleh, however, was still in my ears when I woke up one morning in 2007 on Safi Alishah, a street much grander than my grandfather's in his day but only marginally so today, to the similar twang of a kot-shalvary advertising his suits for sale. His was a hand-drawn cart, and I saw no customers rushing up to him in the brief instant I looked out the window, but his suits could not be much worse than those of the president, who buys his from a shop in Shams Al Emareh (and the suits are commonly and disparagingly known as "Shams Al Emareh" suits for the building that houses the many stores they're sold from), not far from the Tehran bázaar, specializing in locally made and cheap Chinese-made men's clothes. And the president knows it. It must have come as a great disappointment to him when the Western press mockingly referred to the suits provided the British sailors arrested by Iran in the Persian Gulf in 2007 and released two weeks later as "ill-fitting Ahmadinejad-style suits," the assumption being that they were perhaps purchased by the Iranian government at Shams Al Emareh. In fact, the suits came from E Cut, a men's mini-chain that is quite a few steps up from Shams Al Emareh, at least in the minds of ordinary Iranian men, and the government's outfitting of the British prisoners in better suits than the president's was intended to show off Persian hospitality and a little *ta'arouf*: the best for your guest. (Ahmadinejad, like many Iranians who've spent their entire lives in Iran, is blissfully unaware that ta'arouf, or "social ritual," particularly as it's practiced in Iran, is an alien concept in the West.) Based on Western reaction to the drape of its suits, a reaction that can't have escaped E Cut (the name signifying an Iranian fascination with all things technological), the company will have to reprogram its computers for the "electronic cut" of its clothes, at least if it wishes to be considered for any future government gift-giving contracts.

———————

Mahmoud Ahmadinejad's style, sartorial and otherwise, permeates the upper and certainly the lower echelons of his government. The president's office, the Iranian White House if you will, sits smack in the center of downtown Tehran and is in a large compound that shares acreage with the Supreme Leader's office. Unlike his predecessor, Mohammad Khatami, who spent two days a week at Sa'adabad, one of the Shah's palaces in the northern reaches of chic North Tehran and who entertained foreign dignitaries there, Ahmadinejad spends all of his working hours in Tehran in this compound. Only a few days after his inauguration in 2005 and while I was in the country, President Assad of Syria flew to Tehran for a state visit, signaling his country's continued close alliance with Iran despite the somewhat radical change of government. He was greeted by Ahmadinejad on Pasteur Avenue in the bright sun and hundred-plus-degree heat (Sa'adabad is at least ten degrees cooler and sits in an expansive hillside park); Iranians everywhere commented on how uncomfortable he looked, while some claimed to have heard that the Syrians were deeply offended by the very pedestrian reception they received compared with previous visits. But Ahmadinejad had promised to do away with the luxurious and even royal trappings of his office, and that included closing the presidency rooms at Sa'adabad and even evicting Khatami, who had been promised space there for his International Institute for Dialogue Among Cultures and Civilizations by no less an authority than the Supreme Leader himself. Presumably, Ahmadinejad wanted to avoid comparisons drawn between visits to him by foreign ambassadors and leaders and visits to Khatami, who would still be the subject of the occasional courtesy call.

On the winter morning I visited the presidential compound, a light snow was falling in North Tehran, where I had spent the night. I had called a taxi, or *agence*, as hired cars and the agency that employs them are known in Farsi (French words for which there is no Farsi equivalent have more readily been adopted in Iran than English ones, mainly because they are much easier to pronounce for Persian speakers), and was mildly surprised when a slightly overweight woman, probably in her thirties and dressed in all black and a hijab, greeted me on the curb. "Are you the *agence*?" I asked, trying not to sound surprised.

"*Befarma'eed*," she said, gesturing to her gray Iranian-made Peugeot and using one of the most common phrases in the Persian language, one that means almost everything, such as "please take a seat," "come/go," "speak/say/go on," "please help yourself," and "there you are." Normally I sit in the front seat of taxis in Iran, but I hesitated for a moment, thinking I'd better ask before I got in. "However you're comfortable," she said dismissively as she went around to the driver's door. "And where is it you're going?" she asked, buckling her seat belt and putting the manual shift lever into gear.

"Pasteur," I said.

She turned the wipers on. "Downtown," she said. "Where exactly on Pasteur?"

"President's office," I replied. She edged into traffic with a *"Be'sm'allah"* and a *"Ya Ali!"* and turned the wipers off, even though snow was still coming down. In Iran, it seems, many working-class drivers are loath to use anything electrical unless absolutely necessary, and often not even then. A friend told me the reason: lights, wipers, and batteries are expensive spare parts, even in a country with thirty-five-cent-a-gallon gasoline. We drove in heavy traffic in silence while I tried to think of something to say that wouldn't offend. "Unfortunate weather," I said. "Not a nice day for work, I imagine."

"Yes," she replied, "but it's not a problem. You know, the men at work don't want me to work when it snows; *kam-lotfi meekonand*, they're being discourteous, unkind." Apparently, if I correctly understood her, I was being discourteous too, even though I hadn't meant anything sexist by my remark. So much for not offending.

"Of course!" I said. "Why shouldn't you drive when it snows?"

"Exactly. I have to support my kids somehow. Doesn't everybody else drive when it snows?" She turned on the radio and selected a news channel. The snow was turning to drizzle as we descended the steep hills of North Tehran, and she turned the wiper on once to clear the windshield. Between snippets of the day's news read alternately by a man and a woman, an instrumental song, the theme of the network, played over and over, and I struggled to think where I'd heard it before. A bus swerved in front of us, and my driver brought her fist down on the horn.

"Bus drivers!" I said, suddenly remembering where the song was from. It was the theme from *Beverly Hills Cop*, a not entirely inappropriate choice for a news network. "They're the same in New York," I continued, giving away where I live, or so I thought.

"Yes, the bus drivers are really impossible," she said, turning to take a look at the person who claimed to know what bus drivers are like in New York, of all places. "I was going to Jamkaran last week," she continued, "and you should have seen the buses; they nearly ran me off the road a few times!" Jamkaran is a mosque outside of Qom, a two-hour drive from Tehran and an important pilgrimage site for Shias. She paused for a few seconds. "So, you've been to New York?" The beard must have confused her, I thought. Very few ordinary Iranians imagine that an Iranian man who lives in the West might wear a beard. Although common enough in Iran, the beard signifies not style but either government affiliation (and what branch of government depends on the form of the beard) or piety, neither of which should apply, the reasoning goes, to Iranians who've chosen to live in the Judeo-Christian and secular West. I had grown my beard for precisely that reason: so that I wouldn't be immediately identified, as one is by one's mannerisms, dress, and general demeanor, as someone who lives abroad, and therefore someone one might treat differently.

"Yes, I actually live there," I said. "Did you go to Jamkaran with a fare?"

"No," she replied. "I went on Friday [the Iranian and Muslim Sabbath], on my day off. I try to go as often as I can. It's so important." The snow and drizzle had stopped, and she turned the wiper on once more for good measure. "You know it snowed on Christmas," she said, as if searching for something to say to someone who lived among the Christians. "A beautiful, white snow," she continued, "and it made me think that Christians must be good people and God must love them."

"Yes," I said. She downshifted and sped up, almost touching the bumper of the car in front, refusing to let a car cut in front of her.

"Do women drive taxis in America?" she asked. "Have they progressed like us?"

"Yes," I replied. "But most women don't really *want* to drive cabs."

"When my husband died, I had to work somehow," she said. "I have two kids. I could have emigrated, and I even thought about it, but I didn't, because I couldn't leave my mother alone. Perhaps it would have been better if I had." She was quiet for a few moments, as if thinking about a life abroad. "But, no," she finally said, "God knows best." We had reached Pasteur, and she slowed down. "Where do you want me to stop?"

"The president's office," I said.

"Yes, but I can't go any farther than the gate," she said, gesturing up ahead.

"As close as you can get, then," I said. "Traffic was light, wasn't it?"

"Yes, a lot of people don't like to drive when it snows," she said with a knowing smile. My cabdriver, I thought when I got out, hijab and all, can certainly hold her own with any of the laats in her neighborhood.

———————

When one enters the presidential compound on Pasteur Avenue (named after the French chemist Louis Pasteur but, curiously and unlike many other Tehran streets with foreign but not foreign revolutionaries' names, never renamed after the revolution), a street closed to through traffic, one immediately senses that this might be the scruffiest presidential compound of any wealthy country, even some very poor ones too, in the world. After leaving the taxi, I walked along the sidewalk past the car checkpoint, looking for some indication of which of the many buildings lining the street I should be headed for. There were no signs anywhere, so I simply walked into the first building that showed any sign of life, wrongly, it turned out, but—when I emptied my pockets at the metal detector—at least I realized that I had forgotten to check my cell phone at the gate, to the clear disapproval of the guard. No, not the gate, I was told, an office just a few doors down in the direction I came from. "Is there a sign?" No, there is no sign, it's not necessary. Just two or three doors down. Maybe four. I walked out and scrutinized every door as I retraced my steps until I saw a half-opened one and walked into what can best be described as a run-down shack. A Revolutionary Guard, behind a makeshift wooden counter, smiled at me. "Is this where I check my cell phone?" I asked.

"Yeah."

"Do you know where Mr. Javanfekr's office is?"

"No."

"Do you know who Mr. Javanfekr is?"

"No."

"He's in the president's office. Which building would that be?"

"Straight ahead." The Guard handed me a token for my phone, put the phone in a wooden cubbyhole, and then asked if it was off, to which I replied yes. "Can you imagine," he said, "if people didn't turn their phones off before handing them in? I'd go crazy in here!" It was my turn to smile. I headed back in the direction I had just come from, past the building with human activity, or actually a few people dozing in plastic chairs waiting for something or someone, and to the corner of Pasteur, where there was another building with another security guard. "I'm looking for Mr. Javanfekr's office. He's supposed to have left my name at the gate," I said to the guard.

"Who?"

"Mr. Javanfekr," I said slowly. "The president's office."

"Turn left and go to the end of the street," said the guard. I walked out and followed his instructions, walking under towering pine trees and listening to the frequent cries of the hundreds of black crows that seemed to have made the compound, possibly the quietest and most traffic-free part of the metropolis, their home. At the end of the abandoned street there was another gate with buildings beyond, and I nodded to the security guards inside their glass-enclosed booth as one of them activated the switch for the barrier to lift. I paused for a moment and turned back to their booth.

"Do you know which building Mr. Javanfekr is in?" I asked, leaning toward the small window.

"Who?"

"Mr. Javanfekr."

"I don't know. Where are you going?"

"To the president's office," I replied.

"I think you're in the wrong place. Who are you? If you go in through this gate, you can't come back out."

"What?"

"You can go in, but you can't come back." For a moment I could only think of the song "Hotel California," but it dawned on me that perhaps I was trespassing in the Supreme Leader's territory. But why hadn't anyone stopped me? And why were these guards willing to let me go through the gate as long as I didn't try to check back out? Perhaps it was the two-week-old beard that made me look like I belonged; perhaps it was the gray suit and tieless white shirt that identified me as a government official. The suit, incidentally, was a cut above Ahmadinejad's, English bespoke but hardly identifiable as such to any Iranian in Tehran, particularly not to government officials or the Revolutionary Guards. There's an English affectation, picked up by pretentious or merely Anglophile Americans, including myself (although I like to think of myself as more of an Anglophile-phobe), where one leaves one button on the left cuff of one's suit jacket undone, presumably for the sole purpose of showing off the fact that one's suit has working buttonholes on the cuffs and is therefore custom (a trick many ready-to-wear designers who must read the *Robb Report* have employed). In Iran, I found that doing so elicited either comments that I was missing a button or stares from those who noticed but were too polite to point out the apparent scruffiness of this visitor from abroad. Beard, gray suit with one undone button, old loafers on the feet. Yes, I belonged here.

"Can you call someone and find out for me where Mr. Javanfekr's office is, then?" I asked, trying to sound authoritative. The guard picked up a phone and turned his back.

"Go back to the corner building," he said after he hung up.

"But they told me to come here," I said.

"That's the president's office," he said, pointing behind me. "If you go in here, you can't come out." "Hotel California," again. I walked back down the street and stepped into the corner building.

"Mr. Javanfekr," I said to the guard. "I have an appointment, and he's left my name at the door."

"What's his number?" he replied this time, forgetting that he'd sent me on a long detour from which I may not have returned had I not asked where I was going. I gave the guard the extension, and he dialed it. "It's busy. Have a seat."

I sat down on one of three chairs and looked at my watch. The door behind me opened and four men walked in, dressed remarkably much as I was. On closer inspection, their gray suit jackets didn't quite match their gray trousers, their white shirts were slightly graying, and their loafers weren't horsehide. And the buttons on their cuffs were all intact, neatly and immovably sewn into place. *"Salam,"* they said to me one by one, short nods of the head in my direction, the Persian gesture of respect, as they huddled in front of the guard. I was too busy examining their clothes to hear whom they were there to see, but when the guard asked for a telephone extension, two of the men whipped out their cell phones and began dialing. I stared enviously; they must be vastly more important than me, I thought, before realizing that I could have also easily bypassed the cell phone ban by simply coming straight to this office rather than making the unintended stop in the first building.

Whoever they had come to see wasn't in his office either, so they took turns sitting down on the two remaining chairs, dialing their phones every few seconds. Every now and then one would look at me and nod his head again, and I would nod back. I caught the eye of one who was standing long enough for him to feel obliged to follow the nod with a word or two, and he quickly said, *"Mokhlessam,"* or "I'm your devoted friend," a common enough pleasantry in conversational Farsi that would have in the past been a little too informal, too "street," despite how it sounds in English, to hear in a government office. *"Chak-eram,"* I replied in my best Tehrani accent, smiling and bowing my head. "I'm your obedient servant." Even more "street," but the correct retort in the Persian tradition of ta'arouf, a defining Persian characteristic that includes the practice, often infuriating, of small talk, or frustratingly and sometimes incomprehensible back-and-forth niceties uttered in any social encounter. Ta'arouf can be a long-winded prelude to what is actually the matter at hand, whether the matter be a serious negotiation or just ordering dinner, or it can, as in this case, be insincere but well-intentioned politesse. I wondered if he noticed my "missing" cuff button. His phone rang with an incongruous little dance number, the kind of ring tone only Finnish or Chinese designers—and, it seems, also many Iranians—would think appropriate for grown men's telephones, and he stepped outside to take the call.

The guard dialed a number again on his phone and gestured to me with the handset. "It's ringing," he said, holding the receiver in the air. I stood up and took it. Mr. Javanfekr, it appeared, was in his office and ready to receive me. I handed the receiver back to the guard, who, distracted by the other men and now a television crew that had just shown up, took it and nodded his head a few times, gesturing for me to go

through the metal detector. "The building on the left," he said, noticing my inquisitive look. I left the four men and the television crew, almost all chatting away on cell phones, and made my way to the next
building. Another guard, seated at a desk and infinitely more bored
than the last, looked at me with raised eyebrows. "Mr. Javanfekr," I said.

"That door over there," he replied, pointing to an office on the
ground floor. I hesitated for a moment before realizing that no one
would be escorting me, and then I walked straight into Javanfekr's office.

————

Ali Akbar Javanfekr has the unenviable job of being President Ahmadinejad's top press adviser, as well as his most senior official
spokesman. He doesn't work in the presidential press office, and
doesn't sully his days with routine and tedious requests, or with the details of the president's press schedule. But from his large office with
views of the towering pine trees in the compound, he ponders the big
picture—public diplomacy, if you will, for a boss who seems to have
little comprehension of the concept. He is also the president's chief
propaganda adviser, which is a concept his boss *does* have a natural instinct for. A little-known figure in Iranian politics (like many of the
president's other top advisers, who wisely, it seems, prefer to stay in the
shadow of a president who demands top billing everywhere he goes),
he is someone who issues statements only rarely and only on very serious matters, such as his denial that the British servicemen and service-
woman who endured thirteen days of captivity in the spring of 2007
were in any way tortured and, in a clever propagandist moment, his announcement that they were free to tell their stories to the Iranian press
after they were barred from doing so in England by the British government.[5]

Mr. Javanfekr is a slight man with a standard-issue Ahmadinejad
government haircut—thick short black hair parted to one side and par-

tially covering the forehead—and the obligatory, but in his case quite full and quite white, beard. He was examining some faxes when I stepped into his office, but he turned and greeted me in a soft voice. "Please," he said, "have a seat." In Iranian offices, one is never asked if one would like tea or coffee or any other beverage: it is assumed one will drink tea, and usually within seconds the office tea man will arrive with a fresh glass and a bowl of sugar cubes.

Javanfekr sat down beside me on an ugly leatherette couch; he was dressed in navy blue trousers, a white shirt, and a navy cardigan, and with his soft voice and quiet, gentle demeanor he appeared more as a college professor than a top aide to someone who has been likened to, at least in some of the Western media, Hitler. I couldn't help but notice his footwear: he was wearing the ubiquitous plastic sandals that are found by the doors of Iranian homes (for the vast majority of Iranians remove their shoes before entering a house) but not often in offices, and certainly not in important government offices. But Mr. Javanfekr was clearly comfortable in them, as comfortable as the tea man was in his identical pair when he entered the room with a tray balanced on one upturned palm of an outstretched arm. The office tea man, only one rung above a janitor on the personnel ladder, was dressed just like his boss, save the cardigan, and it struck me that the more socialist aspects of the Islamic Republic, indeed Islam itself, were on full view in this quiet and shabby corner office at the heart of the republic's power center. The Islamic Revolution had promised, in 1979, to do away with class and more particularly with any royalist, *taghouti* (which implies class structure) trappings in government and society, and in Javanfekr's office at least, it had succeeded. It was not theater; Javanfekr did not strike me as one to affect a style, as it were, nor was I someone, say, a foreigner, whom the presidential office wished to impress with its overt dismissal of both Western and sometimes Persian pomp and airs. No, Javanfekr and his tea man were simply comfortable with who they were; a generation ago upper-class Iranians would have called them both *dahati*, "peasants," for their appearance. Today some Iranians still do, both inside the country and in exile, and usually with an air of absolute disgust. But it just doesn't matter anymore.

What I wanted to know most from the president's top media adviser was who among the top echelon of government officials had thought, other than Ahmadinejad himself, that organizing a conference on the Holocaust in Tehran (held in the winter of 2006 to wide ridicule mainly outside, but also to some extent inside, Iran) had been a good idea. At least in terms of how the media would see it. Iranians, particularly those who haven't traveled much outside the country and no matter what their level of education, have very little knowledge, if any, of the Holocaust. Contemporary European and American history is not taught much in schools, films and documentaries on the Holocaust rarely make it to Iran, and books on the Holocaust are rarely translated. It was and is still generally accepted by most Iranians that something very bad happened to European Jews under the Third Reich, but because it didn't affect or have anything to do with Iran, not even Iranian Jews, who were mostly unaffected by World War II, the Holocaust was rarely thought about by Iranians until their president decided to make it an issue of great import.

Javanfekr was frozen by the question. He stared at me for a very long time, not angrily, but more with a bewildered look in his eyes. I was impressed that he didn't want to repeat the standard government line, or a denial of Holocaust denial; perhaps he just didn't have an answer that he thought would satisfy me. An Iranian who lives in New York might not, he may have reasoned, understand the subtleties and nuances in his president's pronouncements and actions.

I thought of Fuad, my Jewish-Iranian friend from Los Angeles who had explained to me his perspective on Ahmadinejad's Holocaust denial with no small measure of admiration for what he saw as the finest example of Persian ta'arouf one-upmanship. Ahmadinejad, Fuad reasoned, had in effect said to the Europeans (and, in a letter, to Angela Merkel, chancellor of Germany) that he couldn't believe that Europeans had been or could be such monsters (and this at a time when Iran was being portrayed as monstrous). "You're not monsters," Ahmadinejad was saying. "Surely not? Surely you're a great civilization," a sentiment that could only compel the Europeans, and particularly the Germans, to respond in effect, "No, no, no, we were. We really were monsters. The very worst kind." And by further asking why Israel had had to be created by them, he was essentially getting the Europeans to admit that they were entirely capable of genocide again. It didn't matter, Fuad suggested, that Europeans by and large didn't squirm, for Iranians and Arabs got the message, if only subconsciously. The Westernized and West-worshipping Middle Easterners whom Ahmadinejad loathes with the same passion as Khomeini did could hear the civilization they so admire shout, loud and clear, "Yes, yes, we committed the very worst genocide in history. Only a few years ago, and who knows, we could do it again." And Ahmadinejad must have, Fuad said, derived enormous satisfaction in hearing Europeans indignantly insist that their fathers were mass murderers. But Javanfekr was unwilling or unable to explain the thought process behind a Holocaust conference in Tehran, and maybe Fuad had been too generous in his reading of Ahmadinejad's intentions.

Javanfekr continued to stare at me with blank, almost glazed eyes behind his large, square 1970s-style glasses, unwilling or unable to tackle the subject. I felt a little sorry for him: perhaps it would have been much easier if I had been a foreigner. I changed the subject and we engaged in the kind of polite small talk and ta'arouf that lead nowhere and are one reason for the perpetual paralysis of Iran's bloated bureaucracy: "I am at your disposal should you need anything" (he most certainly wasn't), "Please call if you require anything" (please don't, for if you do, I will have to lie and say I will help when in fact I'd much rather not), and, from my lips, "Thanks so much for giving up your valuable time" (he seemed to have nothing else to do, and no phone calls or messages interrupted our meeting), "You've been very kind and helpful" (when you essentially stared at me the whole time), and "Thank you for your hospitality" (you could at least have worn shoes).

———————

I left Javanfekr's office and headed back to the unrestricted section of Pasteur Avenue to hail a cab. I stopped in at the cell phone drop and handed over my token to the Guard, who reached behind him and handed me my phone. "Thanks very much," I said, turning to leave.

"Excuse me," he said politely. "Can I ask you a question?"

"Of course." I turned back to face him. He had the classic Revolutionary Guard look: a very close-cropped beard with severe lines demarcating where it was permissible to shave for a more professional appearance, that is, the upper cheeks and the lower neck. His cap was pushed back from his forehead, which I suppose gave him a friendlier air than one would expect of a guardian of the Islamic Revolution, one whose uniform's insignia comprised a raised arm holding a Kalashnikov rifle (the same logo that Hezbollah, a creation of the Revolutionary Guards, uses). I wondered what he wanted.

"Where did you get that cell phone?" he asked. "Is it a Motorola?"

"Yes, it's a Motorola, and I got it in New York."

"New York? Wow." He looked at me, as if trying to comprehend what a bearded Iranian who visits the president's office was doing in New York. "Tell me," he continued, "is it any good? Does it give antenna [Farsi for 'work well'] in Iran? It's very beautiful."

"Yes, it gives good antenna," I replied. "No problems at all. I think you can buy them here too."

"Yeah, I think I've seen them in the shopwindows, but I don't know anything about Motorolas."

"They're pretty good, very popular in the United States."

"Really?"

"Yes." I turned to leave.

"Thanks," the Guard said. "Have a good day."

"You too." I left his little room and continued walking toward the main entrance to the presidential compound. I turned on my cell phone and stared at it, waiting for it to "give antenna." I noticed from the corner of my eye various pedestrians heading in the direction I had come from, all of them staring at me, I felt. Was it the beard, the suit, and the phone? *"Haj-Agha!"* I heard a squeaky woman's voice and looked up. *"Haj-Agha,* is this the president's office?" She was enveloped in a black chador and holding it tightly with one hand by her mouth, but I could see that she was quite old. She had an accent, provincial, and I noticed that her chador was stained.

"Yes," I said to her. "Straight ahead, keep going."

"Is he there?" she asked. "I'm going to see the president." She sounded determined and as if she wanted to give him an earful.

"I think so," I replied.

"Thanks very much," she said. She continued walking, her chador flapping with every step. I looked back and watched her for a moment. She walked past the cell phone Guard and disappeared into the first building I had visited earlier. I turned and walked out of the compound, wondering if she would be successful in her quest to deliver a message to her president, a president who had styled himself as a man of the people: a people represented by her, and by those who wear plastic slippers indoors.

———————

Ahmadinejad's "man of the people" image owes as much to his conservative, religious upbringing and his own philosophies as it does to his political mentor, the shadowy Mojtaba Hashemi-Samareh. Officially the "senior adviser to the president," Hashemi-Samareh acts more as a cross between Iran's Karl Rove and a president's chief of staff, although his secretive nature would put Rove to shame. Clearly a ripe subject for an investigative report, or at least an in-depth profile, given that he accompanies the president on every trip and is a disciple of Ayatollah Mohammad Taghi Mesbah-Yazdi (far and away the most hard-line of any cleric in Shia Islam and the dean of the Imam Khomeini Education and Research Institute in Qom), who publishes the archconservative weekly, *Parto-Sokhan*, Hashemi-Samareh has avoided the media glare mostly due to the fact that investigative reporting in Iran can sometimes lead to the curious disappearance of the reporter, particularly if the subject of an investigative report is an unwilling subject, has strong ties to the Revolutionary Guard Corps and to the intelligence services, and is known to have particularly frightening ideas about what comprises an ideal Islamic society. Check all three for Mr. Hashemi-Samareh. Like the president a former member of the Revolutionary Guards, he is believed to have served with Ahmadinejad during the Iran-Iraq war, although it seems impossible to verify this simple fact. It has also been said that Hashemi-Samareh is married to Ahmadinejad's wife's sister, although this too has oddly never been confirmed, or even brought up by the media. What is known is that he is a constant presence at the president's side, in every cabinet meeting and during midday prayers at the office (and on every occasion when I met or saw Ahmadinejad in New York).

Hashemi-Samareh is a slight man, not unlike Ahmadinejad in stature, and has a disarmingly wide smile, almost a Cheshire (and not very Persian) cat grin that, given what is known about him, can send shivers down one's spine. In the early 1990s, when he was sponsored by Ayatollah Mesbah-Yazdi for and quickly appointed to a critical job, director of placements, at the Foreign Ministry, he indeed sent shivers down the spines of not a few diplomats who were subjected to his tests for loyalty and Islamic virtue before they could secure a coveted overseas post. He even published a pamphlet at the Foreign Ministry, one that no one seems to have a copy of but every diplomat swears existed, titled "The Psychology of the Infidels," which could have been subtitled "Forget Everything You Think You Know About How to Be an

Exemplary Diplomat." (A colleague, Saeed Jalili, who rose rapidly through the ranks after Ahmadinejad was elected, published a book titled *The Foreign Policy of the Prophet [PBUH],** presumably also intended as a field guide for Iran's budding diplomats.)

In his pamphlet Hashemi-Samareh apparently laid out the rules for Iranian diplomats' dealings with foreigners overseas, the presumption being that every person an Iranian diplomat comes into contact with is a spy, and included sartorial advice that could have served as a warning of presidential shabbiness to come. In the antithesis of common notions of diplomatic style and sophistication, Hashemi-Samareh believed that Iranian diplomats' trousers could not sport sharp creases, for if they did, it was surely a sign that the diplomats were neglecting their thrice-daily obligatory prayers, which comprise repetitive standing, kneeling, and bowing gestures. For the same reason, he held that Iranian diplomats with polished, lace-up shoes (practically part of the global uniform of diplomacy) could not be counted upon as loyal to the Islamic Revolution, whereas loafers with a heavy crease on the heel, evidence that they've been used as male versions of mules for easy slipping on and off, should be preferred footwear. He didn't need to remind his fellow foreign service officers that in Iran loafers such as he described, particularly if the heel was always left pushed down, were the choice of every laat, jahel, and dahati, the underclass of society.

Hashemi-Samareh hadn't needed to worry about neckties by the time he achieved his position of power at the Foreign Ministry: Ayatollah Khomeini had, early on, decreed that the wearing of them was not only a sign of "West-toxification," *gharb-zadegi,* one of the catchwords of the early years of the revolution, but even a nod to Christianity, for, viewed with an artistic eye, the tie could be said to make the sign of the cross. Naturally, no one in any position of power wished to be thought of as either West-toxified or, worse, nodding to Christ, so neckties rapidly disappeared from men's wardrobes, or at least those of

*Pious Muslims always include the phrase "Peace Be Upon Him" or its abbreviation when writing the name of the prophet (though not necessarily when speaking his name).

men who cared about their jobs. It is a little strange to now see film of
Khomeini and his entourage in Paris plotting the Shah's downfall, or
photos and film of the very early days after the Shah's ouster: other
than the clerics who flocked to his side, some of Khomeini's closest advisers wore ties and in some cases were clean shaven. Mehdi Bazargan,
the first prime minister of the interim government, and Sadeq Ghotbzadeh, foreign minister for the first six months of the hostage crisis,
easily come to mind. Of course Bazargan was quickly shunted aside,
and Ghotbzadeh jailed and later executed for plotting against the revolution, though presumably not for wearing a tie. But Khomeini, or
whoever brought the issue of ties to his attention—and given his apparent early disinterest in the matter, it is unlikely that he gave it much
thought until it was brought to his attention for an opinion—understood that eliminating them from the government wardrobe would
make a unique impression on the world: that Iran wouldn't play by
Western rules.

Indeed, Iran still is the only country in the world whose officials,
including all of its diplomats abroad, are always seen tieless. True, Fi-
del Castro often wore fatigues, and a few other Third World leaders
wear national costumes or appear with open-necked shirts, but the government cadres are always seen in suits and ties. To the Third World
"street," and particularly the Muslim Third World, where Khomeini
wished to have the most influence, even encouraging new Islamic revo-
lutions, the effect was important. First, the message that "real Muslims
don't wear ties" resonated in places where most men, other than the
rich, Westernized, and intellectual classes, didn't wear ties (including in
Iran), and, second, the image projected by Iran, that the country was
independent of the norms and standards of international behavior
(norms that Khomeini believed were created and imposed by the West),
was proof of liberation from the shackles of colonialism. The servants
would no longer emulate, much less listen to, their former masters.
It would be hard to prove, but when I sat at the UN General Assembly in 2006 as the improbable translator for Ahmadinejad's upcoming

speech, only a few feet away from Bolivia's Evo Morales, who was making his first appearance in New York since his election as president and who was wearing a native leather jacket and tieless white shirt, I couldn't help but think that Iran's dismissal of diplomatic etiquette had had some effect on what Third World leaders today thought of as appropriate attire for addressing the entire world.

The sartorial aspects of Hashemi-Samareh's "Psychology of the Infidels" may have become obsolete during the reformist president Khatami's administration, which ushered in an era of relative elegance among government officials to match Khatami's own preference for bespoke garments (though stopping well short of rehabilitating the necktie), but the underlying philosophy became all too apparent in the wake of Ahmadinejad's election. Among his first duties as president, in an act that betrayed Hashemi-Samareh's hand (for Ahmadinejad had no experience in foreign affairs and had probably never even left the country[6]), was the wholesale removal of virtually the entire corps of ambassadors based in the West: an elite group of reform-minded diplomats who not only didn't seem to think the West was all bad all the time but even polished their brogues and pressed their European-made suits from time to time.

Hashemi-Samareh's influence in international affairs became even more apparent when it was he (and not the new ambassador to Paris, whom he undoubtedly had a hand in choosing) who flew to Paris in September 2006 to meet with President Jacques Chirac and deliver a private message from Ahmadinejad. Very shortly afterward, he was appointed deputy interior minister for political affairs, a post he would assume along with his full-time duties as senior adviser. To opponents of Ahmadinejad, and more particularly opponents of Ayatollah Mesbah-Yazdi, it became alarmingly clear that October why Hashemi-Samareh had chosen to take the somewhat higher-profile position in government; as part of his duties he was also appointed head of the election commission, supervisor of the poll for the Assembly of Experts (the body that oversees the work of the Supreme Leader)—an

election where Mesbah-Yazdi and his allies hoped to gain ground
against the more moderate clerics. To his credit, I suppose, and to the
credit of the election process, Hashemi-Samareh must not have inter-
fered with the vote count: his mentor Mesbah-Yazdi suffered a humiliating sixth-place finish in the Tehran municipality (barely squeezing
into his seat in the Assembly), and his and Ahmadinejad's allies generally fared far worse than expected, perhaps contributing to Hashemi-
Samareh's reasons for resigning his post a few months later, in the
summer of 2007, ostensibly to spend *less* time with his family while his
duties as top presidential adviser became all-encompassing, as he
claimed, and allowed him not a waking moment to ponder such pedestrian issues as poll supervision. Persian cats, it appears, when they come
together once in a while, find a way to trim the whiskers of even the
laat cats.

THE AYATOLLAH
HAS A COLD

The Supreme Leader of the Islamic *Revolution*, not Republic, is his official title, but in Iran he is known simply as *Rahbar*, or "Leader." The title betrays two conflicting sides of the national character (plus an emphatic statement that Iran is forever a revolutionary state). Iranians have traditionally, at least in the last few centuries, despised their leaders no matter their character or their deeds, been quick to turn on and mock them, but at the same time yearned for strong leadership and someone to look up to.

Ayatollah Ruhollah Khomeini, the founder of the Islamic Republic and the leader of its revolution, was arguably the first genuinely popular leader in recent Iranian history (except for the democratically elected prime minister Mohammad Mossadeq, whose premiership was short-lived, courtesy of the CIA[1]), but he recognized better than most that the Iranian habit of souring on the subjects of their hero worship meant his dream of a long-lived Islamic state could easily evaporate on the whims of an unruly populace. His concept of *velayat-e-faqih*—"guardianship of the jurist" or "rule of the jurisprudent," depending on interpretation—which he revealed in a published work in 1970 from his exile in Najaf, Iraq, had Shia Islam as its rationale and basis. But apart from the implication that he would be the *faqih*, which also means "leader," it conveniently also envisioned a leadership removed enough from public scrutiny (partly owing to its religious credentials but also because of its inherent aloofness from day-to-day political considerations) that it would not suffer the wrath of the people, should they become wrathful, as other leaders traditionally had. Although some Shia clerics rejected the concept entirely and others have disputed the extent to which the faqih can exercise power—for example, whether he should be limited to purely Islamic questions and issues, or whether he is a "ruler" or "guardian"—it was nonetheless enshrined in the Islamic Republic's constitution after the revolution.

Khomeini, as father of the revolution and someone who was elevated (some argue inappropriately) to Imam, an honorific that has seldom been applied to any Grand Ayatollah, as it implies sainthood of the sort that is the basis of Shia Islam with its twelve Imams, didn't need to worry about his authority and popular support while he was alive, but he was careful to ensure that his successors, who could not be guaranteed to enjoy the same privileges, would have an absolute authority that would entrench the Islamic Republic for generations to come. Today, the *valih-e-faqih*, "Supreme Leader," is Ayatollah Ali Khamenei, the similarity of his name to his predecessor's entirely coincidental but guaranteed, as it has over the years, to confuse Westerners. He has, in the years since Khomeini's death elevated him to the post, carefully balanced his use of what is arguably unlimited power with the cultivation of a public perception that the elected presidents of the republic are responsible for the ordinary welfare and woes of the people, and their general dissatisfaction, if they have any, with their government. It's a difficult balancing act, one that he plays with enormous skill, for when the people are too happy, as they perhaps were in the wake of the initially extremely popular election of President Mohammad Khatami, he has to ensure that credit for that happiness doesn't rest entirely with the elected officials; otherwise his very role might come into question.

Similarly, a certain amount of dissatisfaction, whether from the left or the right, bodes well for his authority as Iran's "Guide," someone who can lead the nation through turbulent times. It speaks volumes about both Iranians' penchant for dislike of the leaders they elect and the Supreme Leader's deft manipulation of the political system that Iranians' disapproval of Khatami's inability to deliver on his promise of reform was blamed not on Khamenei directly, although Khatami and his allies implied as much at every opportunity and most Iranians understood the limits of the president's power, but on *Khatami's* unwillingness to stand up to conservatives and Khamenei, who by the very nature of his job supported the conservative agenda as often as, if not more often than, the president's. Blaming the weakness of their president rather than the strength of the Supreme Leader, then, stands in contrast to Khatami's successor's term, when those Iranians who quickly became unhappy with the state of affairs under President Ahmadinejad blamed him for incompetence and pigheadedness rather than Khamenei for his apparent inability or unwillingness to completely rein him in. The Supreme Leader, it seems, can never lose.

———————

When I arrived in Tehran in January 2007, the world's capital of rumors was abuzz with the mother of all rumors: that the Supreme Leader was either dying or already dead. The elections for the Assembly of Experts, the body that chooses and theoretically supervises the Supreme Leader, were over in December, and moderate clerics had, contrary to some expectations, done extremely well, but there was still some uncertainty as to whom they would choose to succeed Khamenei, who was, after all, a prostate cancer survivor who at sixty-eight looked even older than his years. Many people, even those with close connections to the highest levels of government, spoke in the inimitable Persian way of treating almost any rumor, no, *every* rumor, as fact until it is proven otherwise, and as if Khamenei's imminent demise if not his death were very real. Unlike Cuba, say, where the president's health is a state secret, Iran has no such prohibitions, but it is widely assumed that those in the know would keep the Supreme Leader's passing quiet, particularly at times of sensitive security for the nation, until a succession had been finalized. What led to the rumors were the facts that Khamenei hadn't been seen in public for some weeks, hadn't appeared as he traditionally does at celebrations for the important Muslim holiday of Eid al-Adha (marking the end of the hajj and falling on the last day of the year in 2006), and had apparently been taken to the hospital at some point in late December.

It's impossible to know if the rumor was started in Iran or by hopeful exiles abroad, but Michael Ledeen of the American Enterprise Institute, a notorious neocon, perhaps having picked up some Persian traits of his own through his obsession with all things Iranian, or actually all things Iranian having to do with regime change, declared it as a fact on his Web site and viewed it, as almost every Iranian did, as one of the momentous occasions in the brief history of Iran's Islamic Republic.[2] Ledeen, famous for advocating regime change in Iran *before* Iraq, and an archenemy of the Iranian clerics since 1979, could hardly contain his glee, perhaps believing that a weak Iran temporarily without a Supreme Leader might be ripe for some "shock and awe" courtesy of the Pentagon. For days afterward, bloggers, both in Iran and internationally, competed with each other to either confirm or deny the rumor, but what seemed clear, even to those who denied Khamenei's death, was that business was not as usual where the valih-e-faqih was concerned.

Inside Iran, the question quickly stopped being whether he was dead or not and became who his natural successor was. It was assumed that Ayatollah Ali Akbar Hashemi Rafsanjani, chairman of the Expediency Council (a body that is technically above the president and supervises his work), newly reelected to the Assembly of Experts along with many of his allies, and the de facto number two in the hierarchy of the Islamic Republic, would once again, as he did when Khomeini died in 1989, play kingmaker rather than king. Rafsanjani, from the pistachio-producing town of Rafsanjan, had been one of Khomeini's closest aides and advisers, almost always seen quietly by his side, but his public profile had risen when he became president in 1989 and served two terms until Khatami's election in 1997. Rafsanjani's wealth (and his penchant for accumulating more of it), along with his sons' extensive business dealings and his notoriety overseas (an Argentine judge has issued an arrest warrant for him for his alleged role in the bombing of Buenos Aires's Jewish Center in 1994), many argued, would lead him not to seek the Supreme Leader's office but rather to use his influence and power to put someone else, considerably weaker than himself, in the job.

There was also the unspoken issue of Rafsanjani's white turban: he was not a *Seyyed*, a direct descendant of the Prophet Mohammad who is entitled to wear a black turban, and in the Shia tradition of placing great importance on bloodline in the legitimacy of rule, it might be difficult, at least for some, to accept a non-Seyyed as their Supreme Guide. Seyyed Mohammad Khatami, however, black-turbaned and with the blood of Mohammad coursing through his veins, was a name that kept surfacing as a likely choice. There was, of course, the question of his religious credentials, for even though he was a Seyyed, he was only a *Hojjatoleslam*, a rank below Ayatollah, and the Supreme Leader is supposed to be a *marja-e-taghlid*, or "source of emulation," the Persian definition of a *Grand* Ayatollah. But that hadn't stopped Khamenei from becoming the Supreme Leader in 1989; he was overnight promoted to Ayatollah (promotion to Ayatollah happens by consensus among other Ayatollahs), and soon thereafter was being referred to as "Grand." Those who spoke of Khatami as potential Supreme Leader were genuinely excited by the prospect, and those who dismissed him as a candidate felt he lacked the cunning required to pull off such a feat (in both cases being complimentary to Khatami, for the cunningness of mullahs—or *akhound*, as they are known in Farsi—is considered both legendary and their fundamental character flaw).

———————

As the days wore on with still no public sign of Khamenei, the rumors gathered steam, forcing Iranian diplomats abroad to deny them without offering proof that their Supreme Guide was still giving them guidance. The Supreme Leader's office was mute on the subject, although it is not known to issue press releases or have much of a public face, even in extraordinary times. Maintaining the image of the Supreme Leader as "guide," rather than executive, is part and parcel of the office's job. The Supreme Leader gives no press conferences, never grants interviews, and speaks only at special gatherings, such as an occasional Friday prayer or commemoration ceremonies of one sort or another. The Leader meets with foreign dignitaries (almost exclusively Muslim, with few exceptions) but limits any televised and public words to generalities, such as Iran's support for the country (or entity, in the case of Hamas and Hezbollah) whose emissary he's meeting, Iran's peaceful and Islamic nature, and Iran's eagerness to expand trade and contacts with the friendly country in question. As such, he pointedly does not meet with representatives of Western powers. The Leader does not travel overseas; if anyone worthy wishes to see him, that person must travel to Iran. (Khamenei has been outside Iran, although not as Supreme Leader: during his presidency in the 1980s he even visited New York to attend the UN General Assembly.) He does not travel to Mecca to perform the hajj; having been a cleric his entire adult life, he became a hajji many times over prior to assuming the mantle of Rahbar. But the Supreme Leader is supreme not just because of his religious credentials in an Islamic republic; he's supreme because his position is protected by the nation's most powerful military force, and it's not the army.

———————————

Sepah-e Pasdaran-e Enghlab-e Eslami, or "Guardians of the Islamic Revolution Corps" (now that doesn't sound so bad, does it?), better known as the Revolutionary Guards in the West and, naturally, reporting directly to the Supreme Leader of the Islamic Revolution, are the military force responsible for protecting the velayat-e-faqih and, by extension, the valih-e-faqih. Ayatollah Ruhollah Khomeini created the militia very soon after assuming power in 1979: he had witnessed the supposedly mighty U.S.-equipped army of the Shah, including his much-feared and supposedly elite Imperial Guard unit, the "Immortals," retreat to their barracks and allow his revolution victory with hardly a fight, and he realized that a regular army could not be trusted to protect a regime. In a nation that relied (and still relies) on conscription to man its army, Khomeini wanted an all-volunteer militia that would be fiercely loyal to the regime that created it, and the Pasdaran were born. Pasdaran were recruited from religious and working-class neighborhoods, the base of the Islamic Republic's support, and although initially they were a purely defensive force, defending even the nation's Islamic liquor prohibition, much to the consternation of many an imbibing Iranian, the Iran-Iraq war gave them the opportunity to show their mettle. The Guards fought fiercely, the youthful Basij units their kamikazes, and their strength grew as a parallel force on par with the regular army.

Over time the Guards created their own air force and navy, and of course their foreign expeditionary force, the now famous but quite small Qods (Jerusalem) Force, which the United States accuses of everything from supplying Hezbollah to providing arms to Iraqi insurgents. But the Guards aren't only concerned with security and all things military; they're also concerned with what ultimately assures loyalty to a system beyond pure faith: money. The Supreme Leader has given them much control over the economy of the country, and they willingly exercise it. Revolutionary Guards are involved in everything from oil, such as contracts for drilling and exploration, to the import-export market. It is, I am told time and time again whenever I'm in Iran, virtually impossible to do any kind of large-scale business deal in Iran without the involvement of the Sepah, as they are generally referred to by Iranians. A friend who was working with a European oil equipment company and who had, in 2007 when I was in Tehran, been running around meeting with various officials to try to secure a government contract had his partner meet with representatives of the Sepah, who seemed very interested in getting involved in any deal. A few days later, however, the partner was arrested by the very same Revolutionary Guards, with no real reason given, but presumably as a signal that any deal would from now on *exclude* him and my friend. (The partner was quickly released on bail, and is unlikely to hear from the Sepah again.)

With the very best of the military equipment that Iran possesses in their arsenal (including the mid- and long-range missiles that the army does not possess), with powerful interests in the economy, and with unrivaled career opportunities (virtually the entire top echelon of the Iranian political structure, nonclerical, is filled with former Revolutionary Guards, who seem in this respect to function almost as the Iranian version of the École Nationale), the Sepah-e Pasdaran have every incentive to maintain the political system of their nation, the velayat-e-faqih, at all costs, which of course by definition requires a valih-e-faqih: the Supreme Leader.

The Supreme Leader theoretically wields the kind of political power that would be the envy of any pope (well, perhaps with the exception of the Borgia popes Callistus and Alexander). The Sepah report directly to him, but he is also commander in chief of the regular armed forces. He also has direct responsibility for foreign policy, which cannot be conducted without his direct involvement and approval (he even has his own private foreign policy team, which includes two former foreign ministers), but although he is smart enough to stay above the fray of domestic politics, leaving it to the parliament, the judiciary (which he also directly controls), and the president, he can at any time of his choosing inject himself into the process and "correct" a flawed policy or decision. He also, importantly as far as a nervous West is concerned, controls Iran's nuclear program, as an issue of national security, and has the final say on all matters relating to it. But perhaps the greatest perk of his office, one that would certainly be the envy of the Borgias, is that he can, under the authority of no less a being than God, lie. (Presidents Nixon, Clinton, and Bush, to name just a few, might have wished they were born Shia.)

Shia Islam, which is by its nature political, allows for *taghiyeh*, or "dissimulation," which was viewed as essential in the early days of the split from mainstream Sunni Islam, to protect a minority who were in very real danger of losing their lives as heretics. Although taghiyeh is also accepted by some Sunnis in its strict interpretation, and is theoretically supposed to be lying only for the purpose of concealing one's religion to avoid death, as with other concepts Shia and Iranian (and one cannot separate the two) there is some latitude in its interpretation. A Grand Ayatollah can rule on its permissibility, and the Supreme Leader of Iran is, conveniently, a Grand Ayatollah. Is it to protect one's own individual life, or is it, if you are a religious leader, to protect your larger Shia community from demise? If it is the latter, then the Ayatollah may lie in virtually any instance and claim taghiyeh if and when necessary. He hasn't done so as yet (at least not to anyone's knowledge), and neither did Ayatollah Khomeini, but it must give great comfort to know that one can, and that the explanation will be accepted by one's people.

Still, despite all the political power the Supreme Leader wields, and

despite his religious authority as one among a handful of senior Ayatollahs in Shia Islam, he is decidedly not infallible in the eyes of pious
Shias who choose, as they are quite free to, their very own *marja-e-taghlid*, or "source of emulation," from among those Ayatollahs. In 1979,
when the word "Ayatollah" entered our dictionaries, Khomeini, the
first Supreme Leader of the Islamic Revolution, was viewed by many
(if not most) Shias as a well-established marja whose thoughts, at least
in the religious realm, carried great weight, if not total infallibility.
(His photos still adorn many a Hezbollah supporter's home and office
in Beirut.) If the clerical hierarchy of Shia Islam were more like that of
the Catholic Church, similar though it is in some respects, Khomeini
would have undoubtedly been elected the Shia pope. That cannot be
said of Ali Khamenei, and furthermore it is unlikely to be true of the
next or future Supreme Leader either. The Assembly of Experts, which
is charged with electing the Supreme Leader (it also has the power to
impeach, if necessary), is a body whose members are elected by the regular citizens of Iran (unlike the appointed College of Cardinals), and
the members are more often concerned with who can most effectively
preserve the clerics' domination of Iranian politics and power than
with whoever has the highest religious authority. It is a sensitive and intricate balancing act, for the religious credentials must certainly be such
that the Revolutionary Guards and other religiously minded Iranians
will accept his Islamic "guidance," but he must also ensure that the
Guards' loyalty to the office remains, as the Guards' power grows with
every new missile and every new oil contract, both religious *and* political. It is easy to understand why so many Iranians were captivated by
the question of who that person might be.

In a country where there are dozens of daily newspapers and weekly
periodicals, only some of which are state controlled, news of the
Supreme Leader was scarce in the winter of 2007. It is an unwritten

rule of Iranian public discourse that no one is above criticism except the Supreme Leader and the velayat-e-faqih, and since any mention of the Supreme Leader that isn't completely innocuous can be viewed as critique if the judiciary so decides, no one in the media wished to risk arrest or closure of a paper by mentioning the rumors of his impending or actual death. (Television and radio, which are state owned, had no news of him to report either.) Which of course only fueled those rumors further, to the point where finally Ayatollah Khamenei was forced to publicly issue a statement denying his own death. "Enemies of the Islamic system," he said, "fabricated various rumors about death and health to demoralize the Iranian nation." (Some viewed the statement, along with photos of a visibly weak Leader, as a less-than-ringing endorsement of his health.) He was right about a demoralized nation, but he got the reason wrong, if he even believed it himself (since he can't read about his own person in the papers, it is up to his aides to tell him of such rumors if they believe they are getting out of hand). No one I spoke to, not even ardent supporters of velayat-e-faqih, seemed particularly upset by the rumors, but they were all quite demoralized by UN sanctions, the state of the economy, and the possibility of war with the United States, all of which was blamed on the government of Mahmoud Ahmadinejad. Perhaps it is just that the Supreme Leader does the job of deflecting discontent and blame away from his office so well that the idea of his passing has impact mostly, or only, to the extent that the people wonder if his successor will utilize more or less of his power in setting the government straight.

The Supreme Leader and his predecessor, Ayatollah Khomeini, in separate photos but always side by side, stare down from the walls of every government office and even some businesses. Photos of the president, whoever he is at any given time, are rarely seen anywhere. Unlike in dictatorships elsewhere, the Supreme Leader's likeness need not be dis-

played in the private sector and often isn't; as such, if you're looking at
Khomeini and Khamenei, you are probably somewhere in velayat-e-
faqih territory.

The car-hire office in the neighborhood where I stay is no exception. I found myself there, in the winter of the "big" rumor and continuing rumors of war, looking to hire a car to take me to Qom, the
religious capital of Iran. There are virtually no self-drive rental cars in
Iran; otherwise I would have taken great pleasure in matching my New
York City driving skills against Tehran's impossible drivers', although I
would have undoubtedly ended up a shivering wreck cowering by the
side of the road, too afraid to force my way into a lane of an endless
stream of speeding bumper-to-bumper cars. Without credit cards (U.S.
sanctions make them impossible to administer by Iranian banks) the
car-rental business is probably untenable, but I suspect that the absence
of an Iranian version of Hertz has more to do with Iranian logic than
with credit cards. A logic that dictates that if you need a car, then you
buy one or borrow one from friends or family; if you can't afford it and
no friends or family will lend you one, then why should a rental business trust you with theirs? At any rate, renting a car would be prohib-
itively expensive in a country where there are plenty of underemployed
people willing to give you a ride for a pittance, let alone the thousands
of licensed cabs and car service companies for whom no trip, however
long, is too daunting.

It was mid-afternoon at the car-hire office and what I thought
would be a quiet time. I actually needed the car for the following morning, but I thought a long trip might require some advance notice. The
receptionist was standing, busy answering the two phones on her desk
plus her cell phone, which she had to fish out of her handbag every few
minutes, so I waited and stared at the Ayatollahs. I stared not because
I was fascinated by their photos, the same photos that greet you at
Mehrabad Airport and all over town, but because I didn't want to stare
at *her*. She was wearing a black hijab, every single strand of hair tucked
away out of sight, and an ankle-length black outfit cut far more styl-

ishly, probably by herself, than the shapeless ones I'd seen on the streets outside. Her pale face, bright pink lipstick, and heavily mascaraed eyes under perfectly plucked eyebrows contrasted sharply with the black cloth enveloping her, as well as with the photos of the bearded men I was looking at. She was probably no more than twenty-two—tall, thin, and with long slender fingers that held the two phone receivers. She was, dare I say it, very sexy. When she hung up the phones, she sat down and looked at me inquisitively. "Yes?" she said.

"I need a car to take me to Qom tomorrow. A good car."[3]

"Okay," she said. "Where do you want to be picked up?"

"Just up the street, number 95. Or I can come here."

She studied me for a few seconds. "I'll get you someone *nice*," she said. "Mr. Arab. He drives a Peugeot. Do you want to meet him now?" I realized then that she was the receptionist *and* the dispatcher.

"Sure," I replied.

"Then have a seat and I'll get him." She pushed her chair back and leaned over a wooden partition. "Mr. Arab!" she shouted. "Come to the front!"

She turned back to answer the ringing phones. I waited patiently while she answered phones, plugged her cell phone charger into the wall, and occasionally shouted an order to one of the drivers on the other side of the partition. She glanced at me from time to time, but I tried to avoid eye contact, looking up instead at the photos of the Supreme Guides. "Mr. Arab!" she shouted whenever her eyes fell on me. "Where is he?" she finally said to a driver who stepped into the reception area. He shrugged his shoulders, quietly said he didn't know, and picked up one of the chits she had signed and walked outside to the street. "Where is Mr. Arab?" she yelled angrily across the partition.

"He's praying," a disembodied voice answered meekly.

"Praying?" snorted the receptionist derisively, standing up. "Mr. Arab!" she yelled again. "Come on, even the *akhound-ha* [mullahs] don't pray *that* long!" She turned to me. "I'm sorry," she said. "He'll be out in a minute, I'm sure."

A few minutes later Mr. Arab showed up, apologetic and humble. "This is Mr. Arab," said the dispatcher huffily. "I told the gentleman that you were *nice*," she said to him with a tiny hint of sarcasm. She went back to her phones while I arranged an early morning pickup with the driver, a middle-aged man with a quiet demeanor who assured me that he would be on time, perhaps sensing that I had my doubts about someone who had made me wait and had ignored the dispatcher's frequent shouts. He gave me his cell phone number, just in case, he said, and I walked out, muttering a goodbye to the young woman, who nodded vigorously without looking up at me. This one, I thought as I watched her barking out orders to the much older men through the glass pane, would probably not be amused by reading *Lolita*. In Tehran, or otherwise.

The following morning Mr. Arab was on time. We were to pick up a friend who was going to come with me to Qom, and I tried to make small talk in the heavy Tehran traffic. Small talk has a way of ending up with politics in Iran, and Mr. Arab wasted no time in getting to the subject, starting with the economy and finishing by declaring that Ahmadinejad was ineffective in his dealings with foreigners, which only contributed to the danger of war and the bad state of the economy. Rafsanjani, in his mind, would have been much better. "You see," he said, "Hashemi [as Rafsanjani is referred to in Iran] cuts throats with cotton." He turned and looked at me. "With *cotton*! So that even the victim doesn't know his throat's been cut!" I laughed, nodding my head in agreement. "There wouldn't be any talk of war with Hashemi," he continued, then paused for a moment. "With *cotton*," he repeated with obvious admiration. For a while after we picked up my friend, J. I'll call him, Mr. Arab fell silent. He listened to our conversation and glanced in the rearview mirror, trying, I believe, to figure us out. J. and I of course talked politics, and from the conversation it must have been clear to Mr. Arab that J. was closely connected to one of the hard-line conservative Ayatollahs in Qom. What he couldn't tell was that J. is actually quite liberal himself, for, although religious, he has no patience for intolerance and couldn't care less about imposing Islamic values on anyone. Talk turned to war, and J. was adamant that the United States would never attack Iran. This, apparently, was the cue that Mr. Arab was waiting for.

"Never," he said, glancing in his mirror.

"You don't think so, huh?" I asked.

"They wouldn't dare!" he replied, perhaps emboldened by J.'s nods. "No matter what anyone thinks of the government, the United States knows that if it attacks, everyone will defend Iran."

"Yes," said J. "It would be madness."

"If America attacks," continued Mr. Arab, "every Iranian will take up arms and fight to the death." He was getting excited. "I will take up arms," he declared. "I'm almost sixty, but I'll definitely fight."

"Everyone will," said J., egging him on.

"Yes! I'll fight, my children will fight, the old men will fight. America isn't stupid."

"I understand," I said. "But . . ."

"You'll fight," said Mr. Arab, interrupting me. "Everyone!"

"But . . ." I started again.

"What do they think, the Americans? I'll take up arms and fight them to the last breath," he exclaimed with braggadocio, a true Iranian art if there ever was one, and one that this taxi driver, perhaps mindful of his bearded passengers, was employing skillfully. Boastful exaggeration, or *gholov*, is almost a national trait in a people that has long suffered from deep superiority/inferiority complexes. It alternates and contrasts nicely with the other great national trait, ta'arouf, the exaggerated politesse, modesty, and self-deprecation that Iranians seem to be born with the use of. It is why some fights in Iran will go very quickly from two parties declaring emphatically that they have had sex with the other's mother *and* sister to both sides' insistence that they are the other's obedient servant, or worse.

"*Baleh!*" said J., "yes!" taking a long drag of one of the many cigarettes he had been chain-smoking since he got in the car. The driver momentarily turned around and looked at us. We were passing the heavily fortified Parchin military complex outside of Tehran, a munitions site that is suspected by the West as secretly developing nuclear weaponry. I wondered what Mr. Arab made of us, two bearded men on their way to Qom in the back of his car, one with close connections to the center of religious power. We hadn't broached the subject of the Supreme Leader's health yet, but I felt it was time and I'd had enough of war talk. I wanted to talk to J. about it anyway, and see what he thought of all the rumors now that it was certain that Khamenei was not dead.

"What about the Rahbar?" I asked him. "Do you think he's on his last legs?"

"Na baba," interrupted Mr. Arab, glancing at me in his mirror. "All this talk . . . He's not young, of course." J. nodded, fumbling for another cigarette.

"So you think he's fine?" I asked.

"Sure," said Mr. Arab, with a dismissive wave of the hand. "He just has a cold."

"Yes," repeated J., holding a lighter to the cigarette between his lips. "It happens. The Ayatollah has a cold."

IF IT'S TUESDAY, THIS
MUST BE QOM

On an insufferably hot August afternoon in Qom, the desert town a couple of hours south of Tehran and a great center of Shia learning, I was sitting on the Persian-carpeted floor of the living room of a decrepit old house within a walled garden, a yard really, staring at the stained sheet hung from a rail that served as the summer door while the women—covered head to toe in the cloth known as the chador— served hot tea to the men and an air conditioner, or *cooler*, as the water-operated ones are known in Iran, struggled noisily to make the room bearable. Typical of old homes, nowadays almost exclusively working-class if in poorer neighborhoods (which this was not), the small pond in the yard outside was surrounded by clotheslines, an illegal satellite dish, and an outhouse.[1] Yes, a still-functioning outhouse, and one that reminded me of my grandfather's house in Tehran, where the outhouse stood its ground (and was used by the occupants) long after a Western toilet was installed inside for the benefit of the offspring visiting from abroad.

The owner of the house, a fifty-something man with a slow, nasal twang, missing his front teeth, and extraordinarily polite (other than when he ordered his wife or daughter to bring more tea or his twelve-year-old son to run out and buy some cold drinks), seemingly had nothing to do all day but hang out and play host to anyone who bothered to drop by. I had never met any of the residents of this house: I had come knocking through an introduction, and my back was self-consciously stiff.

A well-built young man, clean shaven and with gelled hair, entered the room in soccer gear and was introduced as the son-in-law; he sat down quietly and stared at me with a furrowed brow as if I had just arrived from Mars. His young bride, the daughter of the house, followed him in, said a quiet hello, and sat down on the floor next to him, also staring, but averting her eyes whenever I glanced in her direction. She switched on the old television set perched on a low table and tuned the channel to PMC, the Persian Music Channel, a satellite station beamed in from Dubai and received illegally by just about every household in Iran. PMC features nothing but Iranian pop music videos from Los Angeles, and the young woman pulled her chador tight across her cheeks as she watched other young Iranian men and women, sans chadors or scarves, sexily cavorting across the Southern California desert in a vintage American convertible.

No one but me in this house seemed terribly interested in the nuclear crisis with the West that was all the news in Europe and back home in the States, and had been a major topic of conversation in middle-class Tehran homes since I had arrived a few days before President Ahmadinejad's inauguration in 2005. Iran had just angrily rejected a European proposal to end the nuclear stalemate and was heading rapidly toward a major confrontation over its plans to restart the uranium fuel cycle, something the United States claimed would lead to nuclear-armed Ayatollahs, perhaps as frightening an image as can be planted, post-9/11, in the minds of ordinary Americans. Ahmadinejad's new hard-line government, perhaps picking up on a cue from President Bush's own lexicon, seemed to be saying, in so many words, "Bring it on" to the entire world. But in this household, there was little concern with the possibility of armed conflict. A middle-class family, religious but educated and wise to the ways of the world, if only through their television screen, they were far more concerned with the more mundane aspects of life, even though they stubbornly continued to live in a house that should have long ago given way to a modern apartment building, with perhaps a nice penthouse for them, the owners of the land underneath.

———————

A noise from the yard signaled the arrival of other guests; an older man and his toothless young companion carrying a heavily crumpled plastic bag pushed aside the sheet and entered the room. Grateful that I wasn't to be the sole source of amusement, I stood up as introductions were made and as the young daughter quickly fled to the safety of other rooms where strange, meaning nonfamilial, men are not allowed. The men shuffled in, the younger one saying his hellos and nodding while the older man gestured, apologizing for the lack of vocal cords, I understood. Although they had been removed recently in an operation, our host told me, the man seemed quite nonchalant about it and even accepted a cigarette proffered by his companion. He sat down on the carpet, lit his cigarette, and began to prepare for what I knew was to be the afternoon activity and part of the reason for the lifestyle of the family: smoking *shir'e*.

Shir'e is made from the charred remnants of previously smoked opium and is the preferred method of drug taking among the hardest of hard-core opium addicts in Iran, who number in the hundreds of thousands. Boiling the burned opium in water, removing the scum, and then straining the gooey residue results in an opiate perhaps tens of times more potent than fresh, raw opium, itself by far the most popular drug in Iran. Always plentiful and almost a part of Iran's heritage (and widely used in the courts of previous dynasties), opium under the fanatically pro-Western and anti-traditionalist Shah was mainly used by provincial Iranians, the lower classes, and a handful of the landed gentry who stubbornly clung to the past and the seductive habit inherited from their forefathers. The modernism the Shah promoted in the 1960s and '70s (along with a huge increase in tourist and student travel to Europe and the United States) meant that among the young at least, Western, and therefore cool, drugs such as marijuana and cocaine replaced the backward, and now plebeian, domestic high. In my maternal grandfather's house in the 1960s, as traditional a household as there could be in Tehran, I had witnessed my great-grandmother, well over ninety years old, eating, yes, *eating*, her daily dose of opium. Her dementia, quite advanced as far as I was concerned since she never seemed to recognize me, not even a few minutes after I told her whose child I was, was noticeably improved after she swallowed the little brown pellets, although I now think it may have been more because she was just too high to be a nuisance to anyone. My mother used to tell me she was taking her medicine, but I heard enough about her *taryak*, "opium" in Farsi, to know better.

My father's father, who died quite young of a heart attack when I was in first grade abroad, was an opium user of some repute in Ardakan, the provincial village he was from: the lengthy afternoon sessions at his *bagh*, or "garden," as grand homes (which are presumed to have extensive gardens) are known in the provinces, were attended by village notables who, like him, were landowners not in need of a day job, I later discovered. But people of my generation stayed away from opium or, if they indulged, preferred to keep it private lest they be viewed by their ganja-smoking friends as hopelessly square. The Islamic Revolution, which inverted class distinctions and frowned upon anything Western, changed things a bit when it inadvertently caused a resurgence in the use of opium as a recreational activity, perhaps because of the ban on alcohol and the ready availability of opium (although illegal) as a substitute, but also perhaps because the old-fashioned, and particularly *Iranian*, customs were now in vogue. Drug use in general, though, has escalated dramatically since the revolution first intentionally created a modern republic without bars, pubs, or real

public entertainment, and unintentionally a birthrate that has produced far more employable youths than the economy can provide jobs
for. And although opium tops the list in terms of favored drugs,
heroin, crack, and even crystal meth, known as *sheesheh*, or "glass," are
becoming commonplace among the working and middle classes. According to the almost boastful headline in an issue of the English-
language daily *Iran News* during my stay in 2005, "Iranians hold the 1st
spot among world countries regarding narcotics consumption. Moreover, 4–6% of Iranians are drug addicts." Yes, "moreover," although
most Iranian experts put the figure as high as 10 percent and some even
at 15 percent and higher.

———————

Shir'e is the traditionalist's hard drug, not too dissimilar from the
heroin preferred in the West. Smoking it is a labor-intensive process,
though: a small homemade paraffin burner is set on the floor, and the
shir'e, a brown paste the color of a Tootsie Roll, is carefully kneaded
onto the tip of a homemade pipe that looks something like an elongated kazoo. (Regular opium smokers often use beautiful pipes, sometimes made to the owner's specifications, and handsome tongs, usually
in pure silver, to lift white-hot charcoal briquettes from extravagantly
decorated ash pits to their pipes.) Lying on the floor, one smokes shir'e
upside down: unless you're an expert, you need an assistant to guide the
inverted pipe to the open flame. One puff and your head starts floating, pain now an adversary that appears vulnerable to conquest; two or
three puffs and you experience a high that is serenely beautiful: problems fade completely away, anxiety and pain surrender, and nothing,
you think, can take away the beauty. Not even a full-scale invasion by
the U.S. military.

When it was my turn at the pipe, I lay down on the carpet and
rested my head on a dirty pillow. The voiceless man painstakingly prepared the makeshift pipe by kneading and twisting a thick paste on its

tip over and over, softening the shir'e by bringing it close to the flame and then quickly pulling it away several times. A gentle prod was my signal that the pipe was ready: I drew the smoke in short inhales until it completely filled my lungs, and then exhaled slowly. The cooler had been switched off to avoid any twentieth-century interference with the purity of the occasion, and although the heat in the room was now the equivalent of a turned-up sauna, I felt surprisingly comfortable. I begged off a third drag and instead moved away and sat up on the carpet, mumbling profuse thank-yous. I tried unsuccessfully to cross my legs, but they were happier stretched out, so I leaned on a big pillow and slowly drank a cup of tea with a few sugar cubes, sugar that I knew would be the only guarantee that I wouldn't throw up, for opium, like heroin, dramatically lowers the blood sugar level—perhaps the one side effect that can diminish the seductiveness of the drug.

The owner of the house was up next. He didn't put down the pipe until he'd taken five good hits of shir'e, carefully exhaling the sweet-smelling smoke in what seemed to me an impressive performance. The TV was still blaring: a long-haired young man was dancing by a tree surrounded by California blondes and Persian girls in skimpy outfits competing for his interest by swaying seductively to his song. I struggled to keep my eyes open, but my eyelids were uncooperative, the opiate seemingly having taken over some of my motor functions, so I decided to give in and quickly nodded off. Not quite asleep, but definitely not fully awake.

After a few minutes, or at least what I thought were a few minutes but could have been much more, I spoke, and with some difficulty managed to ask about the latest news. I was still curious about the reaction in this house—middle-class, although admittedly by no means ordinary—to Iran's threat to resume its nuclear activity, but rather than offer a reply, the owner of the house quietly switched the TV to IRNN, the Iranian CNN, and left it at that. I thought that his fatalistic disinterest in the nuclear crisis, shared by many other Iranians but in his case fortified by the calming effects of the shir'e, could be best understood in the context of faith: "The will of Allah will prevail." The news network offered no new news, and I willingly went back to my altered state between consciousness and deep slumber. Some time later I stirred, and was politely informed by the younger man that it was again my turn at the pipe. By now the TV was back to PMC, and despite my protestations that my delicate Western constitution would surely be overwhelmed by the shir'e, I found it hard to argue with the fact, repeatedly mentioned, that I had only taken two drags so far and a third couldn't hurt. When I finished, not one but two long drags, I again popped some sugar cubes into my mouth and slurped a fresh cup of tea. My eyes closed again involuntarily, and I only half-listened to conversations of lost business opportunities and the general state of economic affairs, which are in present-day Iran characterized by inflation, joblessness, and stagnation. Three hours a day at the shir'e pipe could certainly mean lost business opportunities, I thought, particularly for these men, who seemed like they could use a few extra rials, but I kept quiet. I wasn't sure I could speak coherently anyway.

The conversation continued, and the women of the house occasionally stole into the kitchen to brew a fresh pot of tea. I excused myself to go to the bathroom, and when it was confirmed that there was no indoor plumbing, I went into the yard and entered the outhouse. It was exactly like the outhouse at my grandfather's house, and even the odor, a unique mixture of mud and human waste that I remembered well from my curious visits as a child, gave me a sense of nostalgia rather than disgust.

When I returned to the house after washing my hands under a faucet by the pond, I could infer from the conversations all around me that another guest was due any minute. I sat down on the carpet again and lit a cigarette to keep myself awake. When the curtain was swept aside just a short while later, a tall young mullah walked into the room. He quietly removed his turban and *abba*, or "cloak," and sat down to a steaming-hot glass of tea quickly delivered by the twelve-year-old boy. My astonishment at his presence, for all the Ayatollahs agree that

opium and other drugs are *haram*, "forbidden" by Islam, grew to amazement as I watched him finish his tea and go over to the pipe and burner.
He calmly spent the next hour puffing away, drinking tea, fingering his
beads, and occasionally answering questions of religious philosophy,
none of which I fully understood. And while he was busy pontificat-
ing, the other men, one by one, took the opportunity to perform their
afternoon prayers: facing Mecca, they bowed and kneeled in the
cramped room, carefully avoiding my outstretched limbs, and mumbled
verses from the Koran as PMC blared the latest Iranian pop hit, the
cleric calmly smoked away, and I continued to struggle to stay fully
awake. Eventually, though, I felt the effects of the opiate recede and I
stood up to leave. Despite the protestations of my host, who with traditional Persian ta'arouf insisted I stay for dinner, I managed—after
many exchanges of "I wouldn't dream of imposing," "I couldn't possibly," and "I've already been a tremendous burden on you and your family"—to say my goodbyes, assuring the man that I would be back
sometime to further impose on him but this evening I simply had to
rush to the Shrine of Fatima for a quick *zeeyarat*, or "pilgrimage," before the night was through.[2]

It was my first visit to Qom and my first experience with shir'e, or "extreme opium," as I now think of it. When I was a child, my parents
would never have thought of bringing me here, a city that had very
little to offer other than religious schools, the Shrine of Fatima Masoumeh (Imam Reza's sister), and salty desert water. Back then the only
tourists would have been rather pious pilgrims, and even today there
are few Iranians from abroad who travel there unless it is out of pure
curiosity, and many secular Iranians who live in Tehran avoid the city
as if it harbors the plague. It has, however, become the de rigueur stop
for foreign journalists and writers who understand not only that it is
the spiritual capital of the Islamic Republic but that if Shia Islam is

woven into the body politic as well as the soul of Iran, then Qom is its weaver. Qom of course has always been the most religious city in Iran (probably more so than even Mashhad, which houses a more important Shia shrine), and it merely took on a political significance after the Islamic Revolution of 1979 that it hadn't had in centuries. This was where Ayatollah Khomeini lived before he was sent into exile by the Shah, this is where he resided part-time on his return, and this is where many Ayatollahs, Grand and otherwise, live, teach, and pray. Qom is where legions of young would-be Shia student clerics from around the world, *talibs*, come to study to one day become the religious authorities that hold political and social sway over this nation and, in their dreams, over other Muslim nations too.

Some foreign and Iranian writers who visit Qom come to see and speak with dissident clerics such as Ayatollah Hossein-Ali Montazeri (once heir to Khomeini but later imprisoned for his dissent and now living quietly in a closely watched house) and Hossein (not to be confused with Hassan) Khomeini, grandson of Ayatollah Khomeini who has dramatically broken with the regime (but commands little attention), for clerics who are fundamentally opposed to the political system of Iran make for good headlines, particularly for those readers who want to believe that they are not Islamophobic by nature; but the Islam of the less combative reformist clerics and certainly the more conservative ones and the legions of ordinary people who support them is what really holds sway in this nation. Yes, it's interesting that not all the religious figures in Iran are comfortable with the policies of the Islamic Republic, or even with the concept of velayat-e-faqih, and many of the disapproving mullahs are based in Qom, a city that, as a religious center of study, affords them some protection from charges of treason. But Iran, as one person told me in Tehran, has always been Islamic, if not a republic, and anyone who thinks that Islam entered politics with the 1979 revolution wasn't paying attention to the past fourteen hundred years of Persian history.

What both conservative and reform mullahs share is an understanding of that Islamic history and a strong belief in an Islamic Republic (and even Islamic democracy, however they define it), and contrary to the hopes of secularists everywhere, Islam lite, or a secular society with a nod to Islam, is not a part of anyone's vocabulary. The reform Ayatollahs and even the dissident ones are allowed a measure of freedom to say what they please partly to show off the democratic nature of Islam (and the regime) and partly because the Ayatollahs in actual power know that to mess with another Ayatollah too much, dissident, reform, or otherwise, is to mess with the stability and legitimacy of the regime, to mess with the basic precepts of Shiism, and maybe even to mess with God. And it is Allah who rules Iran and the lives of most Iranians.

There is an overwhelming sense of Shia Islam as soon as one enters Qom. Shia Muslims, believing only men from the Prophet's bloodline should lead the Muslim nation, or *ummah*, revere two martyred Imams above all the others: Ali, who was murdered, and his son Hussein, who died in battle against the prevailing rulers of Islam at Karbala in present-day Iraq. These two deaths play a central part in Shia life, and the concept of struggle, pain, woe, and martyrdom is derived from centuries of mourning for these two souls, whose elaborately painted portraits, contrary to the common Sunni Muslim belief that depicting the human form is forbidden, adorn many a storefront, building, and private home in Shia towns in Iran, Iraq, and Lebanon, but are all the more visible in a town such as Qom. Sunnis, the orthodox of Islam if you will, believe in a strict Islam that takes the Koran as the literal word of God, not to be interpreted by man, whereas Shias, with their clergy, Ayatollahs and others, have, contrary to popular belief, a much more liberal view in that the church can interpret the Koran and the Hadiths (the sayings and deeds of the Prophet Mohammad according to witnesses and scholars who wrote them down) for the masses who might not have the educational and religious qualifications to do so. Qom and Najaf (in Iraq) are the two towns where the clerics go to learn *how* to do so.

One of the first things one notices in Qom—a dusty old city with minarets and mosques visible from a great distance—apart from the many mullahs on the streets (which one would not see in a Sunni town), is that women are barely visible. Women in Qom, unlike their counterparts in Tehran, do not strut about in colorful headscarves and the latest denim fashions from Europe, nor are they seen much behind the wheels of automobiles. The women one does see in Qom seem to venture outdoors only fully enveloped in jet-black chadors, generally scurrying from one errand to another or in the company of what one must presume are their husbands.

Coming by car from Tehran on a hot summer morning, I was stuck in an unusually heavy traffic jam that allowed me much time for observation: a camel had been sacrificed on the road, its neck slit wide open and its blood staining the road a bright red, in honor of a caravan of buses taking pilgrims to Mashhad, the other great Shia shrine, in northeast Iran. Iran's second-largest city, Mashhad is home to Fatima's brother's grave, the Imam Reza Shrine, and pilgrims regularly travel from one city to the other as part of their Shia duties. (When Iraq is stable, and sometimes even when it's not, such as now, Najaf and Karbala, which are the other two holy Shia cities, complete the pilgrimage set, and the truly pious shuttle between the four as often as they can.) Animal sacrifice plays a big part in Islam (more for the purpose of feeding the poor on auspicious religious occasions than for reasons of superstition), but rarely is it on such open display, even in Iran. The culture of Qom, however, is unabashedly medieval. The long line of buses, adorned with religious exhortations such as *"Ya Abolfaz!"* (Imam Hossein's half brother and a man known for his great strength, so invoking his name is an appeal for strength), as well as somewhat less religious slogans such as "Texas," was slowly making its way past the camel (whose flesh would later be donated to the needy), and a crowd of well-wishers had gathered to wave at the caravan.

My first stop on this, my first, trip to Qom, after tiptoeing my way through fresh camel blood, was at the office of Grand Ayatollah Hajj Sheikh Mohammad Fazel Lankarani, a frail archconservative cleric in his seventies and one of the seven Grand Ayatollahs in Iran (there are four in Iraq), a man who rarely met with Westerners (and never any writers) or even, for that matter, any Iranians who weren't his followers. (After a prolonged illness, the Ayatollah passed away in June 2007 in, of all places, a London hospital, ironically on the very same day that Salman Rushdie was knighted by the queen. Ironic because Lankarani was one of the senior clerics who begged to differ with their government and continued to call for Rushdie's death, a duty for all Muslims, he said, even after the Iranian government, in a 1998 compromise with the British government that led to the normalization of relations, promised that it would not act upon Ayatollah Khomeini's fatwa calling for the "apostate" author's murder.)

Although it would seem that Lankarani would have been a strong supporter of the conservative government taking power after Khatami's retirement, he famously refused for weeks to meet with President Ahmadinejad in early 2007 while I was in Iran. It was an open secret in Tehran that Ahmadinejad, beleaguered and under fire from even his conservative base, was attempting a public meeting with the Grand Ayatollah to deflect the conventional wisdom that he had lost the support of the most senior clerics, but he had been constantly rebuffed. The reason, paradoxical as it may appear, wasn't that Ahmadinejad, religiously ultraconservative, had shown incompetence in managing the economy or that he was endangering Iran's security with his foreign policy, nor was it that he had not bettered the lives of the poor, the working class, and the unemployed, the very base of religious support in Iran. No, the reason for dissatisfaction with Ahmadinejad among some senior clerics was that he had had the audacity to interfere in an area they viewed entirely as theirs, that is, Islam.

Ahmadinejad's proclamation in 2006 that women should be allowed into soccer stadiums, a proclamation he made without consulting the clerics, was quickly overruled by them, with an unsubtle message that, as a layman, he should stay out of issues that deal with Islam, Islamic law, and Muslim rules of behavior. And prior to his proclamation on women spectators at soccer stadiums, he had said in a visit to a group of Ayatollahs in Qom immediately upon his return from the UN General Assembly in 2005 that he had felt a halo over his head while he had been giving his speech and that a hidden presence had mesmerized the unblinking audience of foreign leaders, foreign ministers, and ambassadors. This, to conservative Ayatollahs, amounted to blasphemy, for an ordinary man cannot presume a special closeness to God or any of the Imams, nor can he imply the presence of the Mahdi, the disappeared twelfth Imam, who will reappear and reveal himself on earth only at Armageddon, and not, presumably, at an ordinary meeting of the UN General Assembly. The Ayatollahs could not abide the president's halo claim when they, "signs of God" after all, had never made such claims themselves. Needless to say, on his subsequent trip to New York, Ahmadinejad did *not* sense a halo over his head, nor were the delegates mesmerized, but Lankarani and some of the other Ayatollahs were slow to forgive, and in the spring of 2007, when Ahmadinejad publicly kissed the (gloved) hand of his childhood schoolteacher, an old woman in proper hijab, conservatives once again were infuriated by his seemingly lax adherence to their strict rules of modesty.

Lankarani's office was a converted old house with a large drawing room covered in Persian rugs but no furniture. As I sat waiting for him on the floor, I was served a continuous supply of tea and fresh watermelon

slices by an old male attendant. The clock in the room was an hour behind mine. It is, I learned there, a sign of piety in Qom to reject daylight savings time. If the Ayatollahs say it's 11:00 a.m., it's 11:00 a.m.,
for in their world only God has the power to change time, and by the
grace of Allah, I was an hour early for my appointment. An hour later
the room started bustling with activity, men scurrying about, my tea
glass refilled after almost every sip. The Ayatollah's nephew Javad Ab-
utorabian, whom I'd been talking to, suddenly rose and ushered me in
for my audience. The Ayatollah's room was identical to the drawing
room with the exception of two chairs placed by a window in the corner: one for the Grand Ayatollah and one for his highest-ranking disciple. After a few polite pleasantries, I was formally introduced by his
nephew as an Iranian writer from the United States who was looking
to understand Qom and the meaning of Islam in Iranian life, although
I had not actually expressed my reasons for requesting an audience in
those terms.

Lankarani smiled and looked me straight in the eye. "It is very difficult," he said slowly, "to understand."

I remarked that I understood how difficult it was to understand,
and after an uncomfortable silence I suggested that despite the difficulty, I'd still like to ask him some questions.

"Very difficult," he said, chuckling mischievously, "to understand,"
apparently amused by my naïveté.

I smiled at the Ayatollah, trying to come up with some words that
might break the ice, and I even thought about bringing up Salman
Rushdie's name, albeit without mentioning that despite having crossed
paths with him on the sidewalks of the Upper East Side of Manhattan, I had been negligent in my duty as a Muslim to kill him on the
spot. But before I had a chance to form the words in my head, he
turned and sternly looked at one of his aides. The meeting was over.
The aide pulled me aside and explained that the Ayatollah was tired
and sick, and I retreated to the drawing room, hoping I might get another chance to chat after the Ayatollah received the main group of vis-

itors who had started gathering in the room, for Tuesdays are visiting days and noon is the appointed hour. The men—young, old, soldier, civilian—all sat cross-legged on the carpet waiting for their turn to get a glimpse of the Ayatollah. Many of these supporters had traveled from Tehran or other cities just for a chance to spend a few seconds in his presence, and they all seemed serious and eager. When the doors to the anteroom opened, the men made an orderly queue. One by one they filed into the room, kissed the Ayatollah's hand, and walked out, beaming as they left his presence.

Lankarani's followers, indeed the followers of some of the other Grand Ayatollahs in Shia Islam, truly believe in a government of God, and God's representative, their Ayatollah, tells them how to live in God's favor. And they number in the millions, mostly across Iran and Iraq, but also in other countries of the Middle East and Asia, and they give generously to their Ayatollahs. Whether in an Islamic Republic or not, they don't stray from their Ayatollah's teachings, and their faith is inseparable from the governance of their daily lives. I was told by one of Lankarani's aides that day that approximately ten million dollars a month flows into his treasury from his supporters alone. Ten million means either a few very rich supporters or millions of poorer ones; in this case it was a combination of the two. The money was apparently spent on the numerous projects, such as building mosques (a more recent one is in Moscow) and religious schools, that the Ayatollah had going all over the world. The schools, unlike the Wahabi Sunni madrassas that we hear so much about, don't preach hatred for the West or Westerners. But they do preach the supremacy of Shia Islam and for those who believe in a theocracy, as Lankarani did, the concept of velayat-e-faqih, which means rule of the Ayatollahs.

As the Ayatollah quietly left the building, another of Lankarani's aides, sensing my disappointment, suggested that I visit his library and the nerve center of his Web operation in, appropriately, Iran's only city with fiber-optic connections. At a nicely air-conditioned building a few blocks away, a pleasant and self-taught computer-literate young man gave me a tour of the library and explained how Lankarani's Web site operated in seventeen languages, including Swahili and Burmese, for all of his followers. It was updated daily with the Ayatollah's proclamations, fatwas, or religious commands, if he'd issued any recently, and general information, but, most important, it was a place to ask questions: e-mails poured in every day in all seventeen languages and were carefully printed out, one by one, and arranged according to language in mailboxes for Lankarani's Iranian and foreign talibs (Arabic for "students," and where the word "Taliban" comes from) to translate, so that they could be answered by one of the senior staff, such as his son, but always reviewed by the Ayatollah himself. I was shown e-mails in English, translated by hand into Farsi, where the Ayatollah had crossed out an answer and written his own, to be retranslated and transmitted back electronically. Most of the questions in the e-mails I saw related to sex; for example, a sixteen-year-old boy from England had written about his "friend" who had had oral sex with a fourteen-year-old boy and was worried that his prayers would be nullified and that he might be punished by God. The Ayatollah's answer was refreshingly short and simple: repent, and don't do it again. No mention of homosexuality, no judgments—who said the conservative Ayatollahs weren't compassionate? I read the same thing, "repent," page after page, for almost without exception the questioner had committed some kind of sin, or at least thought he had, or claimed to have a "friend" who had. I looked around at the banks of computers and the dark, highly polished wooden mail slots filled with printed e-mails: Digital confession, I thought. The Vatican should get in on this.

———————

The early evening crowd at the Shrine of Hazrat Fatima in the center of Qom was dense, as it is on every other day of the week, 365 days a year. The mosque around which the tomb is built is magnificent, and the crowd, Shia men, women, and children from all over the world but these days including a large number of Iraqis, milled about in the courtyard, either waiting their turn to go inside, touch the tomb with their fingers, and say a few prayers or unwilling to leave quite yet after they had already done so. The truly faithful will spend hours here, sometimes days, praying inside the mosque, touching and kissing the silver and gold latticework encasing the tomb, and pausing only to shop for religious souvenirs at the hundreds of little stores that surround the shrine. Some, particularly those Shias with a strong belief in the imminent coming of the Mahdi, the Messiah, will, particularly on Tuesdays but also on Fridays, the Muslim holiday, make a second pilgrimage to a site a few miles outside of Qom: Jamkaran.

On this Tuesday, before I drove back to Tehran, I also stopped at Jamkaran and visited the gargantuan mosque that had been built on the site of an alleged vision of the twelfth Imam, the Imam Mahdi. (In Shia Islam, the twelfth, or last, Imam is believed to have never died, merely disappeared, and will one day reveal himself to us as the Messiah. The *Muslim* Messiah, that is, and according to believers Jesus Christ will appear at the same time by his side as his *follower*.) On Tuesday evenings the faithful come to Jamkaran to pray and to drop a note to the Imam in a well (near which the vision of or encounter with the "Hidden" Imam actually occurred in 974 C.E.), asking him to solve their problems, as Tuesday is apparently the day the vision appeared and therefore the day of the week that he, although invisible, takes requests. Some also believe that he appears on Tuesdays not just to read the notes but to mingle with the crowd anonymously, which means one is subject to even more intense stares than are normal in a country of starers. (Staring is not considered bad manners by most Iranians, for anyone who ventures outside is considered to have put him- or herself in the public eye, which is partly why men, and even many women, vehemently defend a woman's obligation to cover herself and a man's obligation to dress modestly.)

Tuesday nights at Jamkaran resemble a huge tailgate party where vendors set up in the parking lots and families set up picnic rugs and tens of thousands wander about the grounds as if waiting for a main event to happen, which of course never seems to. There was a long line of pedestrians making their way to the well, the holy spot, as well as busloads and carloads of people, coming from near and far, to pray and to ask a small favor of the missing Imam. As dusk turned to night, thousands, probably hundreds of thousands, prayed outside the over-flowing mosque, women separated from the men in their own special cordoned-off area, and wandered about the grounds, dropping pieces of paper into the well (the women in their own well) and partying with their families. The men's well, which I naturally went to, was crowded with all sorts of people, including Arabs in headdresses and many holding children and babies in their arms, some of whom also dropped their very own little notes into the stone well. Everyone I asked had a story about how a short note to the Imam on a Tuesday night had re-sulted in some kind of favorable outcome for the petitioner. The oc-cultation of the twelfth Imam speaks as much to Shia thought and behavior as the martyrdom of the Imams does, and salvation plays as big a part in Shia belief as it does for evangelical Christians.

President Ahmadinejad, who had only been in office a few days the night I went to Jamkaran and is closer than one might imagine to Chris-tian evangelicals in thought, is a big believer not just in the Hidden Imam (whom he refers to in every speech, including at the UN, plead-ing that he show up as soon as possible) but also in Jamkaran as the site of his coming reappearance. Since his election, Ahmadinejad has do-nated millions of dollars from government funds to the Jamkaran mosque, and expansion projects already started took on an added ur-gency during his presidency. Ahmadinejad also brought attention to a site that was little known outside devout Shia circles, attention that is not always welcome, particularly if it comes from non-Muslims. When I was in Iran in 2007, an Italian photographer friend had just arrived on assignment from *Newsweek*, and he asked what he should see when he traveled to Qom. I immediately told him the highlight of a trip to Qom would be a Tuesday night romp at Jamkaran, and he followed my advice but was allowed near neither the main mosque nor the well, and was in-structed not to shoot any photos in the vicinity. That Jamkaran would become a major Iranian Shia attraction well after a revolution brought the clergy to power is unsurprising, for evenings there resemble a festive party as much as they do a religious ceremony, and the combination is irresistible to believers.

It was not always that way, and my mother, a thoroughly Western-ized but pious woman who has made the hajj pilgrimage as well as vis-ited the Imam Reza Shrine in Mashhad (before the revolution) and is hoping to make it to Karbala before she dies, had never heard of the place until I told her about it. The idea that the twelfth Imam might be roaming about the place on Tuesday nights seemed to her rather ridiculous, even though she believes in him and his eventual return to the realm of the living. (My cousin Fatemeh, far and away the most re-ligious in my family and a woman whose hair I've never seen, whose hand I've never shaken, knows of Jamkaran but has never bothered to visit. She believes in the Savior, the Hidden Imam, but she comes from the educated middle class, surrounded by many relatives who are secu-lar and by clerics who are, like her cousin President Khatami, rather less superstitious, so to her the Imam's presence at Jamkaran is a little too fanciful a notion.)

Before the Ayatollahs and mullahs took over the running of the country, many of the more fanciful concepts of Shiism were largely ig-nored by the masses, religious though they might have been. The idea of a missing Messiah was just that: an idea, and one that few thought to take literally. But with encouragement from the state, no aspect of Shia theology or mysticism is left to the imagination, and an entire generation of Iranians, certainly those from deeply religious families, has grown up with a far more literal interpretation of Shia mythology than previously. To imagine it from an American view: it is in some ways as if evangelical Christians had had their way in the White House, in Congress, in state governments, on the Supreme Court, and in the schools for over a generation. Perhaps not a perfect analogy, for America is far more diverse than Iran and the majority probably less religious, but an analogy of sorts nonetheless. (The fact that little public entertainment exists in Iran might also be a contributing factor to the popularity of, and the carnival atmosphere that surrounds, a site such as Jamkaran on a Tuesday or Friday night, but one supposes that if evangelicals had their way in America, far less nonchurch entertainment might be available there as well.)

One must see Qom and Jamkaran in another light too, not just as places of government-sponsored and encouraged pilgrimage, but as places of hope. The government need not make much effort to persuade an already religious populace that salvation is around the corner, that the Mahdi will solve all their problems, even if only on Tuesdays and Fridays until he decides to take the job full-time. The female cabdriver who took me to the presidential offices on a snowy morning and who braves the errant bus drivers when she drives to Jamkaran, a young widow raising two children and caring for an ailing mother and a woman who mused whether she should have immigrated to a better life, may have little else to look forward to besides salvation. A population that suffered the chaos of revolution followed quickly by a brutal eight-year war—a war that rained missiles down on Tehran and that (oh so!) unjustly killed a generation of Iran's youths—a population that struggles every day with unemployment, financial issues, rampant drug abuse, and the notion that its rights have been trampled, well, this is a population that is somewhat more susceptible to the notion that salvation might be at hand.

When I left Jamkaran in the summer of 2005, after the last evening prayer, there was still bumper-to-bumper traffic on the highway leading to the site. The faithful poured in from Tehran and towns even farther away, and until the sun rose the next day, every man and woman was like a lottery ticket holder the day of a record-breaking jackpot: all winners, all equal, and all full of hope. Earlier that day, I'd picked up a few *noheh* CDs near the shrine in Qom, and on my way out of Jamkaran I picked up a few more from vendors lining the parking lots, at about fifty cents a pop. Noheh, the Shia religious lamentation traditionally sung a cappella on holy days of mourning, is today (at least on CDs) thoroughly modern, with a hypnotic beat provided courtesy of hundreds of young men beating their chests and flailing their backs with chains, and young male singers competing for fame as messengers of woe. Good Shias *feel* the pain. As I listened to the CDs in the car, I couldn't help but empathize with that pain, a pain I had seen on the faces of some at the mosque, hoping their letters to the Hidden Imam would be answered, and on the faces of some of the men who had driven great distances to kiss the hand of their Ayatollah that morning. Just as one doesn't have to be religious to feel and appreciate the emotion of a gospel singer, one doesn't have to be devout to feel the emotion of Muslim religious music, and Shia chants reach into a place deep in the Iranian soul, formed by centuries of cultural DNA and the certain Persian knowledge that the world is indeed a wicked place. Or perhaps it was the blood of Mohammad and his progeny that supposedly runs through my veins, for I had, earlier in the evening in Qom, touched the mausoleum of a saint. A saint who was, after all, my ancestor.

———

I found myself in Qom, at Mofid University, again in the winter of 2007. Friends in Tehran expressed surprise that I wished to return to what most secular-minded Iranians consider a symbol of backwardness: a dull, dreary, and dusty place with nothing to recommend it. They didn't know about the shir'e, of course, but that wasn't the reason I returned. Well, perhaps just a *small* part of the reason. Mofid U, "useful" or "beneficial" university as it would translate into English (and only a Persian could come up with a name as obviously practical, and as boastful, as that), was founded in 1989 by Ayatollah Abdol-

Karim Mousavi Ardebili (head of the judiciary under Khomeini) as an institution dedicated to comparative studies between Islamic sciences and modern humanities, although it has expanded to offer degrees in other disciplines. It was intended as an adjunct to the *howzehs*, the Shia seminaries in Qom, which offer little beyond purely Islamic studies and which Ardebili believed neglected the modern sciences. Hojjatoleslam Mohammad Taghi Fazel-Meybodi, a reformist cleric and good friend of former president Khatami's, is the director of publications at the university, and I sat in his large, somewhat untidy office on a chilly morning drinking tea poured from a large thermos. "You haven't become a *hezbollhahi*, have you?" said Fazel-Meybodi with a laugh, referring, I knew, to the full beard I hadn't had the last time I saw him in Tehran. The beard, it seemed, would always be a point of conversation for anyone who knew I didn't live in Iran. I smiled and shook my head.

"No, no," I said, "it's just nice to not shave, and people who don't know me don't presume I live in the West." And then, without any prodding from me, for this was supposed to be a courtesy call and nothing more, Fazel-Meybodi launched into a critique of the Islamic Republic that, had I actually been a resident of Iran, he might not have imparted with such vigor.

"The things that Ayatollah Khomeini was against the Shah for," he said, "are exactly things we are doing today." At least he said "we," an acknowledgment that he was very much a part of the clerical ruling class. "We akhounds were against Reza Shah [the Shah's father, who started the Pahlavi dynasty]," he continued, "but that was not entirely fair—he did some good things too." My friend Javad, who had driven down with me from Tehran, a nephew of Grand Ayatollah Lankarani's, looked at me with raised eyebrows as he took a sip of tea, holding the glass by his lips for a few seconds longer than necessary. I had introduced him as Lankarani's relative, and the Hojjatoleslam knew how radical his views would be to the archconservative cleric vastly his senior, but he didn't seem to care. In fact, he seemed to be enjoying himself, knowing that there was a chance his views would be recounted later that day to one of the most senior Ayatollahs in all of Shia Islam, and one whose views were the polar opposite of his. "In order to progress, and we *must* progress, we have to constantly step on the akhounds' toes," he said.

"But will progress lead to a secularism of sorts?" I asked. "Surely that's not in the cards."

"Secularism?" said Fazel-Meybodi, somewhat imperiously. "Iran is already becoming secular—it's basically secular—all that's left is the hijab!" Javad glanced at me again, but kept silent. "It's dangerous," continued Fazel-Meybodi, "for religion to be imposed. It's *worse* for the religion." Fazel-Meybodi seemed intent, as some of the reformist clerics are, on making an impression with someone he believed, as a writer, had some influence in the West. It has become almost fashionable, particularly since Ahmadinejad's rise, for reformist mullahs with a sense of public relations to espouse dangerously liberal views, for while their status in the ruling class offers them some protection, their conviction that Iran is inevitably heading toward liberalization and democratization also means that they want to continue to be relevant when other clerics may no longer be. Ayatollahs Sanai and Tehrani, to one degree or another part of the reform camp, also exhibit this tendency, although Sanai will, like Fazel-Meybodi, express extreme and even confrontational views to anyone, particularly foreign, and with an eye to the Western press, who cares to pay him a visit.

It was close to lunchtime, and I was getting hungry for *chelo-kebab*, white rice and lamb skewers and a national lunch dish of sorts. Javad had promised me the best of Qom, a city of akhounds, known for their discriminating palates, healthy appetites, and often portly physiques. Fazel-Meybodi, however, in the best tradition of ta'arouf, insisted that we be his guest at his home, for lunch and a rest from our travels. Traditional hospitality from the days of the caravans has not disappeared from Qom, but I politely refused, insisting that I had much business to do in the city. In the end, after some minutes of back-and-forth insistence and refusal, Meybodi relented but would not hear of us walking the university grounds to the gate: he personally drove us in his car and made us gifts of his most recent books, which he fetched from the overstuffed trunk, before we kissed each other, three times on the cheek in the Islamic manner, and managed to exit "Useful U." Books, but regrettably no souvenir T-shirt.

———————

After lunch, which had lived up to expectations and which I ate in the company of the most turbans I had ever seen in one place, a handful of full black chadors scattered in their midst, I left Javad, promising a rendezvous at the shrine later that evening before our return to Tehran. I made my way to the old house in the center of town, the house where I had spent a pleasant afternoon more than a year earlier and where I had promised to return if I ever made it back to Qom. I saw the house's owner, looking thinner than before and older than his years, on the street outside his door. "Mr. M.!" I exclaimed. *"Salam!"* He had been warned by telephone that I was coming to visit, but he didn't seem to recognize me. "It's me; Majd," I said.

"Oh, come in, come in! I hardly recognized you with that beard." He opened the unlocked door and ushered me into the winter quarters of the house, across the yard from the summer quarters, where I had been the last time.

"I just came by to say hello," I said, "and certainly not to disturb you and your family."

"Don't be ridiculous," he said with the characteristic slow, nasal twang of an opium addict, and I noticed that he may have lost another tooth or two. "Come in and have some tea." I entered a narrow hall-way, took off my shoes, and followed Mr. M. into the living room. Similar to the summer room, it was covered with Persian carpets and pillows, but again, no furniture. He gestured for me to sit, and then yelled for tea. His wife, who had barely spoken the last time, came rushing into the room from behind a curtain, chador flapping, and greeted me as if I were a long-lost relative.

"How *are* you?" she exclaimed. "It's so nice to see you again!"

I stood up, mindful not to extend my hand for a shake, as this was a religious household.

"Very well, thanks," I replied, with my right hand over my heart in a gesture of respect.

"Please sit down," she said. "You'll have some tea." She disappeared into the kitchen and returned immediately with a teapot and glasses already filled on a small tray. I took a glass and a sugar cube and murmured my thanks. Her husband did the same, and to my surprise, unlike during my previous visit, she sat down across from me and beamed. Mr. M. meanwhile made a phone call, and from what I could gather, he was arranging for a delivery. The daughter of the house entered the room, also in a chador, said hello pleasantly, and sat next to her mother. There was no TV in this room, so she just looked at me.

"You have a beard," she said, as a statement rather than a question.

"Yes, that's right," I replied.

"But you live in America?"

"Yes." These were more words than she had spoken the entire time I'd been at the house before.

"Where?"

"New York."

"Oh my God!" she said. "I would love to go to New York!"

"What for?" grunted her father.

"It's so beautiful!" she said, giving him a dirty look.

"Well," I said, "I see the beauty, but it's not really that beautiful *everywhere*, you know."

"Yes, it is," she insisted dismissively, turning to face me. "*Isn't* it?" she demanded, adjusting her chador, pulling it tight under her chin.

"What is it you think is beautiful?" asked Mr. M., drawing out the words.

"The buildings, the modern technology, everything!"

"I hope you'll be able to see it someday," I said. She lowered her eyes and fell silent. Right then her husband, the soccer-playing youth I had seen eighteen months earlier, walked in. I stood up and shook his hand. "How are you?" I asked in as friendly a tone as I could muster, even though I had sensed a little hostility from him the last time.

"Very well," he said, taking my hand in his. "It's nice to see you again." His hair was shorter than the last time and wasn't gelled, and he had a short, uneven beard. He sat down by his wife.

"So what are you up to these days?" I asked. "Still playing soccer?"

"Yes, whenever I get a chance," he replied. "But I'm doing my national service."

"Wow, in the army, eh?" I said.

"No," he said, "I signed up for the Revolutionary Guards."

"You can join the Sepah for your military service?"

"Yeah."

"And how is it?"

"It's easy. I just sit in an office most days, and get plenty of days off."

There was a knock at the door, and Mr. M. went into the hallway. He reappeared moments later with a small bag, and then stepped into the kitchen to pick up the paraffin burner and his homemade pipe. He sat down and began to prepare the shir'e.

"So," said the son-in-law, "what kind of guns do American soldiers carry?"

"Gee, I'm not sure," I said, "but I assume they're given M16s."

"Wow, M16s!" He smiled, his black eyes twinkling with excitement.

"And what do you have?" I asked, sensing he wanted to tell me.

"Kalashnikovs," he said, "although I'm not allowed one. I get to shoot one occasionally for target practice. They're not bad, but they're not M16s."

"Have you seen an M16?" I asked.

"No, but friends have!" He started to absentmindedly pull the short hairs on his chin.

"And you grew the beard for the Guards?" I asked.

"I suppose so," he said, "but my beard isn't really a proper Pasdar beard. I'm not a regular, so it doesn't really matter, as long as I don't shave." His father-in-law had a pipe almost ready, and he gestured for me to join him at his side.

"I can't smoke much," I said. "Last time it really knocked me out."

"It'll be better this time," he said. Indeed, I thought, stretching out and resting my head on a pillow. We smoked for a couple of hours, watched by the rest of the family, who chatted endlessly about matters such as Mr. M.'s unfortunate habit, which had caused him to lose most of his assets and was about to cause him the loss of the house we were in; his siblings' exploitation of his situation by offering to buy the property for far less than its worth; and the daughter's attention deficit disorder, which of course they didn't describe as such but which she oddly seemed quite proud of. Mr. M. had been a senior city government official at one time but had been dismissed following a corruption scandal, and his descent into full-time opium use had taken a greater toll on the family than I had thought the last time I saw them. But unlike working-class addicts who have in many cases ended up on the streets abandoned by their relatives, this family soldiered on, together and intact, and I could only hope that they would continue to do so.

As we lay on the floor, I was often asked my opinion on all their family issues, and I tried to be politely noncommittal, for I found it unnerving not only to be included in what should have been private matters but also to speak on the subject of my host's opium habit while I lay on the floor happily puffing away at his pipe. There was, much as the last time I had visited, no talk of politics or the U.S.-Iran dispute, even with a son-in-law in the Revolutionary Guards who might be called to the front lines of a war someday, for this family, like most in the middle and working classes, had bigger problems and issues to worry about. I hoped that other guests would arrive, to save me from both the uncomfortable conversation and having to, out of ta'arouf, which makes it rude and therefore impossible to do as one really wants, smoke far more than I should, but no one else showed up. I did endorse the idea of the daughter continuing her education, an endeavor she has so far found exceedingly boring, and I also seconded Mrs. M.'s entreaties to her husband not to sell the house (which despite its poor condition was actually quite lovely), at least not for a quick buck. Perhaps it was, I thought, battling my drooping eyelids after a pipe by staring at a picture of the revered Shia saint Imam Hossein on a wall next to a large poster of Ayatollah Fazel Lankarani, that I, the Iranian from foreign lands, was the perfect person for the family to air their issues in front of. I would, after all, be gone soon, possibly never to return, and none of their neighbors knew me. Me and their Ayatollah, it seemed, were the closest to therapy that this family would ever get.

When I finally summoned the energy to stand up and excuse myself for a visit to the outhouse, I heard drumbeats coming from the street. Mr. M.'s young son, now probably thirteen or fourteen and quite a bit larger than when I'd last seen him, came running in from the hall to announce a mourning procession outside. "For whom?" I inquired.

"Zein-ol-Abedeen-e-Beemar," he said, "Imam Sajjad." I must have looked puzzled, for he then added, "The *fourth* Imam!" He must've thought me a complete half-wit. Zein-ol-Abedeen (*beemar* means "the sickly," for he was ill at the Battle of Karbala in 680 C.E. and unable to fight alongside his father, Hossein, the more revered Imam) had a Persian mother, the daughter of Yazdegerd, the last Sassanid Iranian king. Imam Hossein, grandson of the Prophet Mohammad, who married her, and his half-Iranian son, who had her as a mother, hold a special place in Iranian hearts, for they inextricably link Iran and Persian blood to the Arab religion that conquered their land. I followed the boy out-side and watched the marchers, all dressed in black, some beating their chests with one hand while holding colorful banners with the other and some whipping their backs with chains to the rhythm of the drums. Another day, another procession, and even the spectators look-ing on seemed weary. A few women in black chadors listlessly followed the colorful funeral-like procession, and after watching it pass the house, I went inside through the living room murmuring, "Excuse me," and into the yard.

A yellow cat, busily licking the lunch dishes piled up outside the kitchen entrance, froze and stared at me. "Shoo him away!" Mrs. M. shouted through the glass pane of the door. "He's so bumptious, and we can't seem to get rid of him." I made a sudden movement toward the cat, and he gave me what I was sure was a disgusted look before calmly, and arrogantly, walking away. Another neighborhood laat, I thought as I made my way to the outhouse. It was getting late when I returned to the living room, and I begged my leave. Anticipating a few rounds of ta'arouf, I said that I had to make a pilgrimage to the Shrine of Fatima Masoumeh before I left Qom, and that seemed to suffice as both an excuse and a verification of my religious credentials. The daughter left the room as I kissed her father and her husband three times in the Is-lamic manner, and she returned quickly with a small box.

"Here," she said. "This is for you, from Imam Reza's shrine in Mashhad. I picked some up when I went on pilgrimage last month." I opened the cardboard box, and inside was a small string of prayer beads.

"Thanks so much," I said. "I really appreciate it." I knew my mother, whom I'd be re-gifting them to, actually *would*.

"It's auspicious," she said, staring straight at me. "Blessed, because it comes from the shrine." Mr. M.'s daughter, who watches PMC and other satellite television stations, who sees Iranians abroad happily liv-ing luxurious lives, and who might wish, hopelessly, to join them, perhaps takes comfort in believing that she has something many of those exiles don't: faith, and proximity to where the Messiah will appear one Tuesday night to set all the wrongs of the world right.

I put the prayer beads back in the box and into my pocket, taking out my cell phone and turning it on. She glanced at the phone in my hands. "It's different from the last one, isn't it?"

"Yes," I replied. "I got this one quite recently."

"Is it also a Motorola?" she asked.

"Yes," I said, handing her the phone to examine, surprised to learn that she had noticed the make of my phone over a year ago.

"Gosh. It's so beautiful!" she said, caressing the phone. "They make such beautiful things in America," she continued, throwing a glance at her father. I didn't have the heart to tell her that it, like almost all American electronics, was made in China. She handed the phone back to me.

"Is it expensive?" she asked.

"No, not really," I said, "about a hundred dollars: cell phones are pretty cheap in America." She paused, converting the sum into rials in her head. I started for the door, the family following my footsteps as good Iranian manners dictate. I, as manners also dictate, begged them to remain in the room, saying that I would see myself out, but of course they followed me anyway. "Goodbye again," I said, putting on my shoes by the door. "Thank you so much, and I again apologize for imposing on you."

"Please," they all said, Mrs. M. adding the classic ta'arouf line: "Sorry you had a bad time."

"I had a wonderful time!" I said, and I meant it, although they, unaccustomed to anything but ta'arouf, would never know whether my words were spoken sincerely. I noticed the daughter was still looking at the phone in my hand.

"Excuse me," she said, looking up. "Does it give good antenna?"

PRIDE AND HUMILITY

The Iranian Foreign Ministry sits on parklike grounds in the center of downtown Tehran: a visually stunning low-slung building built at the time of Reza Shah but with more art deco and classically Persian flourishes than other government buildings, all of which exhibit the German fascist architecture so popular with the Shah at the time.[1] It is also one of the few large government buildings where you will very rarely encounter a cleric, or even someone not wearing a proper suit, for the Foreign Ministry is where the Islamic Republic gets down to the now critical business of interacting with the outside world at a time when its power and influence are on the rise. Joining the foreign service is the most difficult career choice for would-be civil servants (as it is in most other countries), and the legions of gray-suited men and elegant hijab-wearing women who march purposefully up and down the vast marble-floored corridors of the Foreign Ministry have all, at one time or another, had to endure classes, lectures, and study at the ministry's North Tehran campus: the Center for Research and Education. Nestled in the foothills of the Alborz Mountains on a street named for a war martyr and in the very far reaches of the northern part of the city, the campus is not unlike a college, with numerous nondescript buildings strewn about on acres of parkland.

On a warm winter day in 2007 it was snowing lightly when I arrived at the facility, from a sunnier downtown, twenty minutes early for my appointment with the deputy foreign minister in charge of research and education, and the man essentially responsible for instilling Mahmoud Ahmadinejad's ideology in Iran's diplomats' heads. I decided to linger just outside the gates for a few minutes, and I took shelter under the overhang of the large bookstore accessible to the public, but not yet open for business in the morning. In the windows of the store there were copies of every political tome imaginable, from East and West, Persian authored as well as many translated into Farsi, displayed on stands and stacked in artful piles as they would be in any commercial bookstore in the West.[2] Prominent among the titles, almost center stage in the middle window, was the Farsi translation of *Mein Kampf*, complete with a photo of a serious-looking Adolf Hitler on the cover. A jarring image that I couldn't help but stare at, wondering if President Ahmadinejad had personally directed the ministry to display the book for all to see or if an employee had taken it upon himself or herself to anticipate the president's taste in political literature. I noticed that books on Marx and communism, an ideology that is anathema to the Islamic Republic, were also available, but it was hard to tell from the titles if they were critical of the ideology or merely critiques of it.

It stopped snowing rather suddenly, and the sun shone brightly as I made my way past the security gate and onto the lavish grounds of the center, asking directions to the deputy foreign minister's office, which could have been in any one of a dozen buildings in my view. It was quiet on campus, hardly anyone was around, not even in the building where I finally found myself, and I had to knock on a few doors to find someone who would tell me on which floor and where their boss's office actually was. At the end of one empty hallway near a window I saw a blond young man in jeans, a Briton, complaining loudly into his cell phone about various visa issues and the troubles he was encountering. What an Englishman was doing at the center was a mystery to me, for it's not where foreigners come to extend their visas, but presumably he was a student who, like an English girl I'd met before, had managed to penetrate Iran's normally secretive Foreign Ministry. He turned and looked at me, and I reluctantly moved on, knowing that if I lingered, he'd assume I was spying on him, which I'll freely admit held some appeal to me, especially since my Persian conspiracy-minded opinion was that *he* had to be a spy, or budding spy, himself.

I finally found the office I was looking for at the end of a wide corridor on the third floor of the building, and within minutes I was ushered by an assistant into the cavernous office suite of Manouchehr Mohammadi, Ph.D. (as it points out on his business card), the deputy foreign minister for research and education. (Ph.D. is seemingly not adequately prestigious for Dr. Mohammadi, for his business card also shows his e-mail address as beginning with "professor.") Dr. Mohammadi, dressed in a three-piece suit and the classic collarless white shirt of the Foreign Ministry, stood up and shook my hand, and indicated that I should sit on a sofa some distance from his desk. He sat down on the chair facing his desk and opened a file, presumably mine.

"What can I do for you?" he asked, looking through the papers. I told him that I wanted to chat about various things, that I was a writer, and that I hoped he didn't mind if I took notes. He smiled and waited for the attendant who had walked in with a tray to place a glass of tea on the table in front of me. He waved the attendant away when he approached him with the tray, and looked at the file once more. "Happy to meet you," he said, closing the folder and putting it back on his desk. "I have fond memories of America," he said, "of my time at university there, in Wisconsin."

"Which school did you go to?" I asked.

"Madison," he said. "You know, I've never felt as comfortable anywhere outside Iran as in America."

"Yes," I said, "I think most Iranians feel that way."

"You know, the era of Mr. Nice Guy is over," he suddenly said, seriously, "because it didn't work." He was referring to Khatami, and he must have gleaned from my file that I was close to the ex-president. I thought he wanted to see my reaction, but I showed none except to nod my head and write in my little notebook. "Ahmadinejad is working," he continued matter-of-factly, "and the United States must accept the Islamic Republic as a reality."

"I can't speak for the government," I said, "but I think many ordinary Americans are worried about President Ahmadinejad and the policies of the Iranian government."

"We're not after public diplomacy," said Dr. Mohammadi with a broad and insincere smile. "One and a half billion Muslims have woken up after five hundred years of Western hegemony," he continued, "and we don't want Dick Cheney or Condoleezza Rice to give us orders. We are interested not in *compromise* but in *coexistence*." He had used the English words, and he proudly smiled again as I furiously underlined "no compromise" in my notebook. And as if anticipating my pen strokes, he repeated, "No compromise."

"So how did the Holocaust conference relate to a position of 'no compromise'?" I asked, trying to steer the conversation to that touchy subject. Manouchehr Mohammadi had been the man responsible for organizing the infamous Tehran Holocaust conference of December 2006, on direct orders from President Ahmadinejad. And he had, it seemed, relished the task, beaming in every photo of him at the event.[3]

"Ah," he said, looking at me carefully. "We have a saying in Iran that I'm sure you know. It goes: 'You say something; I believe it. You insist; I begin to wonder. You swear on it; I know you're lying.' The Holocaust conference was an academic affair, looking to find answers to unanswered questions. The West insists—no, swears—it happened, so we wanted to see what we could discover."

"But why would you invite someone like David Duke," I asked, "who has no credibility whatsoever and is a known racist and anti-Semite?"

"Listen," he said, smiling again, "we received a résumé and request to attend from Kiev, Ukraine, from Mr. Duke, and after he arrived in Tehran, there was all this fuss—I think it was CBS News that started it—and he personally came here and told me that it was all Zionist lies and propaganda."

"With all due respect," I said, "David Duke is very well-known in the United States, at least to anyone over a certain age. I myself remember the headlines and the scandal when it was revealed that he was KKK all those years ago, and of course it's not that he's just an anti-Semite; he's a racist ex–Klan leader who actually believes that blacks, and I presume Iranians too, are inferior to whites like himself. Surely that is a problem for the Islamic Republic, a country greatly popular in Africa, even if the Holocaust denial or anti-Semitism isn't?" I really wanted to also ask him whether anyone in his office was aware of Google, but I bit my tongue. Mohammadi stared at me for a few moments, but not angrily. It was as if a realization, that perhaps Duke's racism has additional targets inconvenient to the Islamic Republic's repute, had hit him for the first time.

"Well, we didn't know," he then said with finality, "and when the whole thing happened, I summoned him to my office for an explanation—he sat right where you're sitting—and he denied it, as I just told you, but I had him put on a plane anyway. And I denied his request to meet President Ahmadinejad." We were interrupted by his cell phone, ringing with a Muzak-like soft rock tone, and I unconsciously shifted in my seat. David Duke, after all, had been sitting on the very same cushion only a few weeks earlier. When Mohammadi finished the call, he went into a monologue about how wonderful the hard-line policies of President Ahmadinejad were and how the West was beginning to realize that it couldn't shove Iran around any longer. I stopped taking notes and just looked at him, in a sort of wonderment that the training of Iran's young diplomats had been put under the charge of a person who exhibited about as much diplomatic finesse as John Bolton had as an American ambassador. After a few more interruptions of his cell phone (didn't people know his office number?), he looked at his watch and I took the cue to excuse myself.

"Thanks very much," I said, standing up. "This was enlightening."

"You're very welcome," he replied. "On the Holocaust, by the way, you should know that I conducted my own very extensive research into it. You know I'm a scholar, of course."

"Really," I said, a little surprised that he'd want to revisit the topic.

"And I discovered the truth," he continued proudly. "There was no Holocaust." He gave me a knowing smile. "Sure, some people died," he carried on, perhaps because of my hanging lower jaw and dead stare, "but you see, there was an outbreak of typhus in the prison camps, and in order to stop its spread, the Germans burned the corpses. All told, something like three hundred thousand people died from typhus." Mohammadi smiled again, a little triumphant smirk.

I stood still in disbelief, not knowing what to say. In the space of minutes he had gone from being Holocaust agnostic, like his president, to a full-fledged denier, like Duke. It was, of course, an old theory put forth years ago by various Holocaust deniers, and something he had probably read somewhere in his "scholarly" research. And, although head of research at the Foreign Ministry, he had undoubtedly not availed himself of the ministry archives, archives that might have revealed to him that Iranian diplomats in Paris, from this, his own Foreign Ministry, had taken it upon themselves to issue Iranian passports to Jews escaping the very Holocaust *they* were aware of, but that he now denied. Or he could have simply asked an ex-ambassador or two, say, someone like my father, who knew one of those diplomats himself, a diplomat who had been the uncle of the onetime prime minister Amir Abbas Hoveyda and as such had been a well-known figure in the Foreign Ministry. (An Iranian television historical miniseries a few months later depicted an Iranian diplomat's role in rescuing French Jews, and became the highest-rated show on television in 2007.[4] Presumably the producers did *not* ask for Dr. Mohammadi's input.) But I quickly decided there was no point arguing with him, smiled back at him, and just shook his hand and left.

I felt relieved to be out of his presence, and as I walked across the perfectly manicured lawns outside, I wondered just how much influence men like him could have on Mahmoud Ahmadinejad's thinking. Ahmadinejad may be open to questioning the Holocaust, I thought, but he was a far smarter man than the deputy foreign minister. A few days later, when I was relating my meeting with Mohammadi to President Khatami, he screwed up his face in disgust at the first mention of his name. Moham-madi has held senior positions at the Foreign Ministry even under the re-formists, just as other hard-liners have, and their apparently untouchable status only serves to illustrate that the "Ahmadinejad element," always a factor, will remain a constant in Iranian politics long after he is gone.

President Ahmadinejad and his government deserve much of the scorn heaped on them if for no other reason than his and some of his offi-cials' singular and puerile obsession with the Holocaust, which most Iranians feel has nothing to do with them. But if Ahmadinejad is best known in the West for his outbursts on the Holocaust, Israel, and Iran's more forceful defiance in pursuing a nuclear program, he represented far more to average Iranians the summer they elected him to the presidency.

On a hot night a few days after Ahmadinejad's inauguration in Au-gust 2005, in a comfortably air-conditioned hired car in Tehran, I sat next to the college-educated driver, a clean-cut man in his late twenties who, with his impeccably clean car, manner, and dress, could easily be from the wealthy tree-lined neighborhood in the north of the city where I was headed. When I asked him about the elections that had brought Ahmadinejad to power, the subject of every conversation in Tehran at the time, he pointed to a group of girls in the car next to us: heavily made-up, on their cell phones, and with scarves barely covering their well-coiffed heads. "Some people," he said, "think that freedom means men being able to wear shorts or women to go about without the hijab. Oth-ers think that freedom means having a full belly." He paused for a mo-ment. "There's just more of the latter," he said, forcefully changing gears as if to emphasize the point, which I took to mean that he had voted for the president. When we arrived at the slick apartment building that was my destination, I felt almost embarrassed that to him I must have repre-sented one of the people who, with a stomach about to be made full, felt that freedom did indeed mean that people might dress as they please. But there was no tension in the car, and in fact he enthusiastically engaged in the most traditional form of ta'arouf, which in a taxi ride means having to sometimes beg the driver to take your money. "How much do I owe you?" I asked, fumbling with the thick stacks of well-worn Iranian money in my hands, all of which added up to less than thirty dollars.

"It's unworthy" came the standard ta'arouf reply.

"No, please," I insisted.

"Please, it's nothing," said the driver. Normally, at this stage one more "please" from me and the bill would be settled, usually to the driver's advantage, but this young man was going for a bout of extreme ta'arouf.

"Please," I implored him, counting out some bills.

"Absolutely not, you're my guest," he said.

"No, thanks very much, but really, I must pay you," I insisted.

"I beg you," he replied. For a moment I questioned whether this was not in fact classical ta'arouf but the more sinister form of the art that requires a decisive winner and loser in the verbal sparring, with the winner's philosophical point having been acknowledged by the loser. Was he suggesting that he didn't want to take my money because he was so scornful of the full bellies?

"Please," I implored again, no longer caring if I appeared desperate or if I lost this round. "*Please* tell me how much the fare is." That did it. He had made me really beg, and with a slightly scornful but not malicious smile he said, "Thirty-five hundred *tomans*" (about four dollars), and about five hundred more than the ride should have cost at the time. I paid him without disputing the amount and watched him turn his car around and leave, his smile, a little triumphant, not quite disappearing as he watched me through the window until he stepped heavily on the gas pedal, the car shrieking away down the narrow street.

———

Mahmoud Ahmadinejad had counted on my taxi driver's definition of freedom, or really on the Iranian preoccupation with rights, or *haq*, which define that freedom, in his campaign for president in 2005. And later his history-challenged deputy foreign minister, at least in his encounter with me, seemed delighted in Iran's apparent change of tact in international relations from an emphasis on ta'arouf to one on haq: from Khatami, the master of ta'arouf who had presented a benign image to the world, to Ahmadinejad, for whom ta'arouf cannot exist without a forceful, and unambiguous, defense of haq. Ta'arouf and the preoccupation with the issue of haq form two aspects of the Iranian character that are key to understanding Iran, but are often overlooked or misunderstood by non-Iranians. The concept of ta'arouf goes way back in Iranian history, and if it is true, as some historians maintain, that nations that fell to the Persian Empire were often happy collaborators with their conquerors, perhaps the Persians' ta'arouf enhanced their reputation as benevolent rulers, as did their emphasis on rights (it was Cyrus the Great, after all, who had the world's first declaration of human rights inscribed on a cylinder at Babylon).[5] If Persia later succumbed militarily to the Greeks, the Mongols, and the Arabs, but did not lose its identity as a nation and in fact became home to conquering armies, perhaps ta'arouf played a role in Iranian defense of its culture. Ta'arouf, which can often be employed to catch an opponent off guard, momentarily lulling him into believing he's in the company of a like-minded friend, has been used by Iranians with varying degrees of success ever since. *"I've never felt as comfortable anywhere outside Iran as in America."*

Western observers often define ta'arouf as extreme Iranian hospitality, or as a Persian form of elaborate etiquette, but since Westerners naturally engage in ta'arouf too (as everyone who has ever complimented a host or hostess on what was actually a bad meal knows), it's easy to miss its true significance and its implications in Persian culture. The white lies that good manners dictate we tell in the West and general polite banter or gracious hospitality cannot begin to describe what for Iranians is a cultural imperative that is about manners, yes, but is also about gaining advantage, politically, socially, or economically, as much as anything else. One might be tempted to think of ta'arouf as passive-aggressive behavior with a peculiarly Persian hue, but although it can be, it cannot be defined solely so. American businesses and businessmen are known to succeed with brashness, determination, and sometimes even a certain amount of ruthlessness; Iranian businessmen succeed rather more quietly with a good dose of ta'arouf and in such a way that doors are opened before the ones opening the doors realize they have done so. A friend in Tehran once told me at a dinner, after a frustrating business deal had not yet reached fruition, that "all business in Iran is like first-time sex: first there are the promises, then a little foreplay, followed by more promises and perhaps a little petting." He had a disgusted look on his face. "At that stage, things get complicated—you're not sure who's the boy and who's the girl, but what you do know is that if you continue, you might get fucked." Another guest standing next to him nodded in agreement. "So you decide to proceed cautiously, touching here and touching there, showering the other party with compliments, and whispering an undying commitment, and then maybe, just maybe, it will all end in coitus, but it is rarely as satisfying for one party as it is for the other."

———

Self-deprecation, a part of any businessman's dance with another, is one aspect of ta'arouf, a central theme even, that fits nicely with Persians' admiration of dervish asceticism and selflessness, but in common use is by nature linked with the Persian penchant for gholov, and very much an element in the power plays the two together incite. Purer self-deprecation, perhaps even its root in Persian culture, is evident in a tale told of the Sufi Farid od-Din Attar, one of Persia's greatest poets, who lived in the twelfth and thirteenth centuries and is reputed to have been killed during the Mongol invasion of Persia, specifically by a Mongol soldier who captured him and dragged him about the streets of his hometown of Nishapur. A common version of the story of his death tells us that as the Mongol was leading Attar through the streets, a man came up to him and offered him a bag of silver for the poet's release.[6] Attar advised his captor not to accept, telling him that the price was surely not right. The Mongol, following Attar's advice and encouraged by the apparently high value of his prisoner, refused to sell him and continued on his way, dragging Attar behind him. Soon thereafter, another man approached. He offered the Mongol a bag of straw in return for Attar, who this time advised the Mongol to accept. "Sell me now," legend tells us he said, "for this is the right price and it is what I am worth." Furious, the Mongol beheaded Attar and left his body on the street, aware of neither the lesson of selflessness that Attar had given him nor the ta'arouf that often takes self-deprecation to heights outsiders might consider farcical and absurd. Sufis would undoubtedly disagree with me if I were to claim that Attar was merely engaging in ta'arouf, for his spirituality and mysticism (which by necessity demand extreme modesty) were obvious, but his story nonetheless illustrates that some aspects of ta'arouf, the single defining characteristic of a people that struggles daily with notions of its own superiority or inferiority, have philosophical and spiritual roots.

The Persian form of self-deprecation, perhaps originally an acknowledgment of one's irrelevance in the universe, may have spiritual roots ("Other than God, there was no One"), but it is more often used to flatter another with exaggeration than to make a philosophical point, and can also be a means to lower the guard of a rival or an opponent. It has its practical benefits too—in a country where manners and social intercourse still have a nineteenth-century air about them—when two people of the same class meet in the course of human interaction and ta'arouf requires that each make an effort to elevate the other's rank at the expense of his own. "I am your servant," one might say, and the other might reply, "I am your slave," or "I'm your inferior," both knowing full well that the exaggerations may be meaningless, but they bestow a level of respect on the recipient that may be the only kind of respect or acknowledgment he receives in the course of a day.

Iran was a kingdom for over twenty-five hundred years before becoming a theocracy, which is in itself more akin to a monarchy than any other political system, and was ruled by kings who were happy to make the point whenever they could that every subject was their servant. If a nobleman who had to genuflect and demean himself in the presence of royalty met a fellow nobleman, what better way for them to wash away the bitter taste of their servile behavior in their king's presence, even while seeking some political advantage over a peer, than to engage in a little ta'arouf with each other? If a merchant met a fellow merchant, what better way for them to alleviate the humiliation of daily reminders that they were servants of the nobility? And if two street toughs, laats who'd never know what it was to have a servant, met, how better for them to forget their lowly rank than to engage each other in the art of ta'arouf? In recent times, the laat of Iran injected a vulgarity into self-deprecating ta'arouf that in its waggish artfulness could put literate men to shame. In the back-and-forth banter of self-deprecating ta'arouf, the one who gets the last word wins, even though he has lowered himself the most. In a prime example of lower-class extreme ta'arouf, a laat somewhere, sometime, put an end to rounds of greater and greater expressions of humility by declaring to his companion, *"Beshash sheerjeh beram!"*—"Piss, and I'll dive in!" Gotcha!

Women, of course, also engage in ta'arouf, but theirs takes a slightly different form. Self-deprecation doesn't descend to the depths that it does with men, but women's same-sex banter also often involves expressions of extreme modesty and even unworthiness. Women outside the home, and they have been venturing outside the walls of their gardens for almost a century now, will engage in ta'arouf with men; however, they will generally not belittle themselves; rather, they may compliment the man and elevate his status, but not at their own expense. The ta'arouf that requires that someone providing goods or services always refuse payment at first—the implication, often stated explicitly, being that neither the goods nor the services are worthy—is practiced equally by men and women, as is the insistence by the purchaser that the payment is but a pittance and an unworthy sum for such grand goods or such superlative service. It makes even the trivial buying of a newspaper or a pack of gum a sometimes tiresome transaction when conducted in Farsi, but to Iranians such is the price of civilization.

A traditional expression of ta'arouf, *"pishkesh,"* meaning "it's yours" and uttered when one is complimented on items of clothing, household goods, or any material object for that matter, is also equally utilized by men and women. When my parents were diplomats in London in the 1950s, a time when few Iranians traveled abroad or understood Western culture, a story would be told to every new Iranian arrival as preparation for (and a warning of) the uncouth ways of foreigners. A senior Iranian diplomat and his wife, it seems, once threw a party for their British contemporaries, and at dinner the wife was complimented by an Englishwoman on her Persian silver flatware. She immediately (as would have been correct in Iran) made the offer of pishkesh, but perhaps a little too sincerely in her English translation. The next morning the wife was astonished to find the Englishwoman's butler at her front door, ready to collect the flatware, which the Iranian, out of proper ta'arouf, had to have packaged up and handed to the fellow. The story is probably fictitious (although I remember my mother insisting that it was true), but pishkesh, like other forms of ta'arouf, is not merely about the appearance of generosity and graciousness: had the item being offered been less valuable, the gesture would have been as much about advantage as good manners, and depending on how good one was at ta'arouf, one might gain (in defeat) or lose (in victory) a bauble whose significance, and value, would only later come to light.

While ta'arouf defines Persian social interaction outside the home (and is engaged in only with guests inside), by definition it cannot be employed in anonymity, which perhaps explains some contradictory Iranian behavior. Foreign observers of Iran have often remarked on how demonstrators in the streets, yelling at the top of their lungs about the evil nature of America or Britain, will, when confronted individually, rather sheepishly explain that they're not really anti-American or anti-Western. But this is the essence of ta'arouf: as long as they were anonymous, they could say whatever they wished, insulting though it may have been, but when they are face-to-face with a person who might take offense, politeness takes over. *"I have fond memories of America."*

Any visitor to Iran will also describe Tehran traffic as perhaps the worst in the world with, paradoxically for people known for their extreme hospitality and good manners, the rudest drivers of any country. True, for someone behind the wheel of an automobile, man or woman, is anonymous. There is good reason why Iranian drivers avoid eye contact with other drivers and pedestrians, for if they make eye contact, their veil of anonymity has been lifted, the gates to the walls of their homes have been unlocked, and they must become social Iranians, which means that they must practice ta'arouf. Many a time as a pedestrian I have made every effort to make eye contact with a driver bearing down on me at full speed as I step off a curb, and when I manage to, the car inevitably stops and the driver, usually with a smile, gestures "you first" with his hands. Women drivers, I've found, and perhaps reasonably in a still-sexist society, are the hardest to make eye contact with, and they can be as ruthless as the men in denying a pedestrian the right-of-way or another driver even an inch to maneuver in, but on the occasion a woman's eyes have locked onto mine, even if only for an instant, she has begrudgingly become a polite driver, all the while with her eyes then averted in case further ta'arouf becomes an unwelcome and exhausting necessity.

Although Ahmadinejad, like all Iranians, is a keen practitioner of traditional ta'arouf, he almost invariably balances his more streetlike ta'arouf with assertions of haq. His deceptively blunt language has always been laced with ta'arouf, just as much as it has been an unequivocal defense of haq. Even though it may seem that in his provocative speeches at the UN he has always singled out the United States as an evil enemy, he in fact has not mentioned the United States (or any individual American) by name even once, classical ta'arouf that not only deems it impolite to insult directly (and he might have given a lesson on ta'arouf to his friend Hugo Chávez, at least in 2006, when Chávez labeled George Bush as Satan at the UN) but also can include an obvious, but easily retractable, accusation. When in 2007 Ahmadinejad, contrary to diplomatic norms for nations that do not recognize each other, sat and intently listened to George Bush's speech at the UN (while the entire American delegation walked out on *his*), he was engaging in silent ta'arouf, a ta'arouf that sought to show the world that he was clearly the more reasonable man, and a lesson not lost on his audience back home. But while other Iranian leaders, silver-tongued and not, may have chosen to extend polite ta'arouf to even discussions of their nation's rights, Ahmadinejad generally employed the darker and more subtle form on the international stage.

When Ahmadinejad arrived in New York in 2006 to attend the UN General Assembly, because of his standing up for the haq of Muslims everywhere and because of the recent war in Lebanon, where Hezbollah, openly backed by Iran, had been able to claim a victory of sorts over the Israelis, his stature in the Muslim world, at least on the streets of the Muslim world, was at an all-time high. And he knew it: Ahmadinejad had a hubristic air about him every time I saw him, even while he enthusiastically engaged in ta'arouf that might come across merely as polite behavior to Americans but held greater meaning for Iranians. He had given an interview to Mike Wallace for *60 Minutes* earlier in the summer, an interview where even in America opinion seemed to be that he had (again, thanks to his ta'arouf skills) outmaneuvered the at times frustrated-sounding master of the combative television interview, and according to people close to him he felt supremely confident that he could handle any question posed to him by the media during his brief stay in the United States. Ahmadinejad was, as he always is in public, quite charming. A very small man in stature, though, he is acutely aware of and uncomfortable about his height disadvantage, and he displayed a sense of image control during his television interview with *NBC Nightly News* (where I was present as a consultant to NBC, and not to the Iranians, as I had been on other occasions). Brian Williams and Ahmadinejad were to face each other in armchairs set up in a suite at the InterContinental hotel on Forty-eighth Street, and when I saw the chairs, I knew that the Iranian president would be displeased. Williams, a tall man, would overshadow Ahmadinejad, and indeed, when the president entered the room and sat down, he looked absurd in an *Alice in Wonderland* sort of way, reminding me very much of the music video for Tom Petty's "Don't Come Around Here No More"—all Ahmadinejad needed, I thought, was an oversized glass of water and a floppy top hat, and the image would be complete. Williams immediately saw the comical aspect and sensed the discomfort; he looked at me and, speaking slowly so the president could follow, as Americans are wont to do when confronted with a non–English speaker, suggested that perhaps different chairs should be brought in. Ahmadinejad confirmed to me in Farsi that the chair was a little too big, a ta'arouf-appropriate understatement, to be sure, for he had sunk in and could barely reach the arms or touch the floor with his feet, and the producers scurried about, finally settling on a pair of dining chairs that Ahmadinejad seemed to find agreeable. (He smiled throughout the whole process, almost apologetically, which only made the producers more intent on pleasing him.)

The interview proceeded, and Ahmadinejad was his usual confident and ebullient self, his speech exoteric in contrast with his predecessors' sometimes esoteric wanderings in their public comments. By far the most interesting revelation, though, was not any new explanation of his statements on the Holocaust or his opinion on Israel's fate, but in the clue to his personality, which revealed itself when Williams, in a lighthearted moment, asked the president if he'd like to see more of America, and the president's response was a simple and nonchalant "Sure." Pressed for details about what or where in particular he'd like to visit in America, and perhaps Williams was hoping to elicit an unexpected response such as "Disneyland," Ahmadinejad stuck firmly to generalities, and finally said,

"*Albateh,* esrary *nadareem,*" which was correctly translated as "Of course, we're not insistent." But the actual meaning, and nuance is difficult to translate from Persian, was much closer to "Of course, we don't really *care.*" While Mahmoud Ahmadinejad thought that America might be interesting, it was apparently not *that* interesting, at least to him, but he found a way to say it that was politely insulting. And that remark spoke volumes about Ahmadinejad, a man who had never shown much interest in travel and who believed passionately that Iran had as much to recommend it as any other country, but also volumes about a generation of nationalistic Iranians who often winced at the onetime fawning, beyond-ta'arouf attitude of Iranian leaders, and many of their subjects, toward the West. It was also a classic illustration of the superiority/inferiority complexes that many Iranians suffer from, and it was a signal to his audience back home that he was not about to be seduced, as many of them have been or might be, by the glitter of the West, even though he was, naturally, civilized enough to respond graciously to a question.

Ahmadinejad's personality and image consciousness revealed themselves again when, in another attempt at lighthearted banter, Brian Williams asked him about his attire—a suit (and open-neck shirt) rather than his trademark Windbreaker—and the Iranian president replied, "*Sheneedeem shoma kot-shalvaree hasteen; manam kot-shalvar poosheedam,*" which was translated as "We knew you wear a suit, so I wore a suit." But the phrase is actually much closer in meaning to "We'd heard you *are* a suit, so I wore a suit," a sentiment much in keeping with his ordinary, "man of the people" image, as well as his, and many of his supporters', disdain for symbols of class and wealth, but it was also another example of his employing the darker language of ta'arouf.

———————

Ahmadinejad's darker ta'arouf goes hand in hand with the issue of haq, which is for him a critical political concern (as it is for Iranians of all stripes), whether it is expressed through complex and flowery ta'arouf or the more straightforward language, albeit still infused with ta'arouf, of the common man. Iranians, who've had no history and, until the age of communication, barely a knowledge of Western liberal democracy, do not necessarily equate their rights with democracy as we know it. In almost every noisy public demonstration in recent years, whether it be trade unionists demanding better pay as their *right* (as teachers and bus drivers have done) or the general public protesting gas prices or rationing (objecting to the infringement on their right to cheap fuel, for Iranians believe that the oil under their country's ground belongs to the people), issues such as free speech, social freedoms, and even democratic elections have taken a backseat.

Students at university have been an exception, and their protests have often been violently broken up by the government or quasi-governmental forces (and by Basij fellow students), but, strangely, many ordinary Iranians view the students as hopelessly naive, forgetting that it was students, inside and outside Iran, who were in the vanguard of the Islamic Revolution.[7] The Islamic government, keenly aware of university students' role in bringing it to power and aware of the potential for unrest on campuses spreading elsewhere, has always taken a two-pronged approach to ensuring that a new revolution does not start in academia. The obvious approach has been to crack down on any student movement that has the gall to publicly challenge the government, whether by expelling protesting students, arresting and jailing them, or shutting down their newspapers and limiting their speech. The other approach has been to populate universities with the children of the children of the revolution, with the Basij, and with underprivileged and deeply religious youths from working-class families: exactly the kinds of people that the government can reasonably rely on to counter any threat to an Islamic Republic that has taken extremely good care of its own. And reliable they are, for every time a student pro-democracy movement crops up on any campus, other *Islamic* student organizations are there to challenge it, even violently. (It mustn't be forgotten also that the government mounts its biggest and most influential public gathering, weekly Friday prayers attended by thousands of pro-regime

Iranians as well as every foreign journalist, on the campus of the University of Tehran.) The situation contrasts sharply with prerevolutionary times, when pro-democracy students—and all the Islamic students' organizations were "pro-democracy" then—faced no challenge from royalists (or strict secularists), who either kept quiet in the face of the increasingly overwhelming odds against them or in some cases couldn't believe that their all-powerful Shah might one day be gone.

Students looking to assert their "rights" today face a measure of public apathy as well as the wrath of the government, a wrath that was unchecked even under reformist Khatami's rule. In one of the biggest challenges to the government, at a time when Khatami had ushered in reforms unthinkable to hard-line conservatives, student protests in 1999 led to street riots, causing a level of unrest that conservatives viewed as threatening to the regime. The students themselves were in reality hardly a threat to the regime, for the peaceful protests had started in *support* of Khatami, who after all was a part of the system, and against the closure by the judiciary of a reform newspaper, *Salam*, that was closely associated with him. The protests extended into the dormitories and across the nation's universities, but the police, along with pro-government students and vigilantes, brutally broke up any demonstrations or sit-ins, burned dorm rooms, and made hundreds of arrests. While the violence and unrest continued for a week, resulting in conflicting accounts of numbers killed and injured, a top Revolutionary Guard (who is today the commander of the force) sent an ominous letter to President Khatami warning him that if he didn't crack down on the students, the Guards certainly would. Khatami's enemies saw an opportunity to both reverse some of his reforms and discredit him with his supporters, and Khatami's powerlessness in the face of government brutality—his weak stand on the haq of students—did indeed lead to a loss of prestige for him (but not enough to deny him a landslide reelection two years later) and constant challenges to his policy of promoting his vision of "Islamic democracy" in Iran.

But despite student dissatisfaction, and perhaps a reason for the apparent public apathy toward the student protesters, the Islamic Republic has been astute in understanding what "rights" Iranians cherish above all others, and is careful not to trample on those, as various Shahs' governments did. One important right for Iranians is that of being free to do as one pleases inside the walls of one's home or garden. Other than liquor raids in the early days of the revolution by overzealous komiteh or Basij members, intrusions into private life are extremely rare, and Iranians have no fear of expressing their opinions in what they deem private space, their "movable walls" if you will, which can include a café table or a taxi and which would have been unthinkable under the so-called progressive last Shah.

Publishing is a different matter, for that is public expression, but Iranians who have long been used to very specific codes for public behavior, whether Islamic, cultural, or political under the Shahs, have adjusted to the newer limitations on free speech. They have done so partly by taking to the Internet with hundreds of thousands of Farsi blogs, and partly in the constant game of chicken that newspaper editors play with the government, pushing the envelope to the point of being shut down, only to emerge under a different name, sometimes just days later, often to be closed yet again.

The intellectual elite of Tehran and other big cities chafe under Islamic rules and under suppression of free speech, but for the majority of Iranians they are issues that pale in comparison to their "rights" to employment, a decent wage, or fair consumer prices, rights Ahmadinejad was particularly adept at convincing voters he was the strongest proponent of (while dismissing, with some success, accusations that his religiously conservative side might be tempted to intrude behind Persian walls). Liberal Iranian women, and certainly some Iranian men, would agree with their Western counterparts that their "rights" include dressing as they please when they venture into public space, but I have heard from pious Muslims, including some women, that if that right offends the majority, as some conservatives claim it does in Iran, then it is not an automatic "right." Although the mandatory-hijab question resonates emotionally for some, what resonates more for women activists in Iran is the larger issue of rights as they compare with those of men and fighting discriminatory Islamic laws, which they frame as issues of haq that have sent some progressive clerics searching for Islamic solutions.

Westerners can be forgiven if they often confuse haq with another aspect of Iranian culture that looms large: the much-talked-about "Persian pride." The reason Iranians, even those most opposed to their government, seem to support their country's nuclear program, despite the hardships that they may have to endure in order for it to achieve success, is put forward by many analysts as pure, fierce nationalism and excessive Persian pride, as if Iranians have rejoiced in their scientists' ability to overcome technological hurdles as much as their presidents and other leaders have seemed to. To accept that conclusion is a mistake that betrays a fundamental misunderstanding of the Iranian psyche and of Iranian society. Iranians are indeed proud, sometimes to the point of arrogance, but pride is not what is driving the nuclear issue as far as the majority of Iranians are concerned. The often-mentioned nationalism and pride that Iranians exhibit, much to the discomfort of other Middle Easterners, are mostly related to their history, and the pre-Islamic one at that, rather than any "made in Iran" sentiments. No, the nuclear issue is another matter of haq, basic rights that deeply resonate for a Shia people that has long suffered from inferiority and superiority complexes, often simultaneously.

Iranians deserve their reputation for being annoyingly proud, but they have never exhibited the characteristics of fiercely nationalistic societies when it comes to material goods, and to them nuclear fuel is just another material good. Iranians do not "buy Iranian"; if anything, they go out of their way to "buy" American, European, or even Asian. Billboards in Tehran for consumer goods will often proclaim in big letters "Made in France" or "Made in Korea" as a sign of the obvious superiority of the goods, even when there are Iranian equivalents, sometimes as good and less expensive. Iranians buy Iranian-made cars not out of pride that their nation has a strong automotive industry but because import tariffs mean that a Camry or a Maxima is a luxury car out of reach of ordinary workers, who grudgingly settle for an Iranian-made Peugeot, Kia, or even the completely Iranian-engineered and crudely styled (but well-made) Samand. But goods that are *khareji*, or "foreign," have always commanded a premium as well as bragging rights.

A few years ago in Tehran when I first got into my cousin Ali's car, a Peugeot 206 hatchback, I looked around as I fastened my seat belt and said, "This is a Peugeot, huh?"

"Yes, but this one is made in *France*," he said with great satisfaction, lest I wonder what he was doing driving an *Iranian*-made car.

Much as the government tries to sing the praises of Iranian industry and science, one would be hard-pressed to find a single Iranian who does not believe that foreign-made goods and Western technology are not superior. Even cheap goods from China, such as shoes and clothing that are sold at discount shops, are more popular than equivalent Iranian ones, which sadly are becoming scarcer and scarcer. If the nuclear issue was sold to Iranians by their government as only a matter of pride in Iran's accomplishments, very few Iranians would be willing to suffer economic sanctions or even war as a consequence, and yet the Western media are constantly filled with stories of how ordinary Iranians take great pride in the nuclear program. While the Iranian government has indeed pushed the pride button, most often at rallies and in President Ahmadinejad's speeches (pride is also alluded to at every occasion—say, a tractor factory opening or a new auto assembly plant—that involves Iranian industrial progress), Iranians by and large focus on the other aspect of the issue that is also touched upon by government officials defending their obstinacy on the nuclear question: basic national and, by extension, individual rights.

The question of rights is fundamental to Shia Islam, the very founding of which was a struggle for rightfulness. And Shia Iran, with a history of centuries of perceived injustice toward its religion and sect, and the trampling of its sovereignty by foreign powers, cannot easily accept any attempt to deprive its people of their rights. The sense of rights and justice is so deeply ingrained in the Iranian psyche that when Iranians mourn Imams martyred fourteen centuries ago, as they do during the month of Moharram, they are consumed by paroxysms of weeping, not necessarily for the dead, but for the cruel injustice perpetrated on their saints and, by extension, on them still today. The Iranian government plays up the injustice of the Western position on Iran's nuclear program (which is viewed essentially as to arbitrarily deny them advanced technology), and unjust it is as far as the people—who consider neither themselves nor even their leaders particularly aggressive or violent—are concerned.

———————

Iranians, like all other people, have differing ideas of what their rights are, what constitutes haq, but they do generally agree on the most basic. Thomas Jefferson may have declared that our rights include life, liberty, and the pursuit of happiness, and the French Revolution may have given France the motto *"Liberté, égalité, fraternité,"* but the Iranian motto, if there were one, might simply be "Don't trample on my rights," without defining what those rights are. But the concept of haq is such a part of the Iranian vocabulary, within or without Islam (and Iran is a religious society, after all), that it can sometimes border on the risible.

A man who works for one of my friends in Tehran as a sort of man Friday, doing odd jobs here and there, which have included giving me rides on the back of his motorcycle when Tehran traffic has been at its worst and when I needed to get somewhere fast, is someone who has never set foot outside the country but is nonetheless so obsessed with America and all things American that his nickname for years has been Ali-Amrika-y, or "Ali the American." He naturally quizzes me on all things related to America whenever he sees me, often with the wide-eyed enthusiasm of a child and to the annoyance of his employer, who gently reminds him that he has work to do beyond sitting and conversing with his boss's friend. On one occasion, presumably after something I said must have confirmed to him the absolute greatness of the United States—and he tends to ignore me or not hear whenever I mention anything critical—he shook his head slowly. "I was destined to go to America and become an American, or even to have been born there," he said. *"Haq-e-moon'o khordan"*—"My rights were taken from me" (literally, "My rights were eaten"). I looked at him and started laughing, and he chuckled too, for he realized how absurd his statement was, but I couldn't help wondering how many nights he had spent awake in his bed thinking about how his "right" to be an American had been wrongfully denied him, whether by God, by Iran, or by the United States itself.

Haq-khordan—"trampling of rights"—is a very common expression, and I have heard on many occasions, even from pro-American Iranians, how the United States, whether on the nuclear issue or on others (and certainly in the case of the CIA-backed coup of 1953), has trampled on the God-given rights of the Iranian people. For Iranians, fierce capitalists that they are (which Islam allows, even if only grudgingly), the pursuit of happiness is an important right, as are life, equality (an equality encouraged by Islam with the unfortunate exception of gender equality and, in its attempts at breaking the class system, by the Islamic Republic), and brotherhood (encouraged by Islam). Liberty is the one right that Western democracies view differently, as do some Iranians of course, from the way Iranian governments do. But most Iranians believe that they had defined their liberty under Mossadeq, the prime minister overthrown by the CIA, and had redefined it with the revolution of 1979, which liberated them from the totalitarianism of the Western-supported Pahlavis. Foreign powers, regrettably, often conspire to trample that right in pursuit of their own interests, and their own leaders too, who, as President Khatami once told me, have had little history of or experience with democracy, can exhibit dictatorial qualities rather soon after they've been democratically given the reins of power.

President Ahmadinejad, perhaps better than most other Iranian leaders, made haq the defining concept of Iranian politics both during his

campaign and after he was elected. His obvious resentment of the ruling class was based not just on working-class values but also on his
deep Shia sense of injustice done to the masses, of the violation of
their haq, by their rulers. And to Ahmadinejad, the injustices that Ayatollah Khomeini had railed against were once again taking root in his
beloved Islamic Republic, injustices such as corruption, cronyism,
nepotism, and a stranglehold on power by a handful of politicians. Just
as Khomeini had eschewed the language of politics and diplomacy, so
did Ahmadinejad. He spoke in simple, informal terms, in the language
of the street, with no nuance or obfuscation, and to many it was a refreshing change. His ta'arouf, often self-deprecating, was to present
himself as but a simple man (like Khomeini) who only sought to defend the rights of Iran and Iranians, at home and abroad. His promises to fight corruption, patronage, and privilege while at the same time
redistributing the government's (oil) wealth directly to the dinner tables ("tablecloths," or *sofreh*, as he put it) of ordinary Iranians were believed, and despite the trepidation of wealthy Westernized Tehranis he
started his four-year term with a high degree of popularity.

Ahmadinejad had no religious credentials, but he also managed to
out-believe even the strongest believers in Shia Twelver Islam by constantly invoking the Mahdi's name, which in itself spoke to his obsession with haq and justice, which the good Imam is to deliver to all
believers on Judgment Day.[8] Ahmadinejad not only interprets the story
of the Mahdi's occultation literally but believes it will be during his
presidency that the Mahdi will resurface among ordinary mortals to
once and for all fix the world's problems. I was told by one person present at his inauguration that Ahmadinejad told several people there that
he was only a temporary president, and that the Messiah would relieve
him of the burdensome responsibility in a "few" years, at the *most*.

Despite his Shia fervor, however, Ahmadinejad's acute sense of
what Iranians might consider mundane but essential haq led him to declare less than a year into his presidency, and in the Messiah's continued absence, that women have the right to attend soccer matches (the

announcement cleverly coinciding with the international release of a film, banned in Iran, about a group of girls who disguise themselves as boys to do exactly that, but are arrested by army conscripts[9]). Senior conservative Ayatollahs, who are generally less concerned that the Mahdi will render their work irrelevant in their lifetimes, evidently took exception to their lay president's interpretation of women's rights, and Ahmadinejad's initiative was vetoed immediately.

———

Disappointed female soccer fans aside, Ahmadinejad's inability to deliver either the basic rights of Iranians or the Imam Mahdi began to be felt within a year of his taking office. As the winter of 2006–7 approached, discontent in Iran grew as the economy actually worsened and the prospect of international isolation, attributed largely to Ahmadinejad's style if not his policies, worried the average Iranian. Iranians, like Americans, vote for their president and fully expect him, perhaps as naïvely as we do, to deliver on his campaign promises. Ahmadinejad's promise to fill the bellies of all Iranians with the proceeds of Iran's oil exports had fallen drastically short by that winter, well over a year into his presidency, and after his slate was trounced in municipal and national elections in December, attacks on him in the press, in salons, and in the streets became all too common. Foreign policy, what we were most concerned with when it came to Iran and its unusual leader, was mostly relevant to the Iranian masses only inasmuch as it affected their pocketbooks and, of course, their security. President Ahmadinejad's promises to alleviate Iran's economic woes were no longer believed, and the style of his foreign policy was viewed as having both exacerbated the economic crunch and contributed to the sense of insecurity, even if it continued to defend a nation's rights.

The UN Security Council resolution of December 2006 imposing sanctions on Iran for its refusal to suspend uranium enrichment was viewed in Iran as a foreign policy failure, not because President Ahmadinejad's sometimes belligerent and always defiant insistence that Iran would not give up its rights under the Non-Proliferation Treaty was largely disapproved of, but because the result of that resolution was that certain food staples, such as tomatoes, had, since the passage of the resolution, become unaffordable to the Iranian masses. The Holocaust conference in Tehran that preceded the UN vote was derided not because of its preposterous premise but for its being viewed as having unfavorably swayed the UN vote. The Iranian administration's goading of President Bush and the U.S. government, whether on Iraq, Lebanon, the Palestinian question, or basic issues of Iranian and American power, was viewed not as illegitimate but as having resulted in unilateral U.S. economic sanctions (and undue U.S. pressure on European and Asian allies), which meant foreign letters of credit were essentially unavailable to Iranian businesses that would, if sanctions continued or even expanded, downsize and contribute to Iran's already unenviable unemployment rate.

Iranians inside Iran were neither shy nor fearful in expressing their dissatisfaction with their president, but if his honeymoon with both Iranian voters and the Iranian media had been even shorter lived than President Bush's (his extended by the events of 9/11, as it was), it did not mean that he was politically doomed, nor did it even mean that he couldn't regain his popularity. Foreign policy was indeed inextricably linked in the minds of Iranians to the economy, but it was by no means certain that Iranians, who seemed to generally prefer that their president project a more benign image abroad, were more willing now than before to forgo what they believed to be nuclear independence in order to buy, say, cheaper tomatoes. However, Iranian obsessiveness with a single issue such as the price of tomatoes—and tomatoes were the national obsession for almost two months—was evident in the airtime it received on national television, in a debate in parliament, and in Ahmadinejad's remark on the matter, widely ridiculed, that people should shop in his neighborhood because the price of tomatoes at his corner bodega hadn't increased as much as elsewhere. He was actually not too far off the mark with his quip, which was intended as much as a dig against the elite as a defense of his economy, but his populist tone still wasn't quite putting tomatoes on the tables of the working classes, who naturally deemed it their right to enjoy a meal with that most common of fruits. On weekday afternoons at the Behjatabad bazaar, however, Tehran's chicest (and most expensive) outdoor food emporium, which I visited a few times, tomatoes of every variety were piled high in front of the vegetable stalls, and hawkers beckoned the well-dressed shoppers to sample their wares. The exquisitely red tomatoes, out of reach for most South Tehran residents, were bought by the kilo by men and women with sculpted noses who pulled up in their $120,000 Mercedes and $60,000 BMWs (in a city filled with $8,000 Iranian-made cars), many of whom would go on to discuss the price they paid at dinner parties with the same seriousness they normally reserved for discussing the Dow Jones Industrials or foreign exchange rates.

The Iranian wealthy, certainly the secular, Westernized ones, were taking delight in Ahmadinejad's unpopularity, thankful that at last Iranians from all walks of life were turning against him, but their own lives were actually very little affected by Ahmadinejad's policies. The concern that many had had when he was first elected president—that the social freedoms they had enjoyed under Khatami would be severely curtailed—had not yet materialized, and in Tehran in early 2007 the liberal interpretation of the hijab, along with dating, sex, liquor consumption, and every form of Western influence, continued unabated with the government still turning an, if not blind, then extremely myopic eye.

In the late spring of 2007, however, with an embattled government facing the possibility of further UN sanctions that could harm the already-unsteady economy, the authorities, in what seemed a move to turn attention away from more serious issues, embarked on a far more severe crackdown on liberalization than had been the norm in the past, and Ahmadinejad, despite his earlier statements that the issue of hijab paled in significance to greater issues of haq, did not weigh in on the crackdown.[10] A yearly rite when warm weather, and therefore more revealing outfits, first make their appearance, the public crackdown on "mal-veiling"—

another of the wonderful words the Islamic Republic has given us—made only a small dent in Iranian lifestyles (but received much attention in the West). On the streets, women (and men with exaggerated hairstyles or skimpy T-shirts) were arrested with much greater frequency than in past years, but usually only if they challenged the authorities, who generally first warned them to, and then showed them how to, "correct" their behavior. But apart from the unusual wave of arrests for "un-Islamic behavior," accusations were made both inside and outside Iran that there was a more nefarious aspect to the crackdown, namely, that it had been used as a cover to arrest, imprison, and intimidate opponents of the regime.

Indeed, a simultaneous crackdown on crime and gangs resulted in an unusually high number of executions by the state—a state that is second only to China in the number of its citizens it puts to death—and exile groups made the claim that the government had used the opportunity in enforcing Sharia (Islamic law, which automatically imposes the death penalty on crimes such as murder and rape unless the victims' families agree to receive blood money as reparations) to eliminate some of its opponents. It was an accusation that was difficult to prove, for the most prominent political prisoners, such as labor leaders, student activists, feminists, and, of course, the Iranian-Americans accused of espionage, were not among the hanged, but those the government called "terrorists" certainly were (echoing the Shah's era, when virtually all political prisoners hanged had been first found guilty of "terrorism," and a reminder that the "terrorist" moniker has worked in undermining civil rights in autocracies and democracies equally). They included the confessed assassins of a judge, and a number of men found guilty, having provided less convincing confessions, of acts of terrorism in the troubled regions of Sistan va Baluchestan (bordering Pakistan and where Sunni separatists frequently engage government forces) and Khuzestan (where Arab separatist groups have on occasion resorted to terror tactics and where Iran accuses the United States and the United Kingdom of fomenting unrest).

As horrific as the photographs and videos of public executions that circulated on the Web were, the majority of Iranians support the death penalty for serious crimes, although many, and particularly the reformists, believe that Sharia should be ignored (if not taken off the books) in the cases of lesser crimes (such as adultery, prostitution, and pederasty). The presidency does not control the judiciary, but under Khatami and his influence (including with the Supreme Leader) conservatives had less of a free rein to demand the imposition of the most controversial of Sharia rulings, whereas with the Ahmadinejad administration conservative judges have, to use an American expression, felt free in spending what they believe to be some of their "political capital." Unusually, many executions in 2007 were carried out in public, on the streets and with the hangman's noose dangling from a crane on the back of a truck and often with crowds cheering on, particularly in the cases of confessed murderers. Although Sharia deems that death must come to the condemned quickly and painlessly (and halal regulations even mandate the same for animals destined for the dinner table), Iran's executioners do not seem to have approached hanging—which should result in the instantaneous breaking of the neck—as a mathematical challenge, for some unfortunate convicts have ended up being slowly strangled rather than hanged, either because of an inadequate drop or because the hangmen simply dispensed with the drop altogether, instead allowing the crane to lift the victims by the ropes around their necks.

But despite the arrests and despite the executions (which for those not witnessing them meant very little, since Iranians generally have hardly any sympathy for convicted criminals), Tehran's street scenes, apart from a slight tightening of the headscarf here and there, did not visibly change much in the second year of Ahmadinejad's "return to the values of the revolution," and the vigilance with which authorities initially pursued their public campaign against "mal-veiling" abated somewhat in the face of other pressing issues, such as an unpopular decision to ration gasoline in order to prepare for potential future UN- or unilateral U.S.- and European-imposed sanctions (Iran needs to import gasoline because of a lack of oil-refining capacity, which it in turn blames on years of U.S. sanctions).[11]

———————

Many Iranians, particularly the more secular-minded and those in the diaspora, may insist that Mahmoud Ahmadinejad does not represent the true Iran or Iranians, that he comes from a place few recognize. His political views may indeed be extreme, maybe more so than those of most of the people who voted for him, but the unrecognizable place he comes from is very much a part of Iran and its culture, and many Iranians can readily identify with him, even if they're dissatisfied with his administration's programs. It's an Iran away from the North Tehran that Western journalists tend to focus upon, where nose jobs are few, where humility and ta'arouf share the spotlight with pride and straightforwardness, but, more important, where the all-encompassing Iranian preoccupation with haq is most conspicuous. Ahmadinejad, the commoner elevated to the ranks of the elite by his fellow common man, where he will firmly remain whether in or out of power as long as there is an Islamic Republic, may care or worry less about the trajectory of his political fortunes than other Iranian statesmen. He may also care less about his and everyone else's worldly boss, the Supreme Leader, whoever he may be at any given time, and it perhaps matters less to him that he be right or wrong on any matter, or that history judge him kindly or harshly. He strongly believes that he stands for the haq of the people, and Ahmadinejad, like so many of his fellow citizens who can identify with him and are yearning for justice, deliverance, and their haq, will continue to proclaim himself their champion. Until, that is, the Mahdi takes over his job.

———————

"*Yeki-bood; yeki-nabood.*" A story that embodies both the Iranian obsession with haq and the imbued psychology of ta'arouf is one that may or may not be true, for there is no way of knowing, but the fact that it exists even as a story gives insight into the Iranian psyche. Ahmad Shah, the last Qajar king, of the dynasty that preceded the Pahlavis, in turn the last dynasty before the Islamic Revolution, ruled as a constitutional monarch and left the sorry state of the Iranian economy to hapless viziers to manage. (It is entirely possible that this tale was invented by family and supporters of the Qajars, who were ridiculed by the Pahlavi Shahs and the Islamic governments that followed alike.) The British, who had briefly occupied Iran during World War I and whose influence in Persia was balanced somewhat by Russia, were pressuring Iran to agree to a treaty that would in essence make Persia a British protectorate, on top of the continued concessions in oil and tobacco that they would exploit for decades longer. But the young Shah was resisting. In 1919, on a state visit to London, where he was feted by King George and Lord Curzon, who made separate flowery speeches outlining the future of Persia, he realized that however much he resisted (and his own speeches there reveal, at least in oratory, his cold attitude toward the British plan), the British would have their way, with or without him. One morning, as he was starting to shave, his manservant noticed he hadn't put out his mirror.

"Why, your majesty, are you going to shave without a mirror?" he asked.

"Because," Ahmad Shah replied, "I don't want to look at my *madar-ghahbeh* [son-of-a-whore] face."

Ahmad Shah was ultimately, with the help of the British, pushed aside by a military coup in 1921, self-exiled from his country in 1923, and formally deposed in 1925 (eventually dying in France in 1930). He knew, in London, that he was about to give in to the powerful British Empire because of his and his country's weakness, and be forced to surrender Iran's haq and honor, and little else could describe his feelings of complete humiliation. He was not, of course, a son of a whore, but if the story is true, his ta'arouf was exceptionally fitting.

VICTORY OF BLOOD
OVER THE SWORD

"There was a girl, a young girl, who had already had her leg amputated because of cancer, and she lay dying in the hospital. Her doctor and nurses, who could do no more for her, asked her if she wanted or needed to talk to anyone about any worries or problems she might have. 'I don't even tell *God* my problems or worries,' she replied, 'but I do tell my *problems* about God.' When she died, her distraught father told the doctor, who was trying to comfort him, that it was all right. 'I was unworthy of her,' he said, 'so God took her back to him.' The doctor, a secularist and not religious in any way but impressed by the power of faith, is the one who has told the story many times." Mrs. Khatami finished speaking and looked at me with a smile, her gentle eyes wide and unblinking. She held her floral chador, one she only wears indoors, tightly under her chin with her fist. "You can't explain it, can you?" she said. "But there is *something* about faith and religion."

The story may be corny, I thought, even if it's true, but there was nothing corny about Mrs. Sadoughi, as Maryam Khatami, sister of the former president Khatami, is better known. (Women in Iran keep their maiden names when they marry, including on all legal documents, and use their husband's name only if prefaced with "Mrs.") *"I do tell my* problems *about God."* We were sitting in the living room of the Sadoughi house in the old part of central Yazd, the desert city smack in the middle of Iran where Hojjatoleslam Mohammad Ali Sadoughi, Maryam's husband, is the *Imam Jomeh,* or "Friday prayers leader," and therefore the representative of the Supreme Leader of the Islamic Revolution in the province. It was the start of a busy week for Sadoughi, for this was the ninth day of Moharram, the first month of the Arabic calendar, Tasua, as it is known throughout the Shia world—one of the two holiest days in a holy month of mourning for the martyrdom of the Shia Imam Hossein.

Sadoughi's son, Mohammad, was busy preparing a *ghalyoun,* or "water pipe," for us to smoke Persian tobacco after lunch, and Maryam Khatami and I were having a conversation about the role of religion in Iranian society while her husband, sitting on a couch next to me, listened carefully, nodding his head in agreement from time to time between sips of hot tea. The old Persian doors (or French doors, in the West) of the living room opened onto a completely walled garden with a large, rectangular pond in the center, surrounded by fruit trees and mature palms, and I stared admiringly at the *badgir,* or "wind catcher," the ancient Iranian air-conditioning system—a rectangular tower with slats at the top that "catch" a breeze and accelerate it (thus cooling the air) downward—that served to cool a large shaded patio at the end of the garden used in the summer. The mud-brick house was well over a century old and was as traditional a dwelling as one can find in Iran, albeit unlike many other old houses in that it was restored to perfection and spoke to the Sadoughis' love of all things Persian, including the tobacco we were about to smoke (which is no longer popular, having lost ground to the Arab fruit-flavored tobaccos also found in the West and, of course, cigarettes).

––––––––––

Earlier that morning, I had dutifully arrived at the Hazireh Mosque in front of the Sadoughi house, a house that sits at the beginning of a maze of impossibly narrow alleys that emanate from the main Yazd thoroughfare and is distinguishable from others only by the sole Revolutionary Guard, Kalashnikov casually thrown over his shoulder, standing outside his dilapidated booth. Yazd is a traditional city, a religious city, but is also known for its particularly theatrical public ceremonies commemorating the death of Imam Hossein some fourteen hundred years ago, when the city was the site, as it still is today, of important Zoroastrian temples. Mourning death is a Yazdi specialty, even an art, and death and martyrdom are pillars of Shia Islam. Religion is, at least to me, most interesting in its extreme human expression, particularly extreme *public* expression, and few places compare to Yazd province in that expression, especially in its beauty and emotional resonance rather than what we might think of as fundamentalist character.

The mosque was already almost filled to capacity with men dressed in black; women in black chadors and young girls in black headscarves were relegated to a balcony that ran along one wall and overlooked the expansive Persian-carpeted room, a room so brightly lit by massive fluorescent fixtures that the rows of tiled columns sparkled as if they were mirrors. I was led to a bench just inside the open doors of the entrance on one side of the building where I sat down with a number of mullahs as well as Sadoughi himself, protected by Revolutionary Guards, to watch the proceedings. A path of sorts had been cleared in front of us and extended in a U shape all around the mosque to the entrance on the other side, and an officious, overweight policeman in an ill-fitting uniform stood watch, eagerly anticipating the processions soon to arrive by waving this and that person to one side or another as they entered the mosque. While we were waiting for the ceremonies to begin, we were offered small glasses of tea by an attendant who fetched them from a makeshift kitchen behind us that had been set up to provide tea to any of the hundreds of people who had come in remembrance of Imam Hossein's martyrdom.

I looked around at all the black shirts, thankful that I'd picked one up in Tehran a few days earlier, even though the fit was questionable and the fabric better suited to a ship's sail. I had roamed the Tehran Friday bazaar, looking for an all-black shirt that was cheap but presentable, and had settled on one for five dollars from an old vendor who insisted that it was made of cotton. "Yes, yes," he had told me, "of course it's cotton!" I must've looked unconvinced. "Made in China!" he added, as if that were a strong selling point. "If it wasn't cotton," he continued, "it would be shiny. See?" He was right: it wasn't particularly shiny, but we *were* indoors. I bought it anyway, knowing full well that it couldn't possibly be anything but 100 percent synthetic, and as I was walking away, I heard another vendor shouting, *"Bolouse-e zedeh afsordegi! Bolouse-e zedeh afsordegi!,"* which best translates as "antidepressant blouses," a rather optimistic cry to the female customers who were, perhaps he knew better than I, after all, looking for some new clothes to lift their spirits in this, the most sullen month of the year. But as I suspected, neither the antidepressant blouses nor my black shirt could possibly deliver on their promises. In the bright and hot desert sunshine of Yazd, the shininess of my black shirt was unmistakable, as was the itch, and I suspected rash, developing around my neck as I looked left and right, awaiting with great anticipation the first of the groups of organized mourners who would be marching past me this morning.

And then I heard the drums. A slow beat, and a young man took to the microphone at a stand at the front of the room. In a mellifluous but sad voice, he started singing the praises of the Imams as the men entering the mosque in two columns, marching slowly in step, shouted out a chorus while beating their chests with their right hands in time with the beat. The men around me followed suit, albeit with less vigor, sort of a faux chest beating or really just chest tapping, and I did the same. Following the first group of men came the chain beaters. These men were silent, but each wielded a wooden-handled instrument, something like a feather duster but with metal chain links in place of feathers, and in time to the beat they raised the chains above their shoulders and brought them down on their backs. The swish-swish sound of the chains and the loud thuds they made as they connected with the men's backs provided additional percussive accompaniment, and some of those men, mostly the younger ones with gelled hair, rolled-up sleeves, and tight jeans, beat themselves with such vigor, creating perfect arcs with chains glittering under the fierce lights, that one wondered how they managed to remain expressionless.

The previous day, at my cousin Fatemeh's house in Ardakan, a village thirty-five miles away, I had announced that I wished to participate in the chain beating, *zanjeer-zani*, and had made a few practice swings with a set of chains that were rummaged out of a closet by a relative. They hurt. I'm sure I grimaced when they connected with my back and made facial expressions that must've convinced my family, deeply religious though they are, that I was suffering from a mental illness of some sort, for no sane Westernized Iranian, certainly not one who had lived abroad all his life, could possibly be interested in mourning the death of Imam Hossein with a bout of self-flagellation. In Tehran too, I had been greeted with stunned silence by the more secular Iranians when I would casually say I was going to attend Tasua and Ashura ceremonies, a silence that spoke to their inability to comprehend *why*. But in the end it was explained to me, *after* I tried using the chains, mind you, that I would be unable to actually perform anyway, as the ceremonies were carefully choreographed affairs, not unlike the various parades on Fifth Avenue in New York, and did not allow for spontaneous audience participation beyond symbolic chest beating.

The parade at the mosque continued. Different groups of men, sometimes even very young boys, were marching past me, each group headed by a flag bearer and each group stepping and self-flagellating to a different song and beat. The officious policeman, acting as traffic cop with almost as many hand and arm movements, was thoroughly enjoying himself, although it seemed that his instructions were ignored as many times as they were obeyed. Each neighborhood in Yazd, and apparently many neighborhoods in the surrounding villages, had its own *heyyat*, or "delegation," competing, it seemed, to out-beat and out-sing the others. The Afghans came, refugees first from the Soviets and then from the Taliban who had never returned home, as did the Iraqis, presumably from the Iraqi part of town, near the main square, where they run the cigarette wholesale business and where, much to my delight, I could buy Iranian cigarettes re-smuggled back into Iran from Iraq—where the Iranian government subsidizes their distribution—at half the price of anywhere in Tehran, or about thirty-five cents a pack. Every now and then the parade would stop, someone new would take to the microphone, and the crowd of men sitting cross-legged in the middle of the room would stand and beat their chests with both arms. Arms would be raised high and then brought down, crossing each other in midair and landing heavily on either side of the chest, to a rhythm created by the singer and a chorus repeated by the men. Everyone else in the mosque beat, or in my case tapped, their hearts in time. Everyone, that is, except for the few men I noticed who answered calls on their cell phones, although one did manage to hold a conversation and beat himself at the same time. "Hey, what are you doing, Mamad?" I imagined the conversation. "Oh, nothing much, just pounding my chest."

The women on the balcony watched, some leaning over to get a better look, and at times I felt that the men, the youths anyway, were performing for them as much as for any other reason. If they could (and if it was still legal), some of these men would have used the *ghammeh*, or "sharp dagger," to cut their foreheads and march with blood streaming down their faces. Once a common practice, it was now forbidden by the Ayatollahs of Shia Islam.[1] On the eve of Tasua, in a taxi from Ardakan to Yazd, a newscaster repeatedly advised his listeners (after offering them all condolences on the death of Imam Hossein) that *ghammeh-zani*, "cutting oneself with a blade," was not only illegal but un-Islamic according to the great Ayatollahs, including Fazel Lankarani, Shirazi,

Sistani (in Iraq), and the Supreme Leader himself, Khamenei. The reason, as he quoted the mullahs, was that in Islam it is haram, or "forbidden," to harm one's own body to the point of danger—that is, danger from death due to, in this case, a potential deadly infection. He neglected to mention the Ayatollahs' other reason, one they all agree on and one that has a strong Shia basis: that any act that can be misunderstood, misconstrued, or simply viewed negatively by the non-Shia world must be avoided in order to protect the faith from those who might view it in a negative light or, worse, defame it. Men cutting their foreheads wide open could, one supposes, be viewed negatively by some unbelievers. The practice does continue privately, though (which is why the radio announcer felt it necessary to raise the issue), sometimes in back alleys among small groups of men who just cannot imagine that beating oneself, even shirtless to allow the skin to burst open, suffices as grief. Real men don't just self-flagellate; they *cut* themselves.

There's an old joke in Iran about Moharram, the holy month, one that is told even by the pious who mourn with genuine emotion. A foreigner, it seems, arrives in Iran during Moharram and is witness to the multitude of public grieving ceremonies, the crying, the chest beating, and of course the black flags adorning almost every building and house. "What's happened?" he asks an Iranian. "We're mourning Hossein's death" is the reply. "Oh," says the foreigner, "I'm so sorry. When did he die?" "Fourteen hundred years ago," says the Iranian. "Boy," says the foreigner, "news sure travels slow around these parts!"

On the eve of Ashura, which simply means "tenth" in Arabic and which is the actual day of Imam Hossein's martyrdom, Iranian television is chockablock with religious programming. Apart from showing Tasua ceremonies across the nation, and apart from broadcasting various *Rosehs*, "communal grief gatherings," on a night in 2007 (and as they do every year), reporters on different channels combed the streets of Tehran and other cities interviewing various people on the subject of their love of Hossein. "Why are you crying?" asked one young male reporter of a five-year-old girl. "For Imam Hossein" was the reply. "Do you like Imam Hossein? Why?" asked the reporter. The girl didn't hesitate. "Because he died thirsty!" she exclaimed, as if speaking to an idiot. (Legend has it that Yazid, Hossein's nemesis in the battle for control of the caliphate, cut off Hossein's men from water supplies at Karbala before the final battle and the men died fighting, but never quenching their thirst.) Another asked an older man on the streets of Tehran what he thought of Hossein. "For fourteen hundred years we've been mourning Imam Hossein," he replied. "My one-and-a-half-year-old grandson beats his chest. Why? Because the blood of Hossein boils inside all of us." Indeed. Iranian identity is very much tied up in the story of Hossein, the story of his martyrdom in the cause of justice, and the concept of what is right (and just) and what is wrong (and unjust). *"Yeki-bood; yeki-nabood"*—"Other than God, there was no One." Except, perhaps, Hossein.

Many of the contradictions (or what we think of as contradictions) of Iran play out during the holy month of Moharram. A nation is in mourning, yes; but the Iranian penchant for turning every solemn occasion into a festivity is also on display. Ancient ritual and pageantry, reviled by orthodox Sunnis as paganism and idolatry, are set against a backdrop of modernity and a quest for technology. Public displays of grief, apparently sincere, are quickly followed by sumptuous feasts in the privacy that exists behind Persian walls. Weeks of practicing carefully choreographed mass self-flagellation culminate in an ecstatic, and even at times erotic, display of male machismo. Laughter follows tears, happiness comes from sorrow. And the people often described as the most Western in the Muslim Middle East continue to live their

Western-influenced lives, going to restaurants and cafés, taking the kids to amusement parks, watching movies and listening to music, and surfing the Internet, all the while surrounding themselves with symbolic solemnity. The black flags hanging outside of many homes and offices, even secular ones, are not only for show: inside the home a television may be blaring a European program (even dolorous Iranians, it seems, want their MTV); inside the office there might be a cheerful celebration of a successful business deal; but a certain lugubriousness often punctures the mood, almost as a reminder that without sorrow, happiness cannot be measured.

It was during the month of Moharram that I witnessed another contradiction of Islamic Iranian life, not one directly attributable to the month of mourning, but one I likely wouldn't have witnessed any other time. It is considered auspicious by some to donate blood during the month, and a friend took me to a government donation center in Tehran where we both were eager to spill blood more for our fellow man than for ceremonial purposes. We took numbers from a ticket machine, were given a short form to fill out by a courteous woman behind a desk, and sat down on plastic chairs with a dozen or so others to wait our turn. Our numbers came up within seconds of each other, and we went into separate rooms as indicated by an electronic sign. I closed the heavy wooden door behind me and sat down in front of another woman behind a desk, young and wearing a proper hijab, who took my form and starting making notes. She asked for my national identity card (which unlike my passport gives no clue as to where I reside) and confirmed the personal details I had written down one by one. She finally looked up at me and stared straight into my eyes, holding her pen aloft for effect. "And when was the last time you had sex?"

"Excuse me?" I replied, blushing, I'm sure.

"The last time you had carnal relations?" I had written that I was unmarried, and since sex outside marriage is technically illegal, a government official was asking me to either condemn myself or lie.

"Uh, I'm not sure," I said. "Maybe a month or two?"

"I'm sorry," she replied, after holding my gaze for a few moments, her expression unchanging. "You can't donate blood today."

"Really?" I asked, surprised. I knew that all donated blood is checked for the AIDS virus, so it seemed an unreasonable precaution, particularly since I could have easily lied.

"If you've had sex in the last year and are not married, you can't donate blood." She typed something into her computer terminal, presumably marking me as someone to be rejected by all donation centers for the next twelve months, even if I returned and lied. "Thank you anyway," she said pleasantly, looking me in the eyes again. I couldn't discern any judgment in her eyes, whether she thought I was a sex fiend or whether she was wondering with whom I had managed to have illicit sex.

"Thank you," I also said, standing up and feeling a little embarrassed.

"Have a good day," she replied, pressing the button on her desk signaling the next donor and going back to her computer. I walked out to see my friend sitting on a chair in the waiting room.

"Did you already give blood?" I asked.

"No," he replied. "I was rejected. And you?"

"Me too, for having had sex less than a year ago. I'll tell you, that was embarrassing!"

"Same here. I should have lied, but the girl caught me off guard."

We left the building with our heads lowered, as if others watching, particularly the women, would think us sexual deviants, and hastily jumped into a cab and headed home. Here was the Islamic Republic in all its glorious contradictions, I thought, as we made our way through heavy traffic in silence. A republic that openly recognizes the perils of AIDS (and even hands out free condoms) but that maintains the fiction of Islamic sexual innocence, an innocence that dictates a married man only ever has sex with his wife (and vice versa), that unmarried men only have sex with themselves, and that unmarried women don't know what sex is. And then, to borrow a Ronald Reagan Cold War notion, the Islamic Republic trusts, but also verifies (verbally, and then later scientifically). Apart from the undoubtedly unintentional titillation factor of being asked about one's sex life by a pretty young girl, a girl that if Muslim and unmarried (and I saw no ring on her finger) should not have experienced sex herself, the business of asking about sex appears to serve no purpose whatsoever other than to afford the examinee the opportunity to wonder whether he or she should be truthful or not (for most Iranian men would hardly like to admit, even if it were true and particularly to a young woman, that they had had no prospects for a year, while no unmarried Iranian woman would like to admit publicly that she had succumbed to the advances of one of those men). But in reality it encapsulates the very Persian, pragmatic approach to living under the sexual constraints of Islam: men might all be Muslims, but all Muslim men are, well, *men*. And women, after all, just *might* fall under their spell.

———————

Having been denied the opportunity to shed blood, to self-sacrifice at a time when sacrifice is pondered, on the seventh of Moharram, the day that Hossein's armies were first denied water all those centuries ago, I attended a Roseh at a house in North Tehran. The blood of Hossein boils even in the veins of the Armani crowd, it seems, for my host, a young businessman dressed in a beautiful suit, lives in an upscale neighborhood, Shahrak-e Gharb, in a multimillion-dollar home. The Benzes and BMWs parked outside would have seemed to indicate a more common North Tehran form of entertainment inside: a party with liquor, dancing, and mingling of the sexes, but no, this was Moharram, after all. Businesses and homes all over Tehran, even some in the wealthy and more secular neighborhoods, were draped with black flags and salutations to Imam Hossein, and on the drive north a red neon sign on the top of an incomplete high-rise by the Hemmat Expressway that could be seen for miles proclaimed Iran's love of its Imam with a simple *"Ya Hossein,"* an expression that was also mowed, in huge letters, into the grass embankment of another highway connecting North and South Tehran.

At the house, what appeared to be a huge ten-car garage but was just the covered courtyard entrance to the main house was fully carpeted with expansive Persian rugs, and I sat along the edge of one wall facing a mullah who was sitting and talking to a few men leaning against the opposite wall. Roseh is a tradition I remember from my childhood, when on yearly visits to my grandfather's house my mother would attend the almost weekly women-only Roseh thrown by my grandmother for her friends and family. Roseh is a sort of passion play, actually a passion play *monologue*; the story of Hossein's martyrdom (or the martyrdom of other saints) is recited by a mullah who is an accomplished actor and who deftly manipulates the audience into tears simply by telling them of the injustice of it all.

I remember the shock I felt the first time I saw my mother come out of the living room at my grandfather's house, crying hysterically, and my wondering if someone had died or some other terrible calamity had just occurred. "No, no," my mother had assured me, "it was just a Roseh, and I feel much better now." I must've been five or six years old and fresh from San Francisco, where, needless to say, the handful of Shias who may have lived there in the 1960s did *not* organize Rosehs. I came to understand, even though I wasn't allowed to witness the passion plays, although I did hide outside the closed door on numerous occasions and listen in awe to the mullah's cadences and the spectacular crying of the women, that it served a definite purpose beyond religion and faith, for those who emerged from the Roseh after a heavy round of communal crying seemed to have hefty appetites (all the cakes and biscuits disappeared before we kids had a chance to steal one or two) and left my grandfather's house in great spirits, usually with beaming smiles framed by colorful chadors. My own mother, wiping away tears, always seemed so *relieved*. Hossein's martyrdom was *the* supreme example of injustice: one's own martyrdom (and every Iranian is a martyr) paled by comparison. Go ahead, have a good cry: cry for Hossein, for Abolfazl, and for all the other martyrs, including, of course, *yourself*.

While women often organize a Roseh, hiring a mullah (and the good ones, those who can guarantee tears or your money back, cost a pretty rial) and putting on a party, men also do, usually during Moharram. This house in Shahrak-e Gharb was no exception on the seventh of Moharram, and it was going to be a lavish party. A heavy curtain separated the men from the women, who would be able to hear, but not see, the mullah when he was ready for his performance. Haj-Agha Bayan, the mullah and an accomplished veteran *Roseh-khoon*, or "Roseh reciter," was a portly fellow who, despite the thousands of dollars in fees he commands, was dressed in rather shabby robes. The women weren't missing much. While he waited for the room to fill up, we were served hot tea and fresh dates by our host's servants, and I engaged in small talk, and plenty of ta'arouf, with my host as well as with the men who sat down on the carpet next to me. When Haj-Agha finally rose from the floor and sat down on the only chair in the room, everyone fell silent. A microphone was handed to him, and he began his Roseh. We listened carefully as he began to tell the story of the Battle of Karbala in a theatrical voice, occasionally smiling, occasionally emphasizing one or another aspect of Imam Hossein's beautiful nature, and often employing gholov, the Persian art of exaggeration that fools no one but is accepted as poetic license and as a way of making a point.

The gholov, however, was too much for the gentleman sitting next to me, a religious man certainly but one who wore, of all things, a black necktie with his freshly pressed suit, which indicated some dissent with the notion of what is acceptable menswear in an Islamic Republic. When Haj-Agha told the tale of Imam Hossein's anger at the death of his father, Imam Ali, he said, with much gusto, that Hossein immediately got on his horse and slew, in one continuous action and armed only with his sword, 1,950 soldiers from the Caliph's army. He repeated the number and paused: *"One thousand!* and *nine hundred!* and *fifty!"* he said, unruly white hairs on his chubby cheeks quivering as he looked around the room. *"Can you imagine?"* he asked, before repeating the number once again, seemingly proud of Hossein's ability to exact revenge on an unimaginable scale.

But the man in the necktie could not, apparently, imagine it. He leaned toward me and whispered in my ear. "If you should try to cut *flower* stems with the swing of a sword," he said, "you would fall to the ground exhausted well before you'd even cut a hundred." I nodded, trying to suppress a smile. "One thousand nine hundred and fifty men, indeed!" he snorted in my ear. The rest of the audience looked at Haj-Agha in awe. The story continued: fantastic tales of the absolute goodness of Hossein, the absolute justice of his cause, and the absolute cruelty and absolute wickedness of his enemies, the enemies of Islam. The mullah's tone changed as he spoke of Hossein's suffering, of his men's suffering. "The thirst, my poor Imam Hossein's *thirst!*" he cried. His body started shaking, and then tears started streaming from his eyes. He continued with the story, alternately sobbing gently and then convulsed with grief, his head moving from side to side, his voice straining to tell the world of the injustice of it all.

A man sitting cross-legged in front me, his huge belly covering his ankles, lowered his head into his hands. His shoulders heaved almost imperceptibly, but then, as the mullah shook with grief, he bawled like a baby. He wiped his stubble-covered face repeatedly with his thick fingers, a massive silver and agate ring, the sign of a true believer, glistening with his tears. Other men, young, old, burly, and thin, cried too, loudly enough to drown out any sobs and cries from the women's section. Real Shia men *do* cry. The gentleman with the tie sitting next to me did not shed tears, but he (as did I) beat his chest with one hand when Haj-Agha's tale ended and a group of men sitting in front of him stood up and began the self-flagellation phase of the evening. Haj-Agha, exhausted from his tour de force, had handed the microphone off with a sigh to a young man who immediately launched into a no-heh, the religious song that positively demands physical audience participation, chest-beating claps providing the percussive beat.

Noheh singers are more in demand than even Roseh mullahs, and the very best, often handsome young men with stunning voices who could have been pop stars if they had chosen a different career in music or if their love of the Imams was, say, a little more figurative, command fees for a single short performance that can run as high as ten thousand dollars, and of course their CDs sell in the millions. My old college friend Khosro, sitting a few yards away, also tapped his chest, almost subconsciously, in about as distinguished a way as possible, befitting his princely demeanor as well as his heritage as a descendant of the Qajar kings. Looking straight ahead, right arm resting stiffly across his chest, and his hand moving only at the wrist, he tapped his heart with his palm in perfect time to the beat. The blood of Hossein sometimes boils in the veins of purely secular Iranians too. Western-educated Khosro, whose musical tastes lean to Ella and Billie rather than Sibsorkhi and Helali (famous noheh singers), comes from a family that has, like almost all Iranians, harbored deep religious beliefs for centuries. His father, he once told me, who was educated in Europe before World War II, a time when few Iranians even dreamed of traveling overseas, returned from abroad with his first wife, a Belgian woman. Khosro's grandmother, who took the Muslim concept of what is *najess*, or "unclean," perhaps a little too seriously, would rub clean the dishes and utensils used by the Belgian Christian outside in the garden with mud before washing them with the rest of the china used by the proper Shias of the family. The marriage did not last very long.

The ritual ended in a frenzy of chest beating. The tempo had picked up, the singer's voice reached an emotional high, the men standing and hitting themselves with all the strength of two arms were visibly ecstatic, and the rest of us, myself included, were caught in an almost trancelike state. The most basic (and perhaps basest) human instinct came to the fore: the tribal instinct, the sense of oneness with one's own kind, the sense of pride and power in a small community of men, strangers, yes, but of the same blood. We were a community of Persians, this was *our* cult, and screw the rest of the world, particularly the Arabs, if they didn't like it. Idol worship, the Sunnis say, Sunnis who cannot abide the Shia obsession with one man, a man whose painting adorns many a Shia home and business contrary, they say, to true Muslim belief. No, this was not worship, not of idols or even of God. It was a remembrance, through the story of one man's battle, of the injustices in this world, the injustices we face every day, and of the little bit of martyrdom in all of us. It felt good, almost orgasmic, one might even say. The cigarette afterward, outside on the street while watching servants rush into the room with huge pots of steaming fragrant rice and oversized platters of grilled lamb kebabs, felt even better. Self-flagellation and awakened tribal instincts can work up a real, and carnivorous, appetite.

———————

Two nights later I watched a similar men's Roseh on television. Channel 2 broadcast the event in its entirety, and for good reason. It was a traditional Moharram Roseh attended by the Supreme Leader and virtually the entire Iranian political establishment. Ayatollah Khamenei sat on the only chair, Ahmadinejad sat on the floor on his right, and Rafsanjani sat on the floor on his left. The camera panned around the room, showing Iran's leadership in a state of deep grief. The Rosehkhoon, a bespectacled young mullah who was reciting the story of Imam Hossein, was standing and telling his tale, a tale told a thousand times, into a microphone, beads of sweat visible on his brow. As the story progressed, and as Hossein's plight became apparent, men held their bowed foreheads with their hands, all except Khamenei, who was recovering from a serious bout of flu and looked sickly, and Rafsanjani, who had his usual pained expression on his face. Perhaps Rafsanjani felt that he should have, as the perpetual éminence grise of the Iranian political sphere, been given a proper chair too. President Ahmadinejad, in his trademark beige Windbreaker, soon began to cry. Tears, genuine tears, left streaks around his eyes, and he wiped them away unembarrassed. The mullah started crying himself, struggling to finish his story of woe, and as he described the death of Abolfazl (Hossein's brother and protector, who had his hands chopped off before being killed at Karbala), Ayatollah Khamenei held his forehead, fingers covering his eyes as he shed a tear or two. Rafsanjani, ever the pragmatist even in matters of faith, remained stony faced while listening intently to a story he'd heard, and probably recited, thousands of times before.

The following night, the night of Ashura, state-run television broadcast a virtually identical Roseh, and again Khamenei was seated on the only chair, but this time Gholam Ali Haddad-Adel, the Speaker of the parliament, sat on the floor to his right and Ahmadinejad on his left. Rafsanjani was present, but not by the Supreme Leader's side. If any old Kremlinologists who had diverted their study to mullah-ology were watching, they must've been furiously taking notes. Haddad-Adel and Ahmadinejad both dutifully beat their chests at the appropriate times, and I couldn't help but wonder how the image of the weeping and self-flagellating leadership of Shia Iran could not be viewed by non-Persians in, as the Ayatollahs put it so eloquently, a negative light.

Earlier that day, I had gone to Taft, a village in Yazd province, to observe what is billed as one of the most spectacular Ashura ceremonies in Iran. One of the Imam Jomeh's bodyguards, a former Revolutionary Guard and veteran of the Iran-Iraq war, picked me up in an old Peugeot, and we drove to Sadoughi's house first, to fetch him and his family, before we headed off on the thirty-minute journey into the hills visible in the distance. When I got in the car and after a few bouts of ta'arouf—"I'm sorry to have bothered you, I could have taken a taxi," and "No, no, it's my pleasure, it's my duty"—the bodyguard, who knew I was a guest from foreign lands, asked me whether I thought the United States might attack Iran. "Well," I said, "it doesn't look good. I suppose it's quite possible."

"No," he said forcefully. "The Americans aren't so foolish as to invade a country where ten-year-old boys will strap grenades to their bodies and hurl themselves under tanks." He was referring to the eight-year Iran-Iraq war, and as a veteran he knew what he was talking about. During that war, tens of thousands of young volunteers, Basij, some not even ten years old, did exactly that and committed many other suicidal acts of extreme courage, such as charging the enemy in human waves, knowing they'd be cut down by heavy machine guns, or clearing mines the old-fashioned way—by running over them. The plastic keys given them, keys to heaven that they wore around their necks, have been well reported, but the would-be martyrs were also treated, right before battle, to tales of Ashura, the Battle of Karbala, and the supreme glory of martyrdom. In some cases, an actor (usually a more mature soldier) would mount a white horse and gallop along the lines, providing the child soldiers a vision of Imam Hossein himself on his famous white horse—the hero who would lead them into their fateful battle before they met their God. Witnesses have said that sometimes Iraqi soldiers, seeing the boys charge them in their Hossein-inspired frenzy, would abandon their positions and run away, not necessarily out of fear, but out of shock and amazement. *"If you want to understand Iran, you must become a Shia first."* Rafsanjani's supposed words rang in my head.

Taft is where one can see what could be called full-contact Shiism. Arriving in the Imam Jomeh's car, I was fortunate enough to be driven right up to the entrance to the old square, and even more fortunate to be escorted, along with Sadoughi and his son, by Revolutionary Guards through a narrow and ancient passageway packed with sweaty bodies. In Iran one makes one's way through a crowd the easy way—by forceful shoving—and I struggled with my balance as we squeezed through the men and boys who respectfully tried to get out of the way of their Imam Jomeh but showed no such respect to the rest of the party. Once inside the square, we were greeted by thousands and thousands of men packed tightly together, all wearing black, who turned to see our party make its way to a corner, by a door to a building, where a microphone had been set up on a makeshift lectern. Along the top of the ramparts that enclosed the square on three sides, women and girls, all in black chadors, gathered to watch from the safety of the thirty-foot height. Hanging on the walls immediately below them were large framed photographs of all of the town's martyrs: young men and boys who had perished in the Iran-Iraq war of the 1980s and whose mothers and sisters were undoubtedly still grieving as they stood watch over their portraits.

In the middle of the square sat a huge, two-story-high wooden structure known as the *nakhl*, covered in black cloth imprinted with passages from the Koran and a painting of the shrines at Karbala. The nakhl, which is meant to symbolize Imam Hossein's *taboot*, or "coffin," something he was denied in real death, is peculiar to Yazd province and can range in size from a few feet tall and wide to the size of a three-story building. Muslims use coffins only to carry the dead to their resting place, which is supposed to happen within twenty-four hours of passing, and bury the body in the earth only wrapped in white muslin fabric. Hossein's body, sans head, was famously left in the desert for three or four days, another source of deep anguish for Shias today, some of whom carry as heavy a nakhl as possible to express their sorrow through even more pain, this time on their shoulders, than the chains and their arms have already inflicted on their backs and their chests.

The Imam Jomeh spoke a few words on the importance of Ashura, and then a noheh singer, an older man, probably a local, sang the familiar story of the Battle of Karbala. The entire crowd vigorously and enthusiastically beat their chests on cue, arms raised high in the air, crossed over, and brought down heavily in perfect unison. From my vantage point it was a sea of black—black clothes, black hair, and black beards in the middle of what looked curiously like a Shia version of a synchronized-swimming performance. A passion play began at the far end of the square, too far for me to make out exactly what was going on, but I could see an actor on a white horse wearing a metal helmet circling a tent, and then suddenly, as the man behind the microphone let out a long *"Allahhhhhh-hu-Akbarrrr!,"* the chest beating stopped and the men, perhaps some three or four hundred of them, lifted the monstrously elephantine nakhl onto their shoulders and began running around the square to the encouragement of the onlookers, encouragement that was echoed by the women who threw white long-stemmed roses from the ramparts onto their heads as they passed by. An old man dressed in robes and with the green scarf of Islam around his neck stood on a platform on the nakhl and waved his hands, directing the men who were carrying him on their backs, while the singer continued the Muslim prayer *"Ashadu-allah."* The seemingly endless supply of white roses continued to rain down indiscriminately on the crowd, men carrying the nakhl and those who pressed all around them trying to get as close to it as they could. When they finally stopped and lowered the symbolic coffin to the ground, Sadoughi's guards quickly hustled us out of the square, pushing men out of their way for the Imam Jomeh but leaving the rest of us to fend for ourselves behind him as best we could. I thought that I might be trapped and even crushed, but I fought my way through like the others by pushing and shoving as hard as I could with nary an "excuse me" or "sorry," and I noticed one Revolutionary Guard had kept an eye on me, presumably ready to come to the rescue if I proved to be less than capable with Iranian skills in moving through a crowd.

I breathed easily once outside the square, and near the cars ready to take us home, a group of men, brown mud caking their hair and foreheads and spatters of it on their black shirts, walked past. *"Khak-bar-saram"* was their message—"Dirt upon my head"—the uniquely Persian expression of surprised disapproval, or, if the *khak* is described as upon another's head, of wishing that person, well, *dead.* Dirt, dust, or the earth, all khak (and where the word "khaki" comes from), on any Muslim's head means he or she is dead and buried, and these men, and others I had seen all week with similar mud stains, were proclaiming that they would die for Hossein, that they wished death for themselves rather than the grief Hossein's predicament caused them, and

In a downtown Tehran shopping district, flags and banners in vivid hues are offered to mark the annual Moharram religious festival.

The author's maternal grandfather was a noted Ayatollah and theologian who
taught many of today's Ayatollahs at the University of Tehran, pictured here in the
mid-1960s.

The author's maternal family (his mother is second from left) is pictured taking tea in their typically Persian walled garden in the late 1940s.

The author's paternal great-great-grandfather, Majd-ol-Olama (center), in paisley robe and turban, is pictured with former President Khatami's maternal grandfather on his right, in Ardakan, Yazd province, in the early twentieth century. The two families have been intertwined in marriage for generations.

Former President Mohammad Khatami in his offices in the compound of Iran's first Supreme Leader, Ayatollah Khomeini, North Tehran, 2007

A woman affects a personal style along with her mandatory hijab, Yazd, 2005.

Schoolchildren crossing the street, Yazd, 2007. Schools in Iran are gender-segregated and all girls over the age of nine are required to wear the strict hijab.

Teenagers in recognizably Western dress at an outdoor café in the hills north of Tehran, 2005. Although it is technically illegal for unmarried girls and boys to socialize, Tehran youth comfortably ignore such Islamic regulations, even under a staunchly conservative government like Ahmadinejad's.

The "Bobby Sands Hamburger" stand in North Tehran, 2005. The irony of naming a hamburger stand after a famous hunger striker is lost on most Iranians.

A woman with revealing hijab being given a warning by a morals policewoman in Tehran during the government's annual Spring crackdown, which was more severe than usual in 2007 (Majid/Getty Images)

A typical street scene in North Tehran, 2007, where both men and women continue to stylishly defy Islamic dress codes (Atta Kenare/AFP/Getty Images)

A religious woman viewing decidedly un-Islamic Iranian art, Khaneh-ye-Honar gallery, Tehran, 2005

A female-only car on the Tehran subway. Each train has one car reserved for the exclusive use of women; all other cars are mixed gender. Many women prefer the segregated car for its relative peace and quiet.

A difficult-to-parse but friendly sign at Tehran's Mehrabad airport picturing the founder of the Islamic Revolution, Ayatollah Khomeini (left), and his successor as the Supreme Leader of Iran, Ayatollah Khamenei (right)

A Tehran billboard portraying Khomeini, Khamenei, and a young Basij (volunteer) fighter from the Iran-Iraq war. It says, essentially: "Our mission is to raise a generation of committed basijis." The symbol of Iran's Revolutionary Guards (of which the Basij are a division) is in the bottom-left corner.

A mural in Tehran, one of countless walls emblazoned with the image of Ayatollah Khomeini

A young, rather casual-looking shopkeeper in a store that sells religious flags and banners, Yazd, 2005. The banner on the wall behind him portrays the Shia saint Imam Hossein on his famous white horse.

BELOW: A camel is sacrificed by the road in Qom, the religious capital of Iran, as buses pass by taking pilgrims to Mashhad, home to the Imam Reza shrine.

Men performing their pre-prayer ablutions outside the famous mosque at Jamkaran, site of a vision of the Mahdi over a thousand years ago, Qom, 2005

Women watching Ashura ceremonies from a rampart in the Taft main square, Yazd province, 2007. The photographs are of the boys and men of Taft martyred in the Iran-Iraq war, in which nearly one million Iranians died.

Men self-flagellating with chains, expressing their grief at Imam Hossein's martyrdom, during a Tasua commemoration in a mosque in Yazd, 2007. Unlike in some other countries, here Iranians are not permitted to break the skin when self-flagellating; nonetheless, many of the men whip the chains at their backs with a ferocity that would astound Western onlookers.

Ayatollah Mousavi Bojnourdi, an Ayatollah who begs to differ with his government, with the Iranian delegation at a UNESCO conference, Paris, 2005.

Hojjatoleslam Mohammad Sadoughi (second from right), the Friday Prayer Leader of Yazd and the Supreme Leader's representative in the province, with fellow clerics at a mosque, Yazd, 2007

A ten-story mural on a wall in downtown Tehran, by the side of a major elevated highway. The English is not a direct translation—the Farsi actually reads "*Death* to America." BELOW: The former U.S. embassy in Tehran, now a museum and a Revolutionary Guards barracks, displaying an unsubtle message

Revolutionary Guards at Friday prayers, Tehran, 2007. The Guards, Iran's elite military branch, are recruited from the religious and working classes. They report directly to the Supreme Leader and are fiercely loyal to the principles of the Islamic Revolution (of which they are the guardians). (Scott Peterson/Getty Images)
BELOW: A newsstand in midtown Tehran, displaying the multitude of Iran's dailies on the sidewalk in the morning, giving commuters a peak at the headlines

President Ahmadinejad greets a member of Neturei Karta, the Brooklyn-based anti-Zionist Orthodox Jewish group, with a traditional Muslim kiss, at the notorious Tehran Holocaust Conference, December 2006. (Atta Kenare/AFP/Getty Images)

that they *meant* it. Well, maybe not quite, for Allah rarely grants them their wish.

I rode back to Yazd in Mrs. Sadoughi's car. She had been unable to witness the pageantry, she told me, because it was far too crowded in the women's section for her to make her way to the front. Lacking Revolutionary Guard escorts, or even someone to assist her, Maryam Khatami, wife of the Imam Jomeh of Yazd and sister of the former president, was just another anonymous chador-clad woman in the crowd. Islamic sensibilities, certainly in this case, strangely seem to show a lack of concern for the safety and well-being of the wives of dignitaries, and I witnessed the same situation in New York when President Ahmadinejad's wife, who had accompanied him on a trip to the UN in 2006, wandered about the halls of the General Assembly in a black chador with no Iranian security (but with a lone U.S. female agent) visible. I say "strangely" because the Prophet Mohammad was married to Khadijah, his *boss*, who became the first convert to Islam, and Mohammad's bloodline has been passed down solely through his *daughter* Fatima, wife of Ali, the first Imam of the Shias and their very raison d'être as a sect. But Maryam Khatami seemed unperturbed by the lack of attention given her by any of her husband's guards, who are provided by the state to all Imam Jomehs, and in previous and subsequent conversations with her over tea, a water pipe, and plates of fruit, it was manifest that her view of Islam is formed by her study of the great Islamic philosophers and thinkers and not by blind obedience to the theocracy. Daughter of an Ayatollah, sister of a cleric president, daughter-in-law of a martyred conservative Ayatollah, and wife of the Imam Jomeh on whose thinking she has undoubtedly had quite an effect, Mrs. Sadoughi comfortably holds forth not just on Islamic philosophy but also on Greek and Western philosophy and thought, far more readily than I, and, inside her home at least, is not one to play second fiddle to anyone.

In one particular conversation on Sufism and philosophy, and knowing that I was writing a book, she ventured that perhaps my subject matter was somewhat pedestrian. "You should write a book on your grandfather," she admonished me. "He was a great thinker, and not enough people know his works or know of him."

"You're right," I said, with a modest and embarrassed smile that signified proper ta'arouf.

"Really," she pressed on, "young people especially need to know him."

"I don't think I'm qualified," I said. "I'm by no means an expert on the Philosophy of Illumination, if I even quite understand it."[2]

"You should do some research," she replied. "If you want to do something *good*, write a book on Agha-ye Assar, and get his works translated into English." Her husband listened as she spoke but ventured no opinion.

"Chashm," I said—"Upon my eyes"—another Persian expression of ta'arouf that is the polite and correct way to say "okay." She looked at me knowing full well that it also meant I agreed with her but was in no way promising to actually do anything about it.

"Really," she said softly. She smiled widely, and that was that.

———————

Friday prayers the week of Tasua and Ashura take on added significance, with larger-than-normal crowds showing up at mosque (although it has never been an absolute obligation for Muslims to go to mosque, even on the Sabbath). In 2007, Friday prayers also coincided with the start of the ten-day celebrations of the Islamic Revolution of 1979, commemorating the ten days from Ayatollah Khomeini's arrival in Tehran to the successful victory of his revolt against the Shah, lending the prayers even more weight and gravitas. In Yazd, the assembly on Fridays is held at the Molla Esmaeil Mosque, built by Esmaeil Aqdi, a famous Yazdi scholar and mullah of the late eighteenth and early nineteenth centuries. (The mosque was completed in A.H. 1222, which corresponds to 1807 C.E.) I had discovered two years earlier, and there is no way to verify it because Iranians didn't have surnames, let alone birth certificates or even records of births prior to the reign of Reza Shah in the 1920s, that I am a descendant of his and, more interesting, that he was a Jew: a brilliant mathematician and scholar who not only converted to Islam but became a mullah. In my father's village of Ardakan, moreover, some people apparently still think of my family as "the Jews." During my Ashura week visit to my cousin Fatemeh's house, where a few people I hadn't met before seemed to drop in from time to time, as is not unusual in small towns in Iran, I was introduced to one older woman who asked, "Majd? Ardakani Majd?"

"Yes, Majd-e-Ardakani," I replied, using my grandfather's original name (which just means "Majd from Ardakan," and Majd actually being the single name of my great-great-grandfather).

"Oh," she said. "The Jews."

"I'd heard that," I said after a momentary pause, a little surprised. I looked at Fatemeh's father, my late aunt's ninety-year-old husband and coincidentally also President Khatami's uncle, who had rather triumphantly told me on a previous trip to Yazd that while his family was descended from the Zoroastrians (whom we had been discussing and who have always been a large minority in the region), I was descended from Jews. He said it somewhat gleefully because Iranians, whether pious Muslims or not, take great pride in their Aryan ancestry and revile the ancient Arabs who invaded their land, bringing them Islam, an Islam that they then molded to their Zoroastrian character. Even Seyyeds, descendants of the Prophet Mohammad, take pleasure in noting that their descent is through a Persian princess who married Mohammad's grandson Hossein, whom they so faithfully mourn each year at Moharram. "Your ancestor is Molla Esmaeil," he had said to me, and then he had gone on to explain who Esmaeil was. "God knows why he converted, though!" he had added at the end of his story.

"Yes, everybody knows that," he said, noticing my attention. "But tell me," he continued, "why are you really here? Have you come to do a little spying?"

"No!" I said with a laugh. "I like it here."

"Come on," he said jovially, "nobody likes it here, especially if you're from America. What's there to like?"

"Plenty," I replied, "and of course I'm going to participate in Ashura."

"No. You've come to write a report," he insisted with a broad grin. "Have you written it yet? Did you investigate the uranium plant in Ardakan?"[3]

"Yes, that's right," I said. "I'm finishing my report on it soon." He laughed, and I smiled. I knew he was only half-joking, though, for to someone like him, who has lived all his life in Ardakan and Yazd but has also seen Europe and America, the thought that anyone from those continents would find what he considers a backward place interesting enough to visit more than once, a place that would hardly merit a check mark for "worth a detour" if there were a *Guide Michelin* for Yazd province, was absolutely preposterous.

The Molla Esmaeil Mosque is anything but grand or ornate, although it does have its charms. Tall old walls surround the structure, so it's hard to even see it from the street that runs adjacent to the bazaar. A large crowd, the women separated from the men by a rope that ran along one side of the tented courtyard, had already gathered two hours before the noon prayer, and yet another round of chest- and chain-beating ceremonies by various delegations marched along a path through the crowd kept clear by police and Revolutionary Guards. A man with what looked like an old insecticide sprayer attached to his back wandered around, spraying rose water on the congregants and marchers, one of whom, a toothless old man in clerical garb standing in front of me, was in desperate need of it to mask the body odor that caused me to back away when it hit me. A massive poster on one wall dominated all the other banners strewn about: a picture of a boy, perhaps ten or so and wearing a camouflage T-shirt, holding a photograph of Sheik Hassan Nasrallah of Lebanon and making the victory sign with the fingers of his other hand held in the air. In large black letters underneath were the words "The Party of God Is Victorious." Hezbollah does indeed mean "party of God," although the sentence did not employ that group's moniker, one that has become almost a brand and that has lost its connotation in languages other than Arabic. The sign used the Persian *khoda* for "God" rather than the Arabic *allah*, and spelled out "party of" instead of using the conjunctive *o-*. It couldn't be any clearer that it wasn't a party or a political group or an army that was victorious (in the 2006 war with Israel): it was *God*.

Standing by the rope separating the women, who were all sitting on the floor, some trying to control their young children, from the men, who were preening about hitting themselves, I took out my camera and started taking photos. When I aimed at the women's section, a young woman in full black hijab marched up to me. "Why are you taking pictures of the women?" she asked angrily. Sadoughi's son, Mohammad, jumped in.

"He's a writer," he said. "It's all right."

The woman looked skeptical. "But why is he taking pictures of women?"

"What difference does it make?" said Mohammad. "You don't seem to mind the television crews up there." He pointed in the direction of the state TV cameras in the back of the courtyard. "He's from the media too."

"It's still not right," said the woman suspiciously as she stepped away, still staring at me. She stopped and leaned against a wall, keeping me in her view.

"I'm sorry," I said to Mohammad. "I hope I'm not causing any problems."

"Don't worry," he said, waving his hand. "It's ridiculous. Take as many pictures as you like." I put my camera away and headed for the exit. "I think I'll go outside for a break," I said.

"I'll come too," said Mohammad. We left the tented courtyard through a narrow passageway that led to the entrance of the mosque, a small courtyard drenched in the yellowish light of a fierce desert sun bouncing off the ancient mud and straw of the twenty-foot-high walls that fully enclosed it. Men loitered about, some smoking and others just leaning against the walls, waiting to enter the mosque when the actual prayers would begin.

"Right there," said Mohammad, pointing to the center of the courtyard, "is where my grandfather was martyred." Ayatollah Sadoughi, the current Imam Jomeh's father and a conservative ally of Khomeini's during the revolution, was killed by Mohammad Reza Ebrahimzadeh, a suicide bomber from the Mujahedin-e-Khalq (MEK), on July 2, 1982, during a wave of assassinations and terrorist operations against the Islamic Republic's early leadership in a counterrevolutionary bid to assume power. "My father was standing right behind him," he continued, "and he witnessed the whole thing." Mohammad, who had just been born then, showed no grief, but he was solemn.

"Those days are long past," I said, "and I don't suppose there's much of a terrorist threat these days, is there?"

"No," said Mohammad, fingering his Motorola walkie-talkie, an item illegal for Iranians to own unless they're with the armed forces, the police, or other government security services. "I suppose not."

We lingered for a while; Mohammad went off and sat alone on a ledge built into the wall, and I walked around, thinking about how tenuous the clerics' hold on power had been in the very early years after the revolution.

The Mujahedin had been an armed guerrilla group that were allies of Khomeini in bringing down the Shah, but had resented being excluded from power and had waged a bitter campaign, at first from within but eventually from their base provided them by Saddam Hussein in Iraq, against the Islamic Republic. A number of senior Ayatollahs, and even the republic's second president, Mohammad Ali Rajai, were killed during their campaign, and the current Supreme Leader, Ali

Khamenei, was injured in a bomb attack. Non-suicide operations were often carried out by men who fled as passengers on the backs of motorcycles, the most powerful of which were banned as a result and the reason that today still no motorcycle with an engine larger than 150 cc can be bought in Iran. But the Ayatollahs' system had survived, and it was hard to imagine how anyone could have thought differently, particularly if he had bothered to attend a Friday prayer meeting at his local mosque, and especially during Moharram.

A few minutes before midday, Mohammad and I went inside the mosque, to where the actual prayers were to be held, and Mohammad escorted me to the front row, right in front of the lectern where his father would deliver his sermon. The room was filling up with rows of men kneeling, waiting for the Imam Jomeh to arrive, and making last-minute calls on their cell phones. I wondered what they could possibly be discussing, and it occurred to me that not a few may have been talking to others in the same hall or perhaps to their wives in the women's section, for on Fridays, absolutely no business is conducted in the country and not even newspapers are published. It reminded me, though, to silence my own phone. I sat waiting, saying hello to every man who walked up to Mohammad to pay his respects, until one of Sadoughi's guards showed up and stood right in front of me. *"Befarma-eed vozou, Haj-Agha,"* he said, gesturing with one outstretched arm while holding the other over his heart in the Iranian custom of showing respect. *"Vozou?"* He was pointing in the direction of a private area where dignitaries would perform their ablutions before prayer—the *vozou,* or washing of the hands, forearms, feet, and forehead with water—and he had referred to me as a hajji, someone who has made the pilgrimage to Mecca, which he assumed that I, being of a certain age, certainly had. I was about to stand up when Mohammad held my arm firmly.

"He's going to take photographs," he said to the guard. "He's working." He must have sensed my slight hesitation and wished to spare me any embarrassment, even though I had never told him that I was not accustomed to praying. "He'll pray later," he added, just to ensure that my

Islamic credentials remained bona fide with his father's guards. (Shias, unlike Sunnis, can perform their dawn, noon, or evening prayers either at the time itself or at any time up to the next mandated prayer. Which is one reason why driving around any Iranian city at prayer time, there is no break in traffic. Unlike Muslim cabbies in New York City, many of whom will pull over, usually to a gas station, and pray right on time, not even pious Iranian taxi drivers will pause when their radio broadcasts the thrice-daily call to prayer.) Taking my cue, I took out my camera and stood up. "You can go anywhere with your camera," said Mohammad as the guard excused himself for his own vozou and left us. I was somewhat relieved that I wouldn't have to stay in one place throughout the prayers, mimicking my neighbors' gestures—sitting, kneeling, standing, and muttering, certainly in my case, unintelligible Arabic passages from the Koran.

The Imam Jomeh, Sadoughi, arrived as I started to wander, surrounded by his other guards and trailed by a large group of mullahs. He disappeared into a room next to the lectern and the mullahs arranged themselves on the floor in front, while I stood against the wall with my camera in my hands. When Sadoughi emerged a few moments later, in lieu of the cane he usually walks with, he had an automatic rifle, holding on to the tip of the barrel and bringing the butt down on the stone floor with every step. He positioned himself behind the microphone and held on to the rifle, leaning on it ever so slightly now and then, and began his sermon.

Friday prayer sermons in Iran, the world's only state other than the Vatican that is run by clerics, tend to be more political than religious in nature, and this Friday, falling as it did at the beginning of the Ten-Day Dawn, was doubly so. Sadoughi recounted the story of leaving Paris and arriving in Tehran with Khomeini on his chartered Air France 747, himself sitting in the seat behind Khomeini, and the crowd listened intently. It was a story I had already heard; Sadoughi had told it to me himself with great excitement over tea one day, and I suspect he had also told it in previous years to the very men before us. Khomeini's character, his fearlessness, and the glory of his revolution were the thrust of the speech, as well as his selfless dedication to his people. Women and children, Sadoughi said, were originally barred from the flight, as it was considered too dangerous. The women at Neauphle-le-Château, the suburban Parisian village where Khomeini was based, however, objected strenuously, and Khomeini relented, warning them, however, that the plane could be shot down in Iranian airspace by the Shah's government even though the Shah had already fled into exile. (Neauphle-le-Château was deemed important enough to the revolution to be memorialized by a street name in Tehran, in the neighborhood where I stay and linking two major shopping avenues, but it took me many walks along it to finally decipher the meaning of the street signs, which inexplicably mangled, Persian-style, the village's name to "Nofel Loshato." We may honor a foreign and impure town, the authorities seemed to be saying, specifically to the French, but we'll spell it *our* way.) When Khomeini and his entourage finally circled Tehran's Mehrabad Airport, Sadoughi said, they were initially denied permission to land as they approached, and when the plane banked sharply, everyone thought they might be under attack. Khomeini, however, was calm and expressionless, a testament, the Imam Jomeh implied, to his faith in God's will. Sadoughi also talked about the need for unity in the face of new threats—threats he didn't need to spell out but were clearly a reference to the United States—his rifle with its loaded magazine (I was told) emphasizing the point that he, and other clerics, stood ready to defend the Islamic Republic from any enemy.

He made no mention of Ahmadinejad or the current government, and he didn't need to: as the representative of the Supreme Leader, he was speaking for the velayat-e-faqih, not any elected government that by its nature would be temporary. It wasn't a fiery speech, nor was it angry or hostile, and in fact at times when he talked about Khomeini and the revolution, it was anything but, but then again Sadoughi is not a firebrand and is, after all, close to Khatami, his brother-in-law in whose cabinet he once served as a vice president.[4] However, as we on the outside and those in Iran need reminding every now and then, the most charming (and Sadoughi is certainly a charming man), the most moderate, and even the most liberal reformist clerics are united in their firm belief that the revolution was pure, that Khomeini's views on a political system were sound, and that any democracy in Iran will always be an Islamic one.

When Sadoughi finished his sermon, he handed his rifle to a guard and stood, like everyone else, facing Mecca to lead the prayers. I stood facing him, from behind the lectern he had just vacated, and dutifully took pictures while his guards watched me, occasionally nodding their approval whenever I leaned forward to get a close-up. When the prayers were over, Mohammad stood up and signaled that I was to follow him. We left by a side entrance with his father and the guards, leaving the other mullahs behind, and were driven the short distance to Sadoughi's office, a few doors down from his house. The office, on an impossibly narrow street designed for horses and donkeys and covered by sun-shielding archways over the tall mud walls on either side, had been Sadoughi's father's office and was in a building perhaps two hundred years old. We walked inside and into a square room, the walls covered entirely in intricate hand-carved mirror tiles depicting flowers, birds, geometric Islamic shapes, and calligraphic passages from the Koran. Stained-glass arched windows that touched the ceiling let light in, but allowed no view of the outside. An old attendant rushed to fetch some tea, and then set the huge Persian carpet with a plastic tablecloth and three place settings. "You'll have lunch with us," said Mohammad.

"And you'll have to excuse the meal," said the Imam Jomeh, "but it's *gheimeh* provided by the neighbors." During Ashura week, it is customary for families with means to provide free food in their neighborhood, not just for the poor, but for anyone who wishes to indulge, and in this case a meal had been brought over by them for their spiritual guide. Gheimeh, a stew of lamb and split peas, along with rice, is a dish traditionally prepared during Moharram, and the three of us sat on the floor, cross-legged, eating the watery stew in silence. Sadoughi had had an exhausting Ashura week, and in the morning he had fulfilled his duties as the representative of the Supreme Leader of the Islamic Revolution by giving a speech on the glory of that revolution. Now was a time to eat Allah's gift of food in his martyred father's office, facing a framed photograph of Ayatollah Khomeini prominently displayed on a ledge, and reflect on the suffering of *Ahl'ul'bayt*, the "People of the House," or the Prophet Mohammad's family, for whom the nation mourned. Hossein and his family, grandson and descendants of the Prophet, died by the sword to save Islam, Shias believe. Shiism survived against the odds—Shia Iran is testament to that—and throughout Shia history the shedding of blood, or martyrdom, has been central to the faith and has contributed to its allure.

In Baghdad, the infamous Swords of Qadisiyyah monument (also known as the "Hands of Victory") is formed by two massive swords held by hands resting on the helmets of dead Iranian soldiers, most of them pockmarked by bullet holes. Conceived by Saddam Hussein before his war with Iran ended and intended to serve as a symbol of Iraq's victory over the Persians, which never came, it was, and still is, a reminder for Persians that despite their heavy bloodletting in that conflict, their willingness to sacrifice means that the sword will not always be victorious. Apart from the empty symbolism that most Iraqis recognized at the time despite the propaganda of the Baathist regime, few can help but see that Saddam and his swords are long gone, Iraq is barely a nation, and Shia Iran is more powerful than it has been in centuries. Or, as one Tehran daily, in an attempt to sum up Shia, and by extension Iranian, philosophy for its English-speaking readers, proclaimed, in a bold headline splashed across its front page on the first day of Moharram 2007: "VICTORY OF BLOOD OVER THE SWORD."

PAIRIDAEZA:
THE PERSIAN GARDEN

On March 21, the first day of spring of 1935 and Noruz, the Persian New Year, "Persia" suddenly became "Iran." And Francophones discovered that "Perse" no longer existed. Of course Iran had always been "Iran" to Iranians, or Persians if you prefer, but in the non-Persian-speaking world the country was known by variations on the Greek name "Persis." In 1935, Reza Shah Pahlavi, the semiliterate army officer who had ousted the last Shah of the Qajar dynasty and whose own dynasty would not outlive his son, was in a warm embrace with the Third Reich. A great admirer of Germany, which he thought had far more benign intentions than Russia or Britain in the Middle East, he was also a fierce nationalist and strict fascist for whom Hitler's National Socialism held great appeal. Reza Shah had been busy since his self-coronation hiring German engineers and architects to build Iran's railroad system as well as the government buildings in downtown Tehran, and they still stand today: soaring, pristine fascist architecture—monuments to the resurgent Iranian nationalism of the 1930s.

It is said that Reza Shah's ambassador to Berlin in the mid-1930s, probably with advice and nudges from German ministers, put forth to the Foreign Ministry and his king that Persia should be known to the outside world as "Iran," a word meaning "land of the Aryans" and used by inhabitants of the land since at least Sassanid times (226 C.E.). In an article in the January 26, 1936, issue of the *New York Times*, Oliver McKee stated, "At the suggestion of the Persian Legation in Berlin, the Teheran government . . . substituted Iran for Persia as the official name of the country. Its decision was influenced by the Nazi revival of interest in the so-called Aryan races, cradled in ancient Persia. As the Ministry of Foreign Affairs set forth in its memorandum on the subject, 'Perse,' the French designation of Persia, connoted the weakness and tottering independence of the country in the nineteenth century, when it was a pawn on the chessboard of European imperialistic rivalry. 'Iran,' by contrast, conjured up memories of the vigor and splendor of its historic past." That explanation would come as a surprise to many Iranians today, particularly in the diaspora, for they have the exact opposite view: that "Persia" connotes a glorious past they would like to be identified with, while "Iran," disconnected from that exotic and romantic place in the minds of Westerners, says nothing to the world but Islamic fundamentalism. At the time, however, in the mid-1930s, hardly any Iranians, except for the handful of intellectuals who had some sort of contact with the outside world, really noticed or cared much. Iran was Iran to them, and few, except perhaps for carpet traders in the bazaars, had ever even come across the word "Persian."

This disconnect for many Westerners between Iran and Persia (still prevalent today in many instances) provided cover for not a few Iranian exiles in the early days of the revolution, days that saw Iran hold fifty-two American diplomats hostage, to the obvious disapproval of nearly the entire world. Iran and Iranians now projected an image not only of Islamic fundamentalism and religious extremism but also of violence against Western interests. Iranians in the West, perhaps unduly fearful of a hostile reaction, often said they were "Persian" or from "Persia" to disassociate themselves from the angry flag-burning mobs seen on nightly television broadcasts throughout the world. In America some Iranians—excuse me, *Persians*—went further and changed their first names (unofficially in most cases) to something more English, although for some curious reason, probably a slight sense of guilt at not exhibiting obligatory Iranian pride, they felt compelled to come up with names that were as close as possible to the original, even if that meant only using the first letter of the Iranian name. Mohammads became Moes or Michaels, Hosseins became Henrys or Harrys, and numerous Fereydouns and Faramarzes simply became Freds. Iranian women in the West, who by virtue of their penchant for heavy makeup and a lack of any Islamic-inspired attire in their wardrobe, seemed less inspired to change their names, which at any rate were less identifiably Iranian (or Muslim) than their male counterparts'. I suppose I thought myself fortunate in not having a name that was too obviously Iranian, but I was far too conceited and contrary, I confess, to call myself Persian instead of Iranian, let alone think about changing my name. (One of my American friends did, however, take to calling me Hank, though as more of a joke than anything else.) I do remember admiring the name of an Iranian commentator on the first Iranian television program in the States in the early 1980s: Davoud Ramzi. He could, I thought, legitimately call himself David (Davoud is Persian for David), and a mere change of spelling would render his name American or English. Yes, I thought, what a stroke of fortune to be named David Ramsay, and have it be your real name too!

———————

Perhaps as a defense for having referred to themselves as Persian for so long, some Iranians in the diaspora now argue for "Persia" to return as the English name for their country. It is a debate held almost exclusively outside Iran (for most of those who continue to live in the Islamic Republic generally couldn't care less), but in the age of the Internet the issue reverberates among at least the intellectual classes inside the country as well. Iranian Web sites and blogs are filled with reasons why "Persia" makes perfect sense and why "Persian" should be the language (not "Farsi," the Persian word for it). Oddly, they have never suggested that the Shahs of Persia be referred to as kings, which, after all, is exactly what "Shah" means. Some argue that "Germany" is "Deutschland" in German, "Japan" is "Nippon" in Japanese, and many European countries have different names from those used in English. Of course what's missing from the argument is that the countries that have different names in different languages tend to be the industrialized, powerful nations of the world that do not suffer from a national inferiority complex, one often brought about by the behavior of more powerful nations toward them. Egypt, or Misr, as it is correctly known in the Arab world, is perhaps the glaring exception, but in that case a link to the famous Egypt of the Pharaohs and pyramids is more obviously advantageous, as ancient Egyptian history is almost as well-known in the West as Roman or Greek, partly for biblical reasons and partly because of Elizabeth Taylor. The same cannot be said for Persian history, much to the dismay of Iranians both inside and outside the country, and a critical component of the superiority/inferiority complexes the nation suffers.

All Iranians who study at Iranian schools learn about their great empire and are immensely proud of not only its cultural accomplishments but also its awe-inspiring power at various times throughout history, although in the early days after the revolution teachers were discouraged from delving too far into Iran's pre-Islamic past and were given curricula that emphasized Islamic teachings and history. Nonetheless, even then most students' knowledge of their country's past, supplemented as it was in the home, formed their opinion that Iran was the equal, if not the better, of Rome and Athens. On the other hand, hardly anyone in the West studies Persian history at school, and even study of ancient history at college tends not to include Persian history, other than in its relation to the Greek wars. For this reason, what *has* been written about the ancient Persians and their empires is mostly known through the Greeks, who, as fierce rivals, were not likely to write glowing reviews. Alexander the Great, whom most people *do* know, is sort of an ancient hero in the West and a true villain in Iran, a barbarian who, when he conquered Persia, was such a brute and ignoramus that he burned magnificent libraries along with the greatest city in the world, Persepolis, to the ground. But in a good example of the Persian superiority complex, even this villain is shown to have ultimately had the wisdom to recognize the superiority of the Persians by settling down (until his death) in Persia and marrying a blue-blooded Persian. What could be a better endorsement of the greatest civilization known to man?

Regardless of how Iranians feel about the question of their country's name, and I am willing to concede that "Persian Embassy," "Persian government," and "Persian people" do sound a little better in English, most particularly if "Iran" is, as is sometimes the case with Americans, pronounced "Eye-*ran*." Perhaps it's the "purr-" in "Persian," as soft a sound as anyone can make in the English language, or perhaps it's that most things Persian are beautiful and valuable, such as cats and carpets, to say nothing of the poetry and most things Iranian are, well, we needn't go into that. But one has to wonder if Iran had never demanded that the rest of the world call it by its proper name, and the *Persian* Islamic Revolution had still left a bitter taste in Westerners' mouths, whether *Persians* abroad might not be insisting that they are, in fact, *Iranian.* Despite the country's perceived name change (rather than name *correction*), some things will forever remain Persian in Anglo-American minds: Persian cats (like Siamese, rather than Thai, cats, or Pekingese, rather than Beijing-ese, dogs), carpets, and of course, the least known in the West, Persian gardens.

I use "Persian" and "Iranian" interchangeably, mainly because "Persian" often better distinguishes for readers the Indo-European Iranians from their neighboring Semitic Arabs. It is notable that Arabs, when and if they wish to disparage Iranians, more often than not will also refer to them as Persians: the "other," and, because they're Shia, the infidel. Some Sunni Arabs in Iraq have taken it one step further, calling all Shias, including Iraqi Shias, "Safavids," the name of the Persian dynasty that made Shiism the state religion of Iran, and a clear move in sectarian times to associate non-Sunni Arabs with the non-Arab Persians. Shia Islam, however, because of its beloved saint Imam Hossein, the grandson of the Prophet Mohammad and an Arab, conveniently bridges the Arab-Iranian schism through Hossein's wife, a Persian princess he wisely (as far as Persians are concerned) wed and who bore him the half-Iranian great-grandchildren of the last Prophet of Allah.[1]

The often contradictory Iranian attitudes toward Arabs can be difficult to explain. What can one make of Iranians who shed genuine tears for an Arab who died fourteen hundred years ago, who pray in Arabic three times a day, and yet who will in an instant derisively dismiss the Arab people, certainly those from the peninsula, as *malakh-khor*, "locust eaters"? As one deputy foreign minister once said to me, lips curled in a grimace of disgust and right before he excused himself to pray (in Arabic),[2] "Iranians long ago became Muslims, but they didn't become *Arabs*." His scorn was meant, of course, for desert Arabs who brought Islam to the world, and not necessarily Syrian, Egyptian, or Lebanese Arabs, whom the Iranians place a few degrees higher on the social scale than their desert brethren. The disconnect between Arab and Muslim for Iranians is not unlike the disconnect between certain anti-Semitic Christians and Jews—a disconnect that conveniently ignores not only that Christ was a Jew but also that Christianity, at least at its inception, was a Jewish sect. (The peculiar Iranian disconnect can work both ways, though, for many Arabs today, or at least Arab governments, would rather Israel remain the dominant power in their region than witness, *Allah forbid!*, a Persian ascent to the position.)

The intellectual and fiercely secular classes of Iranian society, a minority limited to enclaves within the biggest cities, are today more likely than ever to embrace their pre-Muslim, their *Persian*, roots for obvious reasons, but there is a sense even among religious Iranians that the Arab invasion that brought them Islam brought them nothing else of any value and may have, in fact, initially hindered Persian progress in the arts and sciences. Compared with Persia and its self-described glorious empire, an empire that had cultivated the deserts of Iran with an underground irrigation system, *qanat*, which allowed them to build their beloved gardens just about anywhere a millennium before the invading Arab Muslims of centuries ago arrived, Arabs, according to Iranians, were an uncultured lot, barely literate, and their brute force persuaded the Iranians to convert to their religion but not their way of life. Why Allah would choose, in His infinite wisdom, to reveal His Word to an illiterate Arab in the desert is not a subject of debate in Iran, but then again, even for Iranians, Allah putatively works in mysterious ways.

Iran is, of course, smaller than an empire but still a geographically large country and counts among its inhabitants many of different ethnicities, including Arabs, who often complain of discrimination and oppression by those who are Fars, from the mid- and southern Iranian province (originally "Pars," but changed because Arabic doesn't have the *p* sound) that was the heart of the ancient empire. Oddly, though the Arabs come in for much derision as culturally inferior and their claims of discrimination are not without merit, they are not, like other ethnicities or even inhabitants of provincial cities, the butt of Persian humor. Much like the Polish in American jokes or the Irish in English jokes, the Turks of Iranian Azerbaijan seem to suffer the most in Persian jokes, followed closely by citizens of the northern city of Rasht, but perhaps it's the real scorn Iranians reserve for Arabs that makes them unworthy even of mockery.

Iranians, as race conscious as any people on the planet, generally describe themselves as Fars, Turk, Kurd, Armenian, Arab, or Jew, although clearly today's Persians are a mixed lot, having suffered invasion after invasion over the millennia, and invasions that often resulted in the invaders putting down roots and taking local women as wives, as Alexander and his armies did, in Persia. But some secular Persian intellectuals (who would absolutely deny that they are in any way racist) will not only exhibit racism toward Arabs or other minorities but reserve a special hatred for Ayatollah Khomeini, not just because he founded the Islamic Republic, but because to them he wasn't even *Persian*. Since his paternal grandfather was an Indian who immigrated to Iran (to the town of Khomein) in the early nineteenth century, some Iranians feel that his "tainted" blood means that a true Persian was not at the helm of the revolution, the most momentous event in their country's modern history, good or bad. And soon after that revolution, when the time came to change the symbol of Iran on its flag from the lion and sun (which the revolutionaries incorrectly associated with the Shahs), Khomeini himself chose a symbol among those submitted by artists—a stylized "Allah"—which his opponents, at least the more race-conscious ones, continue to insist bears a remarkable similarity to the symbol of the Sikhs.

Some of Khomeini's enemies see it as proof of a foreign hand in the revolution, perhaps British because of their influence in India, or, worse, a secret conspiracy by an Indian religion to destroy Persia, and today when Iranian exiles and even some inside Iran want to disparage him, they sometimes refer to him as *Hindi* (which happened to be his grandfather's surname but is also Persian for "Indian"). One such Iranian in Tehran, when he found out where I was staying, insisted that I take a short walk in my neighborhood past the Sikh center of Tehran, a large white compound with a garden surrounded, naturally, by high walls. "Look at the logo on the gates of the walls, and then tell me that Khomeini *wasn't* a Sikh," he said. I replied that I knew exactly what the Sikh emblem looked like (coming from New York, where it is often seen on the back windows of cabs and car service vehicles), but I did as he said anyway, curious about a Sikh center in Tehran, given that the religion is not one of the four—Islam, Christianity, Judaism, and

Zoroastrianism—that is recognized by the state. I found that there was indeed a Sikh center, right in my neighborhood, and the emblem on the gates, I have to admit, does give one pause when viewing it in the Islamic Republic, where its own emblem is ubiquitous. But after a few moments reflecting on the coincidence of its uncanny similarity to the "Allah" of Iran, I moved on, reflecting instead on my compatriots' love of and insatiable appetite for conspiracy theories.

———

Of all the criticisms one might make of Ayatollah Khomeini, his being a descendant of an Indian cannot, despite some of the more racist Iranians' insistence, be included, for if the main criterion for ruling Iran rightfully or for starting a revolution is pure Persian race, then Zoroastrians should be in charge of Iran. They, who still practice the ancient religion of Iran from before the Muslim invasion, can probably claim the "purest" Aryan bloodline of any Iranians, for they rarely marry outside the faith and are excommunicated if they do, but the rest of us are, whether we like it or not, a mixture of all the racial minorities in Iran, including minorities that no longer exist, such as Macedonian and Mongol. And most Iranians do not like it. But what Iranians, no matter their racial makeup, share is a deep cultural tie to the walled garden, figuratively and literally. The four-walled Persian garden, or *pairidaeza* in Old Persian (*pairi* for "around," *daeza* for "wall"), has existed since the time of Cyrus the Great, more than twenty-five hundred years ago, and not only inspired the future grand gardens of Europe but gave its name to our definition of heaven: "paradise."

My own childhood pairidaeza was my grandparents' home in Abbasabad-e-Einedoleh, in downtown Tehran. We visited some summers, and as my parents, who'd been living abroad since the 1950s, didn't own a house in Iran and my father's family was hundreds of miles away in the desert town of Yazd, we always stayed at my maternal grandparents' house, the house my mother was born in. My grandfather Seyyed Kazem

Assar spent most of his time in his rooms, reading or entertaining visitors who came often to see him, either students on a question of philosophy or neighbors for an *estekhareh*, a peculiarly Shia form of a reading, or divining answers to perplexing or simply mundane questions. He was a cleric but also a Sufi, and his estekhareh were well-known, and everyone I met, including my mother, believed with absolute certainty in the divinations. Sometimes he performed the estekhareh by closing his eyes and muttering prayers while he fingered his worry beads, stopping at a particular moment in the prayer and holding the beads up to count how many of them he had moved, thence proclaiming whether whatever was being contemplated was favorable or unfavorable. Other times he would hold a Koran in his hand and pray, again with eyes closed, and at the right moment stop and randomly open the book to a page, whereby he would ascertain from the passage his finger pointed to what answer to give the petitioner.

I always feared becoming sick in Iran, for no matter my malady, my mother would, along with a visit to a doctor, consult her father and his estekhareh, which for me only meant succumbing to the forced drinking of drafts of vomit-inducing tinctures, the tastes of which remain in my throat today and the likes of which I have yet to experience in my adult life. I did come to believe in estekhareh myself, however, or at least the Assar estekhareh, when my uncle Nasser—who also visited some summers from his home in Paris, where he was a painter and to which he had run away after he had finished high school—was cured of a skin disorder on his hands by his father's prescription after a lengthy divination, which neither he nor his French wife believed could possibly help but, given the lack of success by his European doctors, believed would probably not hurt either. For the rest of his stay in Tehran, Nasser would urinate on his hands every day, and his skin cleared up nicely before his return to France.

Kazem Assar, though born of an Iraqi mother and therefore half-Arab, was Persian through and through when it came to love of his garden. Other than during meals, which he sometimes took alone in his library, the only times he seemed relaxed were when he went for his daily stroll in the garden, walking on the stone path in the shade of the walls in his clerical garb and turban, pausing to rest, and I presume reflect, every now and then in front of a mulberry bush or cherry tree. His manservant Ali would wash down the path with a hose every hot, dusty afternoon, briefly cooling the air and adding a very slight and momentary humidity that Tehran normally suffers without. My mother tells me that when my brother, Saman, was born, Kazem's first grandchild, he took great pleasure in pushing his baby carriage around the garden, a novelty pleasure that apparently quickly wore off, for there are no stories, photographs, or memories of him doing the same for me, born a mere eighteen months later.

The garden, surrounded by what I remember as impossibly high mud walls, although they were probably only twelve or fifteen feet, was where my brother and I lived during the summers, playing all sorts of games, trying to climb a pine tree, or taking a dip in the small pond in the center. The purpose of the pond in Persian gardens is twofold: it provides aesthetic pleasure and peaceful tranquillity, and it serves as a place to perform the ablutions required before prayers. For children playing on a hot summer day, it was merely an opportunity to cool down. On the far side of the pond, there was a large stone-paved area under two towering pine trees that extended almost to the back wall of the garden, and it was here that every night wooden beds and cotton mattresses would be set up for the entire family to sleep under the stars. Air-conditioning was rare in those days, particularly in older houses, and quite unnecessary at night in the dry climate, and I remember how exciting it was for an apartment-dwelling child to crawl into a bed in a huge garden and look up at the sky. Almost everyone in the household slept outdoors together during the long, hot summers—beds in a row as if in an army barracks—but I was much too young to wonder about the sex life of the adults and their lack of privacy at night. People must've had sex, but I certainly don't remember hearing any sounds, so perhaps Persian modesty prevailed and sex was quietly confined to daylight hours indoors, or else everyone of an age simply bit down hard on their tongues in the middle of the night.

Sex, of course, was never discussed in my home, but it has always been a major topic of anxiety in an Islamic country with an erotic past. Sex in Iran has had a "don't ask, don't tell" quality about it that is only just beginning to be dispelled, and this despite the common misperception that the Islamic state and the Ayatollahs frown on all matters relating to sex. Shia Islam has always been quite understanding of sexual desire in both men and women; after all, it allows for temporary marriages as short as one hour, known as *sigheh*, for the very purpose of religiously sanctioned fun. Originally intended to alleviate the sexual needs of widows (preferably war widows) as well as unmarried men, it can in fact be a legal device for young men and women to, as we might say, "hook up." It is hardly used, though, and Iranian society, once terrified of sex crawling over the walls of private gardens, today seems to be more comfortable with a rather more open attitude to sex. Condoms are now advertised openly in Iran, and AIDS is not a taboo subject in a country that, under even the progressive Shahs and a Westernized wealthy class in Tehran, was always a society in a state of sexual hypocrisy. Women were expected to remain virgins until they married, and certainly not get pregnant, and yet women did have sex with boyfriends, and sometimes some of them got pregnant. The plastic surgery practice of hymen reconstruction was so common in Tehran in prerevolutionary times that some doctors devoted their practice to it (and hymen-reconstruction expertise followed the large Iranian expatriate community to Los Angeles, where it is still performed), while abortion clinics were plentiful (and still are, discreetly, today). In a society where uttering the words *khar-kosteh*—literally "your sister fucks"—is the very worst of insults, though often merely a statement of fact in the West, men and women know very well that almost everyone has a sexual history, but there is never a reason to allow that history to be exposed outside of the home, and as long as appearances are maintained, all is forgiven.

In 2006 and even into 2007, however, there was a single incident beyond the issue of AIDS that brought sex out from behind the garden walls and right into the street, or, as some hard-line Islamists thought, the gutter. Television's most famous actress, Zahra Ebrahimi, a demure young lady who portrayed a pious, properly Muslim girl on a popular soap opera, was, much like Paris Hilton, the subject of a sex video made by her boyfriend that found its way to every DVD and CD vendor in Iran. She immediately denied that the woman in the video was her, while her boyfriend initially fled the country, and then, when he returned, argued that they had performed a temporary marriage and therefore were not engaging in any illicit activity. Investigations were begun, the judiciary got involved, and then everyone in Iran, of course, had to see the video. Abdolghassem Ghassemzadeh, an editor at large of one of Iran's largest dailies, *Ettelaat*, and the son-in-law of a very senior cleric, told me an anecdote about the affair one afternoon in his offices at the paper. "One day," he said, tapping his pipe on the palm of his hand, "our reporters were excited by the news that the sex video had grossed about four billion rials [approximately half a million dollars] in sales, and at the editorial meeting they were looking for the story to get placement on the front page." He paused while he puffed on his pipe for a few moments. "I said," he then continued, "absolutely not; under no circumstances! The story will be buried deep inside the paper."

"Why?" I asked him, a little confused.

"Because," he replied, "and I had to explain this to the reporters too, if we made the profit on the sex video big news, Iran would be inundated with copycat videos by people hoping to make a killing with their own sex videos."

"Really? So what happened?" I asked.

"It was buried in the paper, but my prediction was right anyway. A few weeks later, a video surfaced in the north of the country, but the couple had been too stupid to hide their faces, so the local police immediately identified them." He chuckled. "The problem was, of course, that they were married, so it wasn't clear if they had actually broken any laws."

"So did they make any money with their video?"

"Yes, of course!" said Ghassemzadeh. "Not as much; but they made money."

Despite the huge scandal and the impropriety in a society where not only Islam but also Persian culture deems that a woman must at least give the appearance of being chaste, the scandal faded away, no one was detained for long, and if the investigation even continued (as the government insisted), everyone, including the conservatives most outraged, lost interest. Sex, it seems, has made its way out of the garden with a big sigh, if not yet in rural Iran or among the poorest and most pious of Iranians, then at least in the urban centers, where Iranians of all classes consume the news with a voracious appetite.

———————

Persian culture, the culture Iranians of all races deem superior to all others in the region and certainly superior to the locust eaters', places a remarkable emphasis on the home, privacy, and private life, and perhaps no other civilization has delineated public behavior from private quite as much. Traditional Iranian houses, with imposing walls surrounding them that afford absolute privacy from roving neighbors' and strangers' eyes, were built around gardens that Persians value as much as the homes themselves. Often, wealthier families built compounds around the gardens that housed extensions of the family or, if there was no room, bought up adjacent lots or houses and connected them if possible. Today in big cities such as Tehran, where houses have ceded much ground to apartments, Iranian sensibilities still exhibit themselves in the thousands of four- and five-story apartment buildings where every unit is occupied by either members of the same family or, at the very least, good friends. High-rise apartment buildings have gained some ground, but they tend to be inhabited by the most Westernized of city dwellers, some of whom own, or have lived in, similar apartments in Europe or America. It is perhaps because of the Iranian concept of the home and garden (and not the city or town it is in) as the defining center of life that Iranians find living in a society with such stringent rules of public behavior somewhat tolerable. Iranian society by and large cares very little about what goes on in the homes and gardens of private citizens, but the Islamic government cares very much how its citizens behave once they venture outside their walls.

Even in the early days of the revolution that brought mandated Islamic behavior to Iran, most Iranians felt secure enough in their homes to do as they pleased, whether it was Islamic behavior or not. Government or quasi-governmental raids on private homes where parties were being held and alcohol consumed were common enough in those days, but the truth is that the way the un-Islamic parties were known to the authorities was that they were loud enough to be heard on the streets or by neighbors, and not because the government was actively spying on the private lives of its citizens. (A bigger problem for partygoers then was the danger of being stopped on the drive home with alcohol on the breath.) Today, despite a deeply conservative government in power, there is no shortage of alcohol- and even drug-fueled parties in metropolitan areas, and there are, despite persistent fears of a crackdown, practically no attempts by the government to breach the walls of the Persian home.[3] And it is behind those walls that one often finds the true Iranian character.

The walls of the Persian garden are, in their figurative sense, movable. Anywhere there is privacy, a Persian feels surrounded by his walls and therefore at ease. And the very top levels of Islamic Iranian officialdom are no exception. In September 2006, former president Khatami made a private visit to the United States, symbolically significant because he was the highest-ranking Iranian official to be allowed into the United

States on anything other than official UN business in more than
twenty-seven years. His first stop was New York, where the Islamic Republic has its only diplomatic outpost (accredited to the UN) in
America, and where he sat in the drawing room of a stately mansion
on Fifth Avenue across from the Metropolitan Museum of Art, just
minutes after arriving, courtesy of a full NYPD and State Department
escort, at Kennedy Airport. The limestone mansion is the residence of
Iran's ambassador to the UN and is a little bit of Islamic Persia in
Manhattan, complete with a flat-screen television in one room broadcasting live Iranian television and fanciful paintings of words from the
Koran or the word "Allah" on the walls that seem to be the artwork of
choice in government offices throughout Iran. The flagpole above the
entrance on Fifth Avenue was bare, an indication of both Iranian hes-
itancy to draw attention to an Islamic Republic not particularly popular in the United States and traditional Persian guardedness when it
comes to privacy behind the walls of the home. Khatami and his entourage, which included a number of his ex-ambassadors, sat on ersatz
Louis Quinze sofas and armchairs, a much-favored Iranian upscale furniture style that for some strange reason never lost its popularity despite a revolution that banished all symbols of grandeur as *taghouti*, or
"royalist," but they were unguarded and relaxed in the privacy of their
Persian home away from home. A number of staff from Iran's UN
Mission were there too, thrilled, it seemed, to be hanging out with a
president whom they had all wholeheartedly supported and who had
probably made their lives easier, at least in terms of relations with other
countries, in the eight years of his two terms.

The conversation was mostly about Khatami's schedule in America,
and what he should or shouldn't agree to do, publicity- and otherwise.
Jimmy Carter had sent a fax inviting Khatami down to Atlanta, and I
seemed to be, as a consultant, adviser, and sometime translator for
Khatami during his U.S. sojourn, the only advocate for a positive response. The Iranian diplomats—worried that Ahmadinejad's government and supporters, who all despised Khatami, would have a field day

in attacking him for meeting with the U.S. president who had allowed the Shah to enter the United States after abandoning the Peacock Throne (what led to the 1979 hostage crisis)—argued forcefully and successfully that the reform movement in Iran would suffer, but Khatami seemed genuinely disappointed.

Khatami's voluntary trip to the "Great Satan" had already come under fierce attack in the conservative Iranian press, and also in the conservative U.S. press and among conservative U.S. politicians, but the reformists hadn't lost their sense of humor or daring, as members of Khatami's delegation explained with some delight. One writer in Tehran, the wife of a senior member of President Ahmadinejad's administration (Fatemeh Rajabi, wife of his spokesman Gholam-Hossein Elham), had published an article decrying Khatami's U.S. visit as blasphemous and had gone so far as to suggest that he be defrocked; in response, the highly regarded reform newspaper, *Shargh*, published a piece the next day subtly pointing out that her views were shared and fully endorsed by the "Zionist" groups in America, a dig that Khatami, who finds his successor's politics somewhat distasteful, savored.

From then on the conversation turned to humor, and as cup after cup of tea was consumed, the Iranian diplomats and former government officials, not known for mirthful expressiveness, howled with laughter at every story told—stories that mostly involved poking fun at the customs of their very own Islamic Republic. One ambassador recounted his days as envoy to Sweden, and his difficulties in explaining to the protocol officers at the Royal Court why he couldn't wear tails to the yearly king's reception, let alone why he would have to refuse to shake the hand of the queen. His tone in describing the ridiculousness of his predicament was what had the others in the room in tears of laughter, presumably because every one of them could relate to the story. Another recalled a colleague, an ambassador in Europe in the days soon after the revolution, who had instructed his junior staff to wear ties. Tehran, furious about reports that Iran's employees overseas were ignoring the Islamic Republic's new dress codes, demanded an explanation. "Don't worry," the ambassador apparently wrote back in a telex, "my senior staff and I still dress like peasants and laborers; however, I have asked my local staff, chauffeurs and the like, to wear ties so that we preserve a little bit of dignity for the embassy." Khatami laughed heartily along with everyone else, and one couldn't help but think of our unfortunate times, when outside the walls of the mansion most Americans believed that officials of the Islamic Republic were a dour, austere, and inflexible lot who did little else but try to undermine U.S. interests wherever and whenever they could. These same people, of course, once outside their gardens, would show a very different face to the world, but it wasn't simply a matter of their toeing an official line in public; it was their very personalities that would be hidden away, reappearing only in the private company of friends and family behind their Persian walls.

In Tehran, those walls have grown even taller since the founding of the Islamic Republic in 1979. While Persians had always made a clear distinction between their public and their private faces, under twentieth-century secular, Westernized, and modernizing Shahs there were fewer and fewer reasons not to bare all outside the home. Except for political opinion, of course, which was the one subject that was absolutely forbidden in those times. Because of a secret police, the SAVAK, that managed, like the Stasi of East Germany, to recruit informers in just about every Iranian neighborhood, Iranians feared speaking out on politics even in the privacy of their own homes. The intelligence services of the Islamic Republic, although sometimes as brutal as the Shahs', spend far less effort in policing free political expression, as long as, of course, that expression cannot be heard beyond the walls, both literal and figurative, of the Persian garden. As a child, and because I lived outside of Iran, I had been unaware of the SAVAK and the fear it could instill in Iranians; but when I reached sixteen or so, the uncomfortable truth, if you will, hit me.

It hit hardest one day when in an embassy car with my mother in Washington, driven by a Guatemalan chauffeur who spoke no Farsi, I uttered the word "SAVAK." My mother turned pale and brought her finger to her lips. *"Shh!"* she whispered loudly. She then made all kinds of ridiculous signs with her hands and eyes, but I understood that she was trying to indicate to me that the car was undoubtedly bugged. And this was the car that was for the sole use of my father, who was the deputy chief of mission at the Iranian Embassy at the time, and his family. I remember being shocked not only that the Shah's government didn't trust even its most senior diplomats but that the privacy I knew Iranians value could be so blatantly violated. When I sat with Khatami in New York years later, in a mansion that is probably bugged by both the National Security Agency *and* the Iranian Intelligence Ministry, I confess that I found myself admiring the Iranian regime: admiring it for at least allowing its officials their privacy to criticize and, yes, even make fun of the foibles of their government.

Inside Iran, I've witnessed many a political discussion behind walls that would have landed everyone present in prison only a generation ago, and many Iranians feel reasonably free to criticize their government beyond their walls as well, albeit without crossing the redlines of disrespect for Islam or the Supreme Leader. But regular social intercourse has retreated fully into the home and gardens, where in Iran anything goes. In the days immediately after President Ahmadinejad's election in 2005, I was invited twice to a Thursday afternoon opium open house in North Tehran. Thursday is the last day of the week in Iran—Friday is the one holiday—and there are many such gatherings in the city. Opium "salons," I like to call them, for the concept of the salon, a very Persian one before the introduction of café society by Westernized intellectuals, has made a strong comeback in the age of enforced Islamic public behavior. At this salon, on a quiet street in an upper-middle-class neighborhood, a stream of friends and acquaintances gathered in a large and well-appointed apartment on the second floor of a modern four-story building. It was a modern household; the women of the house not only walked around without hijab but shook hands and even kissed the men on the cheeks. They did not, however, smoke opium. Opium use is mostly the preserve of men, and men in their thirties and up. It is an establishment pastime that young people are little interested in, and the grown children of the family ventured into the "den," complete with its own ventilation system and a video surveillance system showing the street outside, only to say hello to their father's friends.

Talk was of politics and business, and the news on one Thursday afternoon was the continuing unrest in the Kurdish regions, an unrest little reported in the newspapers but news of which was readily available on the Internet. A nationalist Kurd, Shivan Qaderi, had been shot by state security forces, who labeled him, as usual, a "hooligan," in the Kurdish town of Mahabad on July 9, 2005, and his body had been dragged through town behind a jeep, presumably to intimidate the population. The tactic backfired, and rather than be intimidated, Kurds had been demonstrating for days, causing a government crackdown that had so far resulted in a number of deaths and injuries. Some of the worst violence, even the state-controlled media had to admit, occurred in the town of Saqqez on August 3, the day before our gathering, and Kurdish satellite stations based in Iraqi Kurdish regions (not that I could find any Iranians who'd ever seen them; they seemed to prefer the Persian Music Channel, the BBC, and the Fashion Channel, particularly the lingerie catwalks) were broadcasting news from the front and helping to mobilize more protests. What was remarkable was not that the unrest was little reported but that even among Iranian intellectuals who hungered for news, any news, that painted the government in a bad light, there was very little sympathy for the Kurds, or for the demonstrators killed while protesting. Even a strong hatred of the ruling clergy by some in the room didn't translate into a hatred of their tactics when it came to putting down Kurdish unrest, perhaps a sign of the latent racism so prevalent among Iranians of all stripes, but more likely because it simply could have no effect on their lives.

The other news, of course, was the nuclear standoff. It was the single biggest issue facing Iran, but these Iranians were only interested in how it might affect their wallets. The men in the room seemed to grudgingly accept that the Ayatollahs were right to hold firm on the nuclear negotiations. Perhaps there's something about the idea of a nuclear arsenal that just appeals to a different part of the brain, but Iranians everywhere were pretty united in opposing what they viewed as the arrogance of America in demanding that Iran be denied the nuclear fuel cycle. In 2005 this group of men worried less that the United States might militarily intervene, for the Iraq quagmire was already evidence for them that America had been rendered militarily impotent, and more that the United States might push through UN sanctions that would negatively affect a rather strong economy, or at least strong for the middle class. And of course they were right, for less than two years later all the talk in Tehran was exactly that: a damaged economy, partly because of UN sanctions.

Ahmadinejad, the newly elected president at the time, was the object of much scorn for his unsophisticated manner, but as the upper-middle-class men smoked pipe after pipe, their hijab-less women darting in and out of the room to share a joke or two, it was apparent that these Iranians were against the Islamic Republic and its leaders not so much on the basis of policy as on the basis of class. Iran was supposed to have done away with class distinctions in the Islamic Revolution, but as with almost everything else class consciousness simply retired behind Persian walls. For centuries the class system in Iran, kept intact under successive Shahs, categorized clerics as one rung above the poor and the workers, and almost on par with the *bazaaris*, the men in the bazaar who are the Ayatollahs' benefactors and who to this day, armed with only a 1930s-era Siemens phone and a desk from the same period, control hundreds of millions, if not billions, of dollars of the import-export trade. That these *shepesh'oo*, or "flea-ridden," mullahs had managed to not only rule over them for twenty-six years but also create industry, help generate wealth for their bazaari benefactors, build a powerful military, win successive face-offs with the West, and generally elevate Iran's importance in the world was almost too much to bear for these men.[4] And now, they implied, to make matters worse, an ugly, brutish, and sartorially challenged president had been elected who came from the one class they deemed below the clerics and the bazaaris: the working class. Ahmadinejad, they mused, would be better suited to being a blacksmith, the occupation of his father.

———

A few nights later, I found myself behind the walls of a couple's apartment in the fancy district of Elahieh that had artfully been made to look like a New York loft. "Drink?" asked my hostess right away, and she didn't mean soda. Johnnie Walker, it seems, has fully colonized this part of the world as the British Empire was never able to do. The artists' loft (husband and wife, both young and both artists) could have been anywhere in the West, or at least anywhere there are lofts. As other guests arrived, it was even more so, for along with other Iranian artists who pepper their speech with as much English as possible, there were actually foreign guests.

In Iran there isn't a particularly large expatriate community, for obvious reasons, but the ones who are there are often found at these kinds of parties. A twenty-three-year-old blond, blue-eyed girl walked through the door and said her hellos in perfect, barely accented Farsi. Where was she from, and what was she doing in Tehran? I wondered. She was British, I quickly discovered, living alone in Tehran, and working at the Iranian Foreign Ministry to further her study of international relations. Living alone? Well, not quite. She had a roommate, a male journalist, who as far as her neighbors were concerned was her husband. And did she enjoy living in Tehran? "Love it," she said. "Absolutely *love* it," she continued with a smile, chewing on an olive and slowly enunciating every syllable with her Oxford-tinged accent.

A couple, a French man and his Iranian wife, walked in the door and introductions were made. What, they also wondered, did the English girl do? "She's a spy," I blurted out jokingly, "MI6." The girl simply smiled again, clearly aware of most Iranians' assumptions about the British (that they're never up to any good), and said, "Yes, I'm a spy," and walked away.[5] There was a lot of curiosity about me at the party, as there can be about any Iranian who lives abroad: what I was doing in Iran, whom I had seen, and what I thought of the place. When a cannabis joint was passed around, I begged off, saying I felt that I may have indulged in a little too much opium on this particular trip. The looks of wonder, even disgust, on some of the guests' faces were confirmation that to them opium use was the province of much older men, the bourgeois classes and lower, and not the enlightened artists and intellectuals who were busy puffing away at their very chic Western weed.

Many Iranians in the community of artists and intellectuals believe, as I did, that any Westerners at their parties are spies, or spies in the making, but I found out later that many Iranians are convinced that at any of these gatherings or parties at least one of the artist types is also a spy, but from the Iranian Ministry of Intelligence. Oddly enough, it doesn't affect their behavior, perhaps because they feel so protected behind their walls that they cannot imagine that the state, unlike in the days of the Shah and his SAVAK, would dare to remove the one arena of privacy that allows people a freedom they might otherwise take to demanding in the streets. The spies, one is told, are usually the least obvious men—the ones who fire up the first joint, but also the ones who ask a lot of questions. Like the man, I thought later, who persisted in asking me whom I'd seen while I had been in Tehran. Based on the fact that people rarely get into trouble for attending these kinds of parties, even if they cross every political redline imaginable, as I myself have done, I have to assume that the idea that there are spies everywhere is Iranian paranoia and conspiracy-theory-mindedness, but the idea is intriguing nonetheless and quite to my Persian taste. The Iranian intelligence services certainly monitor their citizens, but if they were to arrest anyone who speaks ill of the government in private, they simply couldn't build cells fast enough to hold their prisoners. It is far more likely that some people *are* watched and carefully monitored—people known for political activism—and any and all evidence, ridiculous or not, of their danger to the state is undoubtedly presented when and if the time comes for them to be tried and convicted.

But there couldn't have been any spies at another party of artists and intellectuals, some of them from the same loft, in the winter of 2007, even though at times I thought there surely had to be if the Islamic Republic deserved its reputation. The party was at a house, a mansion really, of the kind that is simply no longer in private hands in Tehran: on at least an acre or so of land with a huge swimming pool set in the middle of expansive gardens shaded by towering pine trees. Once common enough during the heyday of the Shah's reign, many large properties were confiscated by the Islamic government either in the owners' absence or because of the assumption of ill-gotten gains, and those who managed to retrieve their properties in the courts sold off the land in parcels as Tehran grew—from a population of around four million in 1979 to the current estimate of twelve to fifteen million—both to cash in on the skyrocketing real estate prices and to project a more modest lifestyle in the new Islamic and supposedly classless society. This modernist house, the pool, the view, and the steep winding road leading to its gates, was more Hollywood Hills than Tehran, but then again, so were the occupants, who were among the few who had succeeded in retrieving their confiscated property *and* had decided to live in it, appearances be damned.

Walls surround the property, and two large guard dogs, unclean in Islam and rare in any house, barked up a storm whenever anyone entered the compound. The upper-class gathering included two young men, both born and raised in the United States, who had come to Iran in the last two years to work with their families, and their American-accented and faulty Farsi instantly gave away their background as members of the nonreligious and nonpolitical privileged class, a class that has managed to successfully engage in commerce, or at least successfully enough that these two young men had forsaken America for lucrative opportunities in Iran. Another couple, older and sharply dressed, the man wearing a bold tie, sat with me and told me of their great friendship with and admiration for Ardeshir Zahedi, the Shah's son-in-law, foreign minister, ambassador to Washington, and possibly one of the most hated men of the Shah's era, who is still alive in Switzerland. The husband, busy getting drunk as quickly as he could, explained that he had been in prison since 1992, and this particular evening he was on furlough, or, as they say in Iran, on "vacation" from jail. Although he held U.S. citizenship as well, he seemed resigned to his circumstance, one that he argued wasn't really as bad as all that. "I'm home more often than in Evin," he said.

"Evin?" I asked, knowing that it was Iran's most notorious jail for political prisoners. "That's pretty hard-core, no?"

"Nah," he grunted. "It's like a hotel for us nowadays. Hotel Evin!" He smiled and made a sweeping motion with his arm. "Everything you see here," he said, already slurring just a little, "we have in there: liquor, drugs, whatever you want." As he was a man of considerable means, I didn't doubt his words, for although the expression "Hotel Evin" had been a macabre joke at one time, the government, in an effort to improve its image abroad and to stymie accusations of human rights abuses, had made substantial changes at the prison, at least for high-profile political prisoners. (The Abu Ghraib scandal, CIA rendition cases, and the Guantánamo detention facility gave Iran, but also its prisoners, an unexpected boost in the years after 9/11 in that Iran, in order to show its moral superiority, continually trumpets the treatment of its prisoners as comparing most favorably to those in American hands. Reporters are regularly given tours of the prison, and even Iranian-American political prisoners either released and allowed to travel back to the States or interviewed at the prison have spoken of a rather benign atmosphere in their cells. That is not to say that the less fortunate—Iranians unlikely to command any attention on the outside—are not treated as harshly as they always have been, including with alleged bouts of torture.)

"Really?" I said. "So when do you officially get released?"

"Who knows," he said. "I've been told any day now for the last fifteen years."

"And why were you arrested in the first place?" I asked, assuming it was for some sort of political or antirevolutionary infraction.

"Some business issues," he said. "I was told, before I came back to Iran in '92, that I'd be okay, but obviously I wasn't." A friend leaned over to me and explained that he had been a rather wealthy and successful businessman during the Shah's era and that his businesses were taken over by the government when he fled during the revolution, apparently with quite a large sum of cash. "When I escaped prison the first time and went to the United States—"

"Wait a minute!" I interrupted him. "You escaped Evin and went back to the United States?"

"Yeah," he said. "I just left during one of my 'vacations'—"

"Wait," I interrupted again. "Why on earth did you return, then?"

"To *fuck* these people's mothers!" he exclaimed. "Why else?" I looked around uncomfortably, his wife blushed, and he burst out laughing. "Eighty percent of all Iranians born after Khomeini came to power will have to be killed," he continued in a more serious tone, but one that reflected both a bitterness and a tacit admission that Iran, with most of its population born after the revolution, is unlikely to ever change in the way that he and his contemporaries may wish it to. *"Eighty percent,"* he said loudly, as if to emphasize the impossibility of his political dreams, and he headed to the dining table, rather stoically, I thought, despite his advancing state of inebriation.

If there's any Thursday afternoon salon where the Iranian intelligence services must absolutely be present, even behind the garden walls, it would have to be at the home of Sadeq Kharrazi, nephew of the former foreign minister Kamal Kharrazi, a former ambassador to Paris himself, and a key member of the nuclear negotiating team under President Khatami. Kharrazi's distaste for Ahmadinejad and his ilk is well-known; he is one of the most vocal of former government officials in openly criticizing the current administration to anyone who will listen. A charming, highly intelligent man with sophisticated tastes, he was a principal author of the infamous Iranian "proposal" to the White House in 2003, a proposal for steps Iran would be willing to take in order to normalize relations that was rejected by George Bush out of hand; and, if for no other reason than his efforts to reach out to the United States, the present government reserves for him a particular loathing.[6] But Kharrazi is a child of the revolution too, from a clerical family (and his sister is married to the Supreme Leader's son), and unless he strays too far from the principles of the Islamic Republic in his views or actions, Ahmadinejad can do him no harm.

Kharrazi's house is, naturally, in the far reaches of privileged North Tehran, on a quiet street of unseen mansions behind the tall walls that surround their gardens. The entrance, a nondescript and very ordinary white metal door, properly disguises, as Persian tastes dictate, what has to be one of the finest homes in the capital: a house that could easily grace the pages of any American or European shelter magazine; a fully and authentically remodeled old Persian house, filled with Persian art and antiques, old rescued tile work on the interior walls and arches that look onto large, manicured gardens hidden from prying eyes by their tall walls. Kharrazi's library, up a winding staircase that leads to the traditional second-floor formal quarters, and which he showed me on a short private tour, is possibly the largest antiquarian Persian library in private hands, with shelf after shelf lined with irreplaceable volumes of Iranian poetry, literature, and religious texts from before the printing press to more contemporary times. (Kharrazi donated some ten thousand contemporary Iranian books to the newly created Institute for Iranian Studies at the University of St. Andrews in Scotland in late 2006.)

The salon here, in 2007, is not about opium or indeed any other vice, for the guests are all from the revolutionary elite even if they're not in power at present, and they cannot boldly exhibit un-Islamic behavior in each other's presence. They do, however, relax with tea, coffee, and Cuban cigars, a favored status symbol of the more progressive among the establishment. Progressive, reformist, and even quite Westernized in some ways they may be, but there are no women (who must be hidden somewhere), for all the work of serving tea and sweetmeats, emptying ashtrays, and such is performed by two houseboys. It could be a Persian house of a century ago, except the houseboys are the most modern of the men, with long, gelled hair, fashionable jeans and T-shirts, and, unlike the guests, clean-shaven cheeks. Talk is almost always of politics and, with a number of Foreign Ministry types always present, of foreign relations, but the houseboys take no notice, only occasionally smiling if a ribald joke is inserted into the conversation by one of the guests. Despair at what everyone considers the sorry state of Iranian politics is evident in the conversation, and one guest, a former top official with extremely close ties to the Revolutionary Guards who has been written about in the West, even suggests that Iran would be better off without elections. "*This* is what happens when you let people vote," he says emphatically. "The idiots elect an idiot." He then turns to a colleague with banking connections and whispers, loud enough for me to hear a few feet away, "Do you think you can help with a $120 million transaction?" His colleague seems momentarily taken aback. "For the Guards, of course," he adds nonchalantly, taking a puff from a long Cohiba. (Recent UN and U.S. sanctions against Iranian banks had made dollar transactions in Tehran somewhat problematic.)

If any of the fifteen or twenty men who drifted in and out of the house on a Thursday afternoon were indeed informants or intelligence agents, they'd have much to report, I thought, but nothing that could be particularly actionable. The judiciary and the intelligence services, independent of the executive branch, may indeed be the more conservative and hard-line bodies in the Islamic Republic, but they know better than to do anything more than listen in a gathering such as this. Populist presidents like Ahmadinejad, they know, will come and go, but the political elite (reform-minded or not but all with close ties to, if not relatives of, the clerics) and the Revolutionary Guards, of course, are the constants that the republic needs to survive.

———————

In Iran today, the Iranian intelligence services are generally far more concerned with plots against the state, real or imagined, and political activism that spreads to the streets than with the conversations of Iranians behind closed doors, whether they be doors belonging to prominent citizens known to the state or more unassuming ones behind which anonymous middle- and working-class Iranians grumble about the country's state of affairs. It is perhaps for that reason that some political activists have, consciously or unconsciously, taken their activism behind movable Persian walls, away from the prying eyes of the state.

One of the better-known groups who have done so are women campaigning for change in the discriminatory laws of the Islamic Republic (but who are careful to emphasize in their materials that what they are calling for is not against the laws of Islam) who come under the banner of "Change for Equality."[7] A campaign to gather one million signatures to present to parliament began in mid-2006, after a women's demonstration was broken up by police and its leaders arrested (most received suspended sentences and were subsequently released), but the way the campaigners went about gathering the signatures and pursuing their activism made it almost impossible for the authorities to clamp down on their activities without breaching the figurative walls that Persians erect wherever they can. Women's hair salons, for example, became places to promote their campaign, as did subway cars, buses, factories, and even picnic grounds, places not normally patrolled by government agents looking for treasonous activity, and although many women sympathetic to the cause were unwilling to put their names to a document out of concern that they might endanger themselves, by the summer of 2007 over a hundred thousand signatures had been compiled, an impressive number if one considers the handful of women who were active in collecting them and the lengths to which they went, including knocking on the doors of private homes, to do so.[8] A million signatures, or even a hundred thousand, the organizers must've reasoned, could be a far more effective call for change, change in Iran's laws that has the moral, if not vocal, support of many politicians and even clerics, than a public demonstration of a few hundred women that would immediately be broken up by the authorities and quickly forgotten, as such events always had been in the past.

———————

While political activists of all stripes continue to devise imaginative ways to further their causes and agendas, whether by retreating behind walls they believe the authorities can't or won't breach or by challenging the government publicly but with caution, they know they have to tread lightly as their names become known to the security services, who are at all times suspicious of any activity that might lead to a revolution, "velvet" or otherwise. Iranians who are of little or no interest to agents of the Islamic Republic are Iranians who, despite privilege, wealth, Western appearance, and generally secular ways, live their lives quietly behind the walls of their homes and have neither real political influence nor ambitions. As long as they can continue to make a living, maintain their wealth, travel freely, and party as they please in private, the members of this secular elite are generally unwilling to jeopardize their comfortable lifestyles for the sake of any form of political activism. They have political opinions, of course, and they express them openly among friends in the privacy of their homes, but they seem uninterested in any real activism—the kinds of efforts that would include attending or organizing protest rallies or marches—and they are no threat to the Islamic Republic.

On New Year's Eve 2005, I was invited to a party in North Tehran,

one of many being held by desperately Westernized Persians, for whom
their own calendar, firmly stuck in the fourteenth century, provided little excuse to show off their European ways. The ride to the wealthy part
of town took me past grand embassies, smart shops with Christmas
decorations, and a brightly lit Apachi burger joint on Shariati Avenue.
The "Apachi" is, as one can denote from the logo, indeed meant to be
an Apache, or at least a cartoon depiction of a tomahawk-wielding Native American, another indication that racial sensitivity has never been
the Persians' strong suit. Crawling along the boulevard at rush-hour
pace despite the late hour, I could see the inside of the burger joint
teeming with youngsters of both genders, and they were hanging out,
just as teenagers do in small-town and rural America, where the Dairy
Queen and the bowling alley are the only places to meet girls or boys.
And although the signs above the registers—big enough to be read from
a passing car—begged the customers to be respectful of and follow Islamic dress laws, the diners inside seemed more intent on testing the
boundaries of exactly what those laws were. This night, at least, the Islamic Republic was allowing the walls of the fast-food restaurant, even
its glass ones, to be a private barrier not to be breached.

I heard the music before I spotted the building. Bass, heavy bass, and
all I could think was that the whole neighborhood knew there was a
party going on. My cabdriver sensibly zeroed in on the source and let
me out. "No, please, it really was very worthy," I said a few times, trying to hand over a few banknotes to his ta'arouf protestations. Inside
the fancy apartment liquor flowed, the music was loud, the women
were not only bareheaded but mostly bare, and I thought that there was
nothing Islamic about this little part of the republic, with the glaring
exception of the person who was serving drinks. She was a tall woman
in head-to-toe chador with no hint of makeup, and stood in stark contrast to the heavily mascaraed, rouged, and lipsticked ladies, most with

décolletages that would be considered provocative by Parisian standards, all around her. Her little daughter in the kitchen was helping out
with the food: she couldn't be more than ten, but she was also wearing
a full head covering, a hijab, tightly contoured under her chin. What, I
wondered, did the mother-and-daughter domestic team make of all
this? Wasn't the mother offended by the bacchanalia? Especially in
front of her daughter? Wasn't she going to call the morals police?

The women danced to nauseating Los Angeles–produced Iranian
pop, and every now and then one of them would shimmy up to me
provocatively, breasts heaving, and encourage me to join in. "Can't
dance Persian," I would say, but they were really insistent. "Really, no,"
I would insist, but ta'arouf extends to the dance floor and "no" really
means "ask me again." Other men, all wearing ties as symbols of their
disapproval of Islamic dress codes and hearty approval of all things
Western, succumbed to their charms rather more readily and flailed
about hopelessly while the women who enticed them from their chairs
all but ignored them, happier to show off their own dancing and their
seduction skills to anyone who cared to notice.

Eventually the chador-clad housekeeper elbowed her way through
the gyrating bodies to place food on the dining table, but she kept her
head down in either submissiveness or denial, I couldn't be sure which.
My eyes followed her back to the kitchen and watched her pick up the
phone. Perhaps she had had enough; perhaps she *was* calling the vice
squad. But no, nothing happened. She was behind the walls of her employer, after all, of her own free will, and she might explain it that way
to her young and impressionable daughter. The men and women, obliv-
ious to them, danced the night away as if they were in New York or
London, and the housekeeper and her daughter were driven southward
home, a home behind their own more *najeeb*, or "virtuous," walls, by the
husband she had called. A home where the Islamic Republic lived up
to its name, and where it would have no reason to ever come knocking.

THE AYATOLLAH
BEGS TO DIFFER

Arriving in Tehran from Qom late at night on the last day of Mohammad Khatami's presidency, I switched on the car radio. A sweet-voiced
female presenter read an ode to the president as my car passed by a
huge mural depicting an American flag on the side of a building facing an overpass—stars represented as skulls, and stripes as the trails of
bombs falling. Her voice was sorrowful with a hint of trepidation. The
next day Mahmoud Ahmadinejad would be installed as the new president of Iran by the Supreme Leader, Ayatollah Ali Khamenei, and
Tehran seemed to have suddenly become collectively nostalgic for a
man it had all but abandoned, if not openly mocked, in the last years
of his eight-year presidency.

All week I had witnessed a sort of melancholy mood; Iranians, even
those who voted against the reformers, heirs to Khatami's politics,
seemed now saddened to see him go. He had been the soft face of the
nation for a long time, a period of growth and international outreach
for the Islamic Republic, and despite frequent criticism from both left
and right he had, many Iranians agreed on the eve of the archconservative Ahmadinejad's inauguration, performed his duties as honorably
as any man could. Slowly, middle- and upper-middle-class Iranians

seemed to be coming to the realization that perhaps their lives, at least their social lives, could be in for a change, and not for the better. Khatami had challenged the system, if not changed it, in a way that no high-ranking official had, for although Iran had had its share of dissident mullahs, none had been permitted to advance their careers within the system as Khatami had. Strictly speaking not a dissident, for Khatami was a product of the revolution and was dedicated to its promise, he was nonetheless someone who differed with many of the leading senior Ayatollahs, and certainly with their conservative followers in government, on issues as far-reaching as the place of Islam in society and relations with the outside world, including the United States.

My friend Fuad once joked to me, after I had spent time with President Ahmadinejad in New York, that I should persuade the president to go to dinner at his house in Los Angeles, implying that he—and perhaps some other Iranian Jews—would politely give him a piece of his mind, certainly while employing some particularly challenging ta'arouf. I half-jokingly replied that although I thought that was an impossibility, perhaps I could persuade Khatami, who had told me he very much wanted to go to California the last time he toured the East Coast, to have dinner with him instead. "Listen," Fuad said in all seriousness, aware of my relationship with Khatami, "if you could arrange that, believe me, it would be a greater honor for me than if Ben-Gurion himself came to dinner! Please tell him that; I really mean it." Over a year and a half after leaving office, Khatami still had his fans.

———

That Khatami would still be relevant in Iranian politics today, particularly after a stunning loss in the presidential elections of 2005 by his would-be successors (Mehdi Karroubi and Mostafa Moin, the reform candidates in the first round, finished third and fourth, respectively), is not particularly surprising. Iranians have very little experience with political parties (the Shah having outlawed all except his own, Rastakhiz, to which membership was mandatory for not only all civil servants but practically the entire country), and few identify themselves with one or another of the parties that have existed legally under the Islamic governments that followed. Most Iranian voters wouldn't know to what party a particular candidate belongs anyway, and as such, personality plays a large role in elections, as does, naturally, where a candidate falls in the political spectrum: liberal, pragmatic center, or conservative. Khatami was the first true liberal (by the standards of Iran, or indeed the Middle East) to become president, and under his leadership noticeable changes occurred in Iranian society. Not only were laws on public behavior relaxed (or ignored, mostly), but Iran's isolationist policies were almost completely reversed, leading to an opening for Iranian businesses and even tourism that changed the character of the Islamic Republic. Iranians abroad, after years of staying away from their homeland partly out of fear and partly because of the obstacles Iranian consulates would erect for dual-passport holders, were actively encouraged to return to Iran, if only for yearly visits, and the normally dour and even rude officials in charge of issuing passports to Iranians were transformed, by direct order from Tehran, into charmingly polite, ta'aroufing, and helpful fellow citizens.[1]

The kinds of changes to Iranian society that were made under Khatami have proven very difficult to undo, even when conservatives have tried their utmost. (It is important to note that during his populist campaign, Ahmadinejad convincingly dismissed, usually with a giggle, as ridiculous any notion that his administration would clamp down on press freedom, questionable hijab, or the Internet, all of which of course he then proceeded to attempt to do with varying degrees of success.) It is probably safe to say that a majority of Iranians, perhaps commensurate with the percentages that voted for him, share a political philosophy with Khatami—that is to say, a philosophy of moderation and real political change that doesn't subvert the Islamic underpinning of the state. (It should be noted that the Revolutionary Guards, thought of in the West as monolithically and ideologically hard-line, also voted for Khatami with about the same percentages, over 70 percent, as the general population.) Naturally the more left-leaning and liberal Iranians were greatly disappointed by the pace of change and by Khatami's unwillingness to take on the real hard-liners when it most counted, and there are those in the diaspora who are reluctant to countenance anyone who works within the Islamic system, but leaving aside economic factors (which Ahmadinejad played to his advantage), few Iranians, including members of the Guards, would describe themselves as being philosophically much to the left or the right of Khatami.

The desire for reform, both economic and political, is very much alive in Iran, no matter whom one talks to, and the broader reform movement seems to be awaiting a leader to emerge before the presidential elections of 2009. In every election since Ahmadinejad became president, the moderate and reform candidates have—much with the same majority that Khatami attracted—won decisive victories. A senior Iranian diplomat (and relative of an important cleric), in the days after Ahmadinejad's election, described to me what he believed to be Khatami's, and ultimately the reform movement's, biggest fault. "He didn't designate a successor," he told me, "and that doomed the reform candidates. If only he had groomed someone, if only he had properly endorsed one of the candidates, that person would have won easily, and we wouldn't be stuck with this idiot, this *ablah!*"

———

A few days before he was to hand over power to his successor, I met with Khatami at Sa'adabad Palace, his part-time office in the less polluted and more secluded part of the city, and he seemed relieved to be leaving office, happy to be able to devote his time to what he truly believed in—working for dialogue among civilizations. Khatami, a mid-level cleric, a Hojjatoleslam (meaning "expert on Islam" or "proof of Islam") and not yet an Ayatollah, told me he was forming an NGO to pursue his dialogue initiative, and I got the sense that he thought he might actually be more effective outside government than in it, for he had, over the years, been thwarted by the clerical leadership in trying to implement many political and societal changes he thought necessary to the healthy development of "Islamic democracy." He also had a fatalistic view of the future of politics in Iran, hinting at the probability of a painful future for democracy-minded Iranians under a strict right-wing regime not known for its tolerance of liberal or, in their minds, un-Islamic thought.

Khatami seemed saddened by the Bush administration's attitude toward his country; he told me of his brief encounter with Bill Clinton at the pope's funeral that April, a mere nod of the head, and wistfully said that things would have been much different the last few years had America been under a Clinton presidency. He reminded me that Clinton had been the first U.S. president to sit through a speech by an Iranian official (his, at the UN) since the founding of the Islamic Republic (U.S. officials normally stand up and walk out as protest when an Iranian leader begins a speech at the UN), a sign to him that had there not been an American election in 2000, or had the Supreme Court decided its outcome differently, Iran and the United States might have found a way toward normalization of relations. Fundamentalists in both countries, he said, contributed to the animosity between the United States and Iran, and now, he implied, the situation could only get worse. I don't think he was quite aware of the irony that the "fundamentalists" he spoke of in America were closer in philosophy to Muslim fundamentalists, his political enemies, than to anyone else in the West. It strikes me often while I am in Iran that were Christian evangelicals to take a tour of Iran today, they might find it the model for an ideal society they seek in America. Replace Allah with God, Mohammad with Jesus, keep the same public and private notions of chastity, sin, salvation, and God's will, and a Christian Republic is born.

During the last few days of Khatami's presidency, there were a number of farewell events planned by his supporters and, on an official level, the state. On the Sunday night of the biggest event, dubbed *"Salam Khatami!"* (*salam* can mean both "goodbye" and "hello"), traffic around the Interior Ministry, where it was held, was snarled, and the main conference hall itself was packed. As I walked to my reserved seat, I passed many dignitaries I could recognize and some I couldn't. The Chief Rabbi of Tehran was conspicuous in the front row, as were the Bishops of the Armenian Church and the Assyrian Church, and the Zoroastrian priests who were scattered about the first and second rows in prominent and television-dominating seats, no doubt reserved for them on explicit instructions by Khatami himself, who had made interfaith relations a priority of his presidency. Ayatollah Khomeini's grandson Hossein sat in the front row, center, next to Khatami's brother Reza, the ultraliberal politician disqualified from running for any office by the Guardian Council, who sat with his wife, Zahra Eshraghi, Ayatollah Khomeini's granddaughter. This was the liberal face of the Islamic Republic, even with Khomeini descendants in the crowd, and die-hard conservatives chose to stay away. The evening began, as all official functions in Iran do, with a piercingly loud recitation of the Koran. It sounded not unlike the call to prayer to my ears, but every time I thought the orator was finished, he'd leap into another verse. It was hauntingly beautiful, for Khatami's people had chosen a man with a mellifluous voice, though I still couldn't help but wonder as it went on and on with no end in sight whether the rabbi and the priests were thinking the same thing I was: that sometimes the *Islamic* part of the Islamic Republic can be, shall we say, a little overbearing.

When the recitation was finally over, speakers from all walks of life—artists, professors, doctors, and students—took to the stage and spoke proudly of Khatami's accomplishments and what he had meant to them and the nation. The highlights of the evening were two young students, one man and one woman, who, with a nationalistic fervor that would have been more appropriate at a fascist rally than at a gathering of liberals, poured poetic praise on the great nation, the great people, and the great leader they had had. The Khatami cheerleading section behind me broke out in chants, raised their banners, and enthusiastically jumped but not quite danced (for public dancing is prohibited in the Islamic Republic, especially for women), even as the applause died down. The speeches and the cheering momentarily threatened to turn the event into a dangerous celebration of a cult of personality, but I was confident that Khatami himself, who forbade government offices to display his photograph while he was in office (although many ignored his request), would ensure that it would not.

Khatami, elegant as ever in his summer cream-colored linen robes and perfectly wound black turban, rose from his front-row seat to renewed thunderous applause and an audience of millions watching on live TV. He hushed the crowd with gestures and launched into a speech that was self-congratulatory and yet somehow modest at the same time. How often, I wondered, had he wanted to give this speech, to tell an ungrateful nation that they didn't have it so bad, that without him they wouldn't have enjoyed even the modest freedoms they now took for granted? He spoke at length of two Islams—*his* true Islam and the Islam of extremism and fanaticism: the Islam of the Taliban. Both, he daringly said (for the strictly Sunni Taliban were Iran's archenemies and are reviled by almost all Iranians, including all the mullahs), exist in Iran, a veiled reference to the likes of Ayatollah Mesbah-Yazdi, Ahmadinejad's archconservative patron, and to what might come under the new regime. A few people shouted, "Death to the reactionaries!" but Khatami quickly silenced them. "'Death to,'" he said in so many words, "'is *so* over."

The president defended the progress made under his administration, listing his accomplishments one by one, but what was notable about his almost hour-long speech was that he referred to the Rahbar, or "Supreme Leader," only once. No public figure in Iran would ordinarily dare to exclude his ultimate boss, Ayatollah Khamenei, from a major speech, but Khatami was, now that he was leaving office, showing his contempt for the ruling class that had made his job difficult during his presidency. The only other reference to Rahbar (which simply translates from Farsi as "Leader," but is also Khamenei's title) during the evening was when the MC, in a flourish of Persian ta'arouf that combined flattery for one and insult for another, referred to Khatami as the "Rahbar" and, after an almost perceptible pause, "of the dialogue among civilizations." Wow, I thought, *that* did not go unnoticed by the conservative supporters of Khamenei watching at home. At the end of his speech, and a moment that I found out later had been cut away from on television, a man shouted from the floor, "What about Ganji?," referring to the hunger-striking political prisoner Akbar Ganji languishing in Evin prison at the time. Khatami smiled and called back, "Okay, okay," as if he intended to answer, but the MC, a tall, imposing woman in a cream-colored manteau (ankle-length lightweight coat) and hijab, intervened quickly and brought the rally to an end, allowing Khatami to be conveniently whisked away by his security contingent. Don't push it, she wisely must have thought, and as I looked behind me, I was relieved to see the man walk away unmolested by any government security agents undoubtedly mingling with the crowd.

Seyyed Mohammad Khatami was elected president of the Islamic Republic of Iran by a landslide in 1997. It had been eighteen years since the revolution of 1979 had wiped out over twenty-five hundred years of monarchy and the Shia clerics of Iran had solidified their power in forming the only functioning theocracy of the late twentieth century. Iran had suffered a brutal eight-year war with Iraq in the 1980s, a period when immigration to the West resulted in brain drain on a scale Iran had never seen, and those who remained committed to living in Iran (out of either necessity or unwillingness to start a new life elsewhere), from all classes in society, were ready for a change. The austere, rigidly controlled society had already started opening up under Ali Akbar Hashemi Rafsanjani, the pragmatic and fiercely capitalist previous president, but Iranians were growing tired of the establishment that he and other clerics represented—a corrupt establishment given to cronyism—and voted overwhelmingly to give power to the relatively obscure former culture minister Khatami, someone they knew had at least allowed far greater freedom from censorship and a freer press and had expressed liberal views on Islamic democracy during his tenure as minister of culture and Islamic guidance—more so than any other public figure had dared to in the past.

Khatami had studied Western philosophy at university in Isfahan, but after receiving his bachelor's degree and while still studying for a master's at the University of Tehran, he moved to Qom to further his education in Islam. He completed his studies, *ijtihad*, at the seminaries, achieving the status of *mujtahed*, or "scholar," the equivalent of a divinity Ph.D., before moving to Hamburg, where he became chairman of the Islamic Center in the German city. He returned to Iran after the revolution of 1979 and immediately became involved with the government, first as a member of parliament, then as culture minister twice, once from 1982 to 1986 and then again from 1989 to 1992, when he resigned. He then went on to become the head of the National Library, reflecting his taste for all things academic, until his election as president in 1997. He was also (and still is) a member from its inception of the beautifully named but actually liberal-leaning Association of Combatant Clerics, not to be confused with the hard-line Combatant Clergy Association, both of which conjure up images of Monty Python's "Spanish Inquisition" skit from the 1970s, though only some of those in the latter group espouse philosophies bearing any similarity to the Bishops' of the Python troupe's fantasies. The "combatant" (or *mobarez* in Farsi, which can also be translated as "resistant") clerics of neither association, however, are ninja Ayatollahs who might, with robes flying, soar across a room to land a deadening blow on those they do combat with, but they are politically minded senior clerics who have chosen one side or another, reform or conservative, in the ongoing struggle for the soul of their beloved Islamic Republic.

There are some in either camp who agree on many issues, and Hassan Rowhani, for example, the chief nuclear negotiator under Khatami and by no means a staunch conservative, is in the opposing camp to his, as is Rafsanjani the pragmatist, who leans to the reform side in Iranian politics, particularly if the conservatives are ascendant. Both clergies, extremely influential with the Supreme Leader, have, under a continued onslaught by Ahmadinejad and his allies, grown even closer to Khatami and the liberal reformers, perhaps hoping to derail any possibility of hard-line conservatives staying in power after the next presidential election in 2009 by uniting in their opposition to them.

———————

Khatami was born in Ardakan, in the desert province of Yazd, in 1943, and so, unlike some other clerics, he has spent most of his adult life under an Islamic Republic. Ardakan is my father's hometown, and at the time of Khatami's youth was a backwater small village where everybody knew one another and a handful of families, probably no more than four or five, were wealthy landowners and the acknowledged elite. These families intermarried, naturally, and two of Khatami's mother's siblings, a brother and a sister from the Ziaie family, married my father's older sister and brother, thus making my many first cousins on that side of the family first cousins to Khatami as well. I had never met Khatami himself, however, until well into his presidency, but I had met his brother (and chief of staff during his second term) Ali Khatami in the late 1970s, when we were both in college in Washington, where he roomed with his cousin Mohammad Majd, also my cousin.

Iranian small-town values aren't diluted by years in the big city or even abroad, or by elevated status, and President Khatami welcomed me in Tehran in 2004 as a *hamshahri*, a "fellow from the same hometown," and as though I were a long-lost relative. I saw Khatami twice on that trip at his offices at Sa'adabad Palace, a former palace of the Shah's used mostly for entertaining foreign dignitaries and assigned to the presidential office under Khatami for essentially the same purposes. Khatami was most concerned at the time with finding a solution to the nuclear issue, and his government had suspended uranium enrichment research and processing while negotiating with the Europeans. But he was adamant that Iran had no plans to develop weapons and was incredulous that many Americans, especially members of the Bush administration, didn't believe *him*, even if he recognized that they might have a harder time trusting some of the other members of Iran's ruling class.

On my subsequent trip, in 2005, I met with him again at Sa'adabad, once while he was still president and once a few days after Ahmadinejad took office but while Khatami was still ensconced in his palace offices, which had been promised him by the Supreme Leader for his post-presidential career. (Ahmadinejad quickly convinced the Leader that that arrangement needed to end and evicted him within weeks of taking over, perhaps as payback for Khatami's barring him, when Ahmadinejad was mayor of Tehran and as was customary for the mayor, from attending his cabinet meetings.) Ali Khatami would normally arrange for a car to pick me up, but on my second visit, when Khatami had been out of office for a few days, there were no cars available from the presidential pool, so I jumped in a taxi and asked to be taken to Sa'adabad.

My driver was a chatty fellow, and we got into a conversation about war, mainly because, with Ahmadinejad taking over the presidency, *le tout* Tehran was coming to believe that conflict with the United States was a distinct possibility. I asked the driver if he had served in the military, compulsory for Iranian males at eighteen or after college, and he replied in the affirmative. "I was wounded in battle," he said, "which is why my arm doesn't work properly." He lifted his right arm in the air, although it was impossible to detect any injury.

"The Iraq war?" I asked.

"Not exactly," he said. "It was at the tail end of the war, and it was the battle with the Mujahedin." I felt a chill, for he was referring to the Mujahedin-e-Khalq, the Iranian resistance group, the MEK, which had attacked Iran from its base in Iraq in July 1988 and had been ambushed by waiting Iranian troops, who decimated the small army, leaving some two thousand Mujahedin dead. My childhood friend and the son of one of my father's oldest friends, Payman Bazargan, who had joined the Mujahedin out of college in the United Kingdom, was one of those killed.

"Did you shoot any of the Mujahedin?" I asked, wondering if my driver could have fired the shot that killed my friend.

"Well, I fired my rifle, but I was wounded almost immediately and evacuated from the battlefield. Those poor bastards, they didn't stand a chance. We knew they were coming, and we just mowed them down."

"And how did that feel?" I asked. "I mean, killing fellow Iranians?"

"Just as bad as killing anyone, I suppose," he replied. "It's all awful, this business of war, no matter who's fighting. I hope it never comes here again."

I was silent for a while, but didn't tell him that a friend had died in the battle he had described. I blamed Payman's death on the Mujahedin anyway, for as far as I was concerned he had been brainwashed by the cultlike organization, which had no business sending amateurs to fight against an army such as the Islamic Republic's. Payman had been a press officer for the Mujahedin; his British-accented perfect English had been useful to them until they had decided that in their biggest military campaign against Iran, pompously named Forouq-e Javidan— or "Eternal Light"—every able-bodied member of the organization would have to fight. Fight they did, and die they did. I had lost contact with Payman from the time he had joined the resistance group, but our families are very close, and his death had a large impact on our lives.

In Iran, former *monafeghin*, or "hypocrites," as the MEK are called by the government, are usually given amnesty if they repent and pledge allegiance to the Islamic Republic—in fact, the Iranian media make a fuss over every former MEK member released from prison as a show of Iran's leniency—and I wondered as I sat in a cab heading to see a president of Iran whether Payman, if he had survived, would today have wanted to take advantage of the government's largesse. He would have recognized by now, I like to believe, that if there's one thing almost all Iranians inside Iran, and most outside, agree on, it is particular disdain for the most organized and militant of the exile opposition groups, the MEK. Although individual members have been in the forefront of a struggle against the Islamic government and have brought a good measure of deserved pressure on the regime, the fact that the group allied itself with the hated Saddam Hussein—an Arab tyrant who, unprovoked, rained Scud missiles on Tehran and whose soldiers massacred untold hundreds of thousands of Iranians—and then actually fought on the Iraqi side during the long war, is an unforgivable crime in the minds of most. Even Iranians most strongly opposed to the Islamic Republic cannot abide the MEK and its leaders, Massoud and Maryam Rajavi, who were allies of Khomeini in the revolution that toppled the monarchy but broke with the regime, it is widely thought, not because of any discomfort over its interpretation of democracy, but because they were excluded from power by the clerics. Deep in thought, I looked out the window as my driver took me on a route I didn't recognize and came to a stop outside gates that were unfamiliar. "Sa'ad-abad," he said triumphantly.

"This isn't it," I said.

"Yes, it is," he replied indignantly. "The museum entrance is right there, past the gate."

"But I don't want the museum," I said, realizing that I'd have to tell him whom I was going to visit. "I need to go to the offices."

"Which offices?"

"Khatami's office."

The driver turned and looked at me. "President Khatami?"

"Former president," I said. "But his offices are still where they were."

"I think that's all the way at the other end," said the driver as he turned the car around. He looked at me suspiciously, wondering what business I could possibly have with the former president of Iran. When we finally pulled up to the correct gate, manned by soldiers and Revolutionary Guards holding machine guns, fingers on the triggers, he seemed nervous. "What should I say?" he asked me.

"Just stop right in front of the gate," I said, rolling down my window and smiling at the soldiers as we slowly came to a stop.

"Are you going to see Khatami himself?" the driver asked, seemingly unconvinced, after I paid him.

"I think so."

"Then tell him *damesh-garm!*" he exclaimed, grinning, a Persian expression difficult to translate into American English but oddly very close to the Australian "good on you."

Khatami was as usual gracious when he met me at the door to his office, despite my being late because of the detour with my driver, and seemed even more relaxed than ever. We talked in general terms about his presidency and his plans for the future. He asked me if I understood his speech at the *"Salam Khatami!"* function; he seemed proud of his "two Islams" reference, although he wouldn't go into more details or launch a more direct attack on the new leadership in Iran. His goal now, he said, dismissing an invitation to critique the hard-liners taking over, was to further the understanding of Islam and Iran in the West, but also to further the understanding of the West in the Islamic world. He felt perfectly suited to the job. And, a year later, at the end of August 2006, in keeping with that job, he made his first trip to the United States as a private citizen and, more important, as the most senior Iranian official to visit the United States, outside of a trip to the UN, in the history of the Islamic Republic. He was serious, it appeared, about his new role and what he believed were his responsibilities. I traveled with him to Chicago, Washington, and Boston, and spent time with him in New York, and throughout the trip he was energized and frankly amazed at the goodwill he experienced at every stop, whether by Americans or Muslim Americans who hosted a number of functions for him. He was genuinely embarrassed by the level of security provided him by the State Department, a level normally reserved for the highest-profile visiting heads of state and one that attracted much attention, and by the end of the trip had become friendly with the security detail assigned to him, so much so that jokes and pleasantries, in halting English on his part, were often exchanged with his minders, who told me they had really enjoyed working with and learning from Khatami and his entourage. "Axis of evil," it seems, was the furthest thing from their minds.

———————

President Khatami had arrived in New York on August 31, at almost the exact hour that Ambassador John Bolton declared the deadline would pass for Iran to comply with the UN resolution on enrichment. As ludicrous as it sounds, there had been some question as to whether it would expire at midnight New York time or Tehran time; in the end, it seems, Tehran time, seven and a half hours ahead of New York, won. And Ambassador Bolton's own State Department met Khatami's Austrian Airlines jet at Kennedy, on the tarmac, with a full contingent of security provided by the department's Bureau of Diplomatic Security (along with the New York Police Department and the New York State Highway Patrol). The president was whisked to the residence of the Iranian ambassador to the UN on Fifth Avenue, and he settled in for a quiet day of rest before his tour of America began in earnest. The Bush administration had already forbidden contact between current government officials and Khatami (not counting the security contingent), and for domestic Iranian political reasons he couldn't have met with anyone from the Bush administration anyway, but there were apparently many former government officials who were keen to see him, along with countless other influential Americans, such as George Soros and Richard Blum (Dianne Feinstein's husband), who flew into Boston on his private jet to have a private meeting with Khatami in his hotel suite. Blum, who is close to Jimmy Carter, again offered Khatami (I was interpreting for them) to help set up a meeting between the two, suggesting his jet could be available should it be necessary for logistical reasons. Khatami declined graciously, and I pointed out that not only was his schedule full but his special visa allowed him to visit only the cities that had been preapproved by the State Department. Atlanta was not on the list.

At the end of President Khatami's private U.S. trip, the question of whether it was sanctioned or not or even ordered by the leadership in Tehran, as some American political figures claimed, seemed to fade away, at least to those of us who were along for the ride. The symbolism itself of an Iranian president in America was important, yes, but outside of the media reports and what could be gleaned from the interviews and the questions Khatami answered publicly, there were moments that gave real hope to those who were looking for signs, any signs, that a conflict with Iran could be avoided, even with a far more obstinate government in power in Tehran. Khatami's U.S. visit began on a day when Iran defied the UN and the world by refusing to abide by a resolution, and ended on the fifth anniversary of September 11, a tragedy that, he often pointed out on his trip, he was one of the first world leaders to condemn. Many of the Americans he met, evidently impressed by him, expressed the wish that he was still the president of Iran rather than the incorrigible Mahmoud Ahmadinejad, but the same is probably said often enough to Al Gore about the Bush administration and almost certainly privately said to Bill Clinton as well. Khatami, who still has the ear of the Supreme Leader and will remain influential in Iranian politics for years to come, was himself influenced by traveling around the eastern United States, always on commercial flights (including a Jet Blue one-class-service flight from Boston to New York, where the security agents accompanying us managed to get seats in the middle of the aircraft, much to the surprise and trepidation of some of the passengers who, when they saw the bearded and turbaned Khatami and the half-dozen bearded men with him—to say nothing of the SWAT team, machine guns at the ready, surrounding the jet on the tarmac—asked to be let off the plane).

He was already a man who admired the United States for some reasons, all the while discounting its "liberal" democracy as a model for his own country, but on more than a few occasions he told Americans an anecdote that gave a clue as to what he most admired about that democracy. "Erdogan," he would say (referring to the Islamist prime minister of Turkey, Recep Tayyip Erdogan, at the time), "was once asked by angry Islamic nationalists why he sent his daughter to the United States to attend college. And he replied, 'Because in America she can wear her hijab at university.'" (In Turkey, a strictly secular, albeit Muslim, state, the headscarf, or hijab, was banned in academic institutions until 2008 and is still banned in government.)

———————

Mohammad Khatami was neither the first nor the only cleric to differ with the ruling establishment of the Islamic Republic on matters of democracy, affairs of state, or even interpretation of Islam. Shia Islam allows for a wide range of opinion on virtually every issue, religious or political, which is partly why Iran feels it needs a Supreme Leader, an Ayatollah ostensibly senior to others, to guide the nation and its policies. Khomeini was certainly senior enough, and by virtue of his leadership of the revolution he would have had the title anyway, but Ali Khamenei is, despite his designation as a Grand Ayatollah, not universally recognized by Shias as the most senior of the clerics. Grand Ayatollah Hossein-Ali Montazeri, once Khomeini's designated successor, subsequently disgraced for criticizing him and the government, placed under house arrest in Qom for his dissent, and finally freed during Khatami's presidency, qualifies as perhaps the first Ayatollah to differ with the ruling establishment on political and religious matters, and was far senior to Khamenei at the time of his ascendancy to the position of all-powerful leader of Iran. Grand Ayatollah Ali al-Sistani, the most senior cleric in Iraq, who is actually Iranian, is also considered senior to most other Ayatollahs, although, because he differs with his Iranian peers on the matter of velayat-e-faqih, "rule of the jurisprudent," he would be automatically disqualified from any governmental role even if he tried to use his Iranian passport to gain entry to the corridors of power (he doesn't hold Iraqi citizenship). While most Iranian Ayatollahs, certainly those deemed "Grand," and even most Hojjatoleslams, the next rung down in the Shia hierarchy, agree with the concept of "rule of the jurisprudent," they often differ as to the interpretation of "rule." Some, like Khatami, believe strongly in the operative word "guide" and feel, for good reason in Khatami's case, that the role of the Supreme Leader should be limited to one of a guide in matters mostly confined to the religious, leaving the president of the republic, democratically elected, to administer the country with little interference from above.

Reformists, keen to bring Iran into the twenty-first century in terms of social progress, all agree, but it is important to note that without the power the Supreme Leader wields, a government such as Ahmadinejad's, also democratically elected, would undoubtedly harm Iran's political and social development to a far greater degree than it has. The Supreme Leader, a sort of one-man Congress and Supreme Court rolled into each other, provides something of a bulwark against extremism from any side, and although a different Supreme Leader might swing more to the left or to the right, it is unlikely that a Leader elevated to the position by the Assembly of Experts—a sort of College of Cardinals that is popularly elected and reflects the diversity of

Iranian political opinion—would not understand that his and his government's stability and survival depend very much on his performing the balancing act with finesse. (The first and only chairman of the Assembly of Experts, Ayatollah Meshkini, died in the summer of 2007, and while one or two extremist members made a bid for his position, they were easily defeated when the body elected the pragmatic and far-from-extreme Rafsanjani as its chairman.)

Iran's second Supreme Leader, Ayatollah Ali Khamenei, listens to his constituents, the Iranian people, he listens to all sides of the political spectrum, he considers public and world opinion, and then he makes decisions that annoy one or more parties but keep the Islamic Republic somewhat on an even keel. Democracy it is not, at least not by Western standards, but, as has often been stated to me by supporters of the system inside Iran, supporters who dislike being lectured to by Americans or even Iranian-Americans on the niceties of democracy, neither was the Supreme Court's decision in 2000 to award the presidency to George Bush "in the interests of the country" despite his second-place showing in the popular vote and a very questionable victory in the electoral college. But reformers are convinced, as they might be in any democracy, that in a truly free system the people would choose them, the liberals intent on empowering the people, rather than conservatives who would limit their freedoms. They believe that Iran would not have produced a president such as Ahmadinejad had they not been unfairly blamed for the limitations of the political system, a system that meant they had to compromise with and even yield to the Supreme Leader and the more conservative politicians at every turn.

—————

One of the leading and most senior Ayatollahs closely allied with Khatami and known for his liberal views is Mohammad Mousavi Bojnourdi, head of the Imam Khomeini Center for Islamic Studies. He was present at almost every public event that Khatami attended, even traveling with him on his trips abroad (I met him for the first time at a UNESCO conference in Paris in 2005), and provided Khatami with some serious Islamic cover, for although Khatami himself was a cleric, he was, and is, far more vulnerable to attack by hard-liners than an established Ayatollah ever would or could be.

In addition to calls from extremists on the right for Khatami to be censured or even defrocked for traveling to the United States in 2006, there were renewed attacks on his Islamic piety when news surfaced in Iran in the late spring of 2007, via video on YouTube, that Khatami had shaken the hands of women on a visit to Rome, where he had met Pope Benedict, a few weeks earlier. YouTube is blocked in Iran, as are many other foreign Web sites, and it is often impossible to fathom the reasons behind the censorship (the Web sites of the *New York Post*, the *Baltimore Sun*, and the *International Herald Tribune* are blocked, for example, but those of the *New York Times*—which owns the *International Herald Tribune*—*Haaretz*, and even the conservative and rabidly anti–Islamic Republic *Jerusalem Post* aren't), particularly since it is common knowledge in Tehran that proxies are used to gain access to blocked sites. Naturally the government censors block the proxies as well as soon as they become aware of them (using U.S. software, much like the Chinese censors), but new proxies pop up on a daily basis, and Internet-surfing Iranians will often call each other in the mornings, as I have often done, to pass around the latest proxy addresses that enable them to freely navigate the Web. As such, and without too much trouble, the YouTube Khatami video and downloaded versions of it made the rounds of Iranian computers with lightning speed. Although the clip clearly showed him shaking hands with female admirers, he was forced to first issue a denial, and then say that in the crowds he encountered, it was far too difficult to see whether an outstretched hand belonged to a man or a woman.[2]

His denial was reminiscent of another denial he was forced to make while he was still president—that he had cordially chatted with Moshe Katsav, president of Israel at the time, at Pope John Paul II's funeral in 2005, also in Rome. (What is it about the Eternal City that comes back to haunt him?) Ali Khatami, his chief of staff, had told me a few days prior to attending the funeral that they were making arrangements with the Italian government and Vatican officials to ensure that Khatami, representing Iran, would not be seated too close to Katsav, representing the alphabetically adjacent Israel, in the viewing stands, but it had been impossible to separate the two by more than a few chairs and a few feet. Khatami's problem was not so much that he might be forced to cross paths with an Israeli leader, who under normal circumstances would have wanted to shun the leader of Iran anyway, as that Katsav was an Iranian by birth, spoke fluent Farsi, and, moreover, was from the same hometown as Khatami. As such, and with Katsav's inherent knowledge of ta'arouf, the danger that he would say hello was real, particularly to someone such as Khatami, who was known, even among the Iranian community in Israel, as a mild-mannered mullah who harbored none of the prejudices of some of his fellow clerics. (Under Khatami, Iranians who lived in Israel, for example, were quietly allowed to reclaim their Iranian citizenship through the Iranian Consulate in Istanbul and travel back and forth—again, usually through Turkey—unmolested, a practice that continues today, despite Ahmadinejad's anti-Israel rants.)

As it happened, Katsav did apparently say hello, at least according to him, perhaps offering up proof to Iranian Jews that his ta'arouf skills had not diminished, speaking in Farsi and reminiscing for a few moments about their hometown of Yazd. Foreign newspapers published photographs that showed Khatami and Katsav standing very close to each other, apparently engaged in conversation, although it was impossible to prove that they actually uttered any words, and upon his return to Iran, Khatami simply flatly denied, despite Katsav's assertion, having had any contact whatsoever with the Israeli president. The issue died quickly, in all probability because the Supreme Leader, who had no desire to see his president in the kind of hot water that might lead to a destabilization of the republic, ordered the dogs off, but Khatami's enemies made a mental note that apparently remains archived in their memories.

Khatami was and is by no means a friend of Israel, and he shares the Iranian leadership's view that the "Zionist" state is an illegal one, but he has told me on many occasions that he strongly believes that Iran under any leadership would abide with whatever the Palestinian people decided on their future, implying that if the Palestinians made peace with Israel, then Iran's position might change. As president, if on a foreign trip an Israeli reporter tried to ask him a question at a press conference, Khatami would, as other Iranian officials do, refuse to take the question, but at Harvard University in 2006, as a private citizen, he had no qualms about politely answering the questions of a few Israeli students who quizzed him on the Holocaust (he said of *course* it happened), on Israel, and even on the topic of Ron Arad, the missing Israeli pilot who bailed out of his crippled Phantom jet fighter over Lebanon in 1986 and was captured by Shia militias, but is believed by some to be held alive in Tehran. One question, on the issue of Ahmadinejad's "wiping Israel off the map," left Khatami distancing himself from his successor's remarks but pointing out at the end that "Palestine has been wiped off the map for sixty years," a quip that drew cheers from many in the audience and, surprisingly, no jeers. It is difficult to dislike Khatami, even, apparently, if one is an Israeli at Harvard.

I met with Ayatollah Bojnourdi for the second time in Tehran after Ahmadinejad took office and the reformers he was close to had suffered a stinging loss at the polls. Bojnourdi, who with visible pride told me of his audience with Pope John Paul II, is known for his progressive views on women's rights in Islam, although his front office was staffed with women fully enveloped in black chadors, not scarves. One of them served us tea and Persian sweets while we sat and chatted, or, more accurately, while I sat and he chatted, but at least women were present, I thought, even if they didn't shake hands with men—unlike in Qom, where senior Ayatollah offices are all-male enclaves. Bojnourdi himself doesn't have a strong feeling on men shaking hands with women and believes it to be a nonissue, although he himself would not shake the hand of a woman not his wife, sister, or daughter (*mahram* to men in Islam, which means women who can be uncovered and one can physically touch, while all other women, even cousins and aunts, are *na-mahram*, and therefore even their hair mustn't be seen).

An endearing and disarmingly laid-back rotund man, the Ayatollah launched into a spirited defense of Khatami and his policies, policies that he claimed had the full support of the people. Barely giving me time to comment, he then jumped to a defense of Islam: *his* Islam. Islam, he said, is based on logic, Islam is based on friendship and love, and Islam's ideology is the ideology of freedom. "The twelfth Imam will come [it appears that all Shia roads lead back to the Mahdi], and he will bring the Islam of dialogue, not of blood!" he exclaimed. But what about the lack of certain freedoms in the Islamic Republic? "In Shia Islam, anyone has the ability to disagree. In the West, and even in Iran, things are done in the name of Islam that are not Islamic," Bojnourdi said, implying but not specifying his view that many of the freedoms curtailed in his country have no basis in his religion. "Islam made a point of peaceful dialogue fourteen hundred years ago," he pointed out. "Islam teaches character and morality. There is no ambiguousness about that," he continued. What about the role of women in Islam? I asked. "Women have all the God-given rights. A woman can certainly be president," Bojnourdi added, referring to the argument before every presidential election when women are automatically disqualified from running, despite registering freely as candidates in the initial stages of the process. That opinion on women's rights alone puts him at odds with many fellow Ayatollahs, has enhanced his stature among Iranian females (and activists quote him), and perhaps accounts for the all-female staff in his front office.

It could be argued that Bojnourdi's stance on female presidents is a clever distraction from the larger issue of gender equality in Islam, for although women in the Islamic Republic enjoy rights that women in some Arab countries can only dream of, they are hobbled in achieving parity with their male counterparts by interpretations of Islam that vary widely among the clerics of Shia Islam, and "God-given rights" is, after all, a rather ambiguous phrase. How to challenge Islamic law that states, for example, that a woman's testimony carries half the weight of a man's, or that a woman can inherit only half of what a male sibling can, is an issue on the minds of feminists who are generally careful to not be seen as un-Islamic, and opinions from Ayatollahs such as Bojnourdi are crucial to the advancement of their cause. A nation that churns out hundreds of thousands of college graduates each year—60 percent of them women—many of whom end up either jobless or working in fields below their qualifications (such as running a taxi service or even driving a cab), will have to deal with the question of gender equality sooner rather than later, and Bojnourdi's pronouncements on female presidents, distraction or not, are seen to be a step in the right direction. For if a woman can be president, it surely follows that she can also be a judge (a position denied the Nobel laureate Shirin Ebadi), and if she can be a judge, then perhaps more liberal interpretations of the law, on issues such as divorce, child custody, and spousal rights, might soon gain favor. And if a woman can be president, then surely she would no longer need her husband's or her father's permission to travel abroad—a law that dates from the time of the Shah, who, despite his Western ways and progressive reputation, was as sexist and misogynist as some of the Ayatollahs—unlike Bojnourdi, who is a voice of reason in an often unreasonable debate.

The Shah, who had divorced two women he claimed to love for their inability to produce a male heir, when asked by Barbara Walters in an interview in 1977 about his earlier sexist comments to the journalist Oriana Fallaci, didn't deny them, and in fact went further in dismissing equality of the sexes and betrayed his misogyny by saying that women hadn't even been able to produce a famous and great chef (he must not have heard of Alice Waters, whose reputation and restaurant were in their infancy at the time). Walters's follow-up question, with the Shah's wife, Farah, looking on, was whether he believed that Mrs. Pahlavi could govern as well as a man, and he replied that he "preferred not to answer." I remember feeling sorry for the empress, whose tear-filled eyes were clearly visible even on my small portable TV. But in the context of the kinds of questions on women's rights that have been debated in Iran since before the revolution, it is easy to see why the issue of the hijab, a flashpoint for liberals in the West but an inconvenience that pales in significance compared with other gender issues in Iran, is not a battle that women are keen to fight, at least not yet.

In my meeting with Bojnourdi, I was also curious to hear him speak about the notion that an all-encompassing Islam has smothered the Iranian character, the soul of the nation. "Not at all," the Ayatollah replied indignantly. "Islam is a way of life and part of the Iranian soul," he said, "but so is poetry, music, and Iranian art. Hafez, Sa'di, Rumi, and all the Sufi poets are more widely read and taught now than before the revolution." Bojnourdi wasn't quite being disingenuous, but in naming Sufi poets, he was touching upon another of the infuriating contradictions of Islamic Iran, for Sufism has always been viewed with great suspicion by some of the Ayatollah's fellow clerics as a potential challenge to their supreme, and more orthodox, religious authority. Not all Sufis (who owe a philosophical allegiance to and are disciples of a master of an order, rather than an Ayatollah) are poets, but nearly all the great poets of Iran were Sufis. The authorities, though, know better than to disparage Iran's national heroes, the great poets of centuries past, and most will extol their virtues as humans—pious Muslims at that—as well as recite their poetry at the drop of a turban. Bojnourdi, to my relief, did not recite any ancient verses to make his points (for that would have required me, if I were to be considered at all literate, to respond cleverly in kind), but this gentle Friar Tuck–like

figure left me with no doubt that he would, with his religious authority, remain a powerful force for would-be reformers of Iran. That he,
and even a few of his fellow clerics, bearded men in eighteenth-century
garb, would hold views more progressive on some issues than even the
Shah (yes, she *can* govern!), a king and leader beloved and even glorified
by every U.S. administration since FDR (and who did not live to see
either Nigella Lawson or the Food Network), may seem counterintu-
itive, but it provides more than a glimmer of hope for Iranians struggling to effect change within the constraints of an Islamic society.
Undoubtedly disliked for his views by the Supreme Leader and the
band of conservative mullahs and their supporters whose Islam he
clashes with, in some cases severely, Bojnourdi nonetheless is one of the
Ayatollahs they can't mess with, for messing with a "sign of God" is
fraught with risk in a country ruled by, well, God. And thank Allah for
that.

I saw Mohammad Khatami twice when I was in Tehran in early 2007,
this time at his offices in Jamaran. Having been evicted from Sa'adabad
by Ahmadinejad when he took office as president, Khatami must have
seen it as sweet revenge to land at Jamaran, the name of a neighborhood, once a village but now part of the urban sprawl, in the far
reaches of North Tehran, but best known as home to Ayatollah
Khomeini while he was still alive. Ahmadinejad, who after all cam-
paigned on bringing back the purity of Khomeini's revolution and
whose feelings toward the founder of the Islamic Republic border on
hero worship, could not have anticipated that Khomeini's family and
the Khomeini foundation, with the full backing of the Supreme
Leader, would provide offices to Khatami and his International Institute for Dialogue Among Cultures and Civilizations in one of their
compounds at Jamaran. In a way, it's far more appropriate for Khatami
than the royal palace of Sa'adabad, as it shields him from accusations

that he is enjoying an imperial lifestyle and puts Khomeini's imprimatur onto his organization, an advantage that I'm confident he doesn't take lightly in the always turbulent political atmosphere of Tehran.

On the second floor of a stately villa behind tall walls and an imposing gate, manned by security guards, Khatami sat in his thousand-square-foot office in mid-January, preparing for a trip to Davos and the World Economic Forum. Word among former and present high-ranking government officials was that Ahmadinejad, verging on apoplexy upon hearing that Khatami would be hobnobbing with the likes of Tony Blair and John Kerry, demanded from his foreign minister, Manouchehr Mottaki, that he be invited too. Mottaki came up, needless to say, empty-handed, but it is doubtful that he took the opportunity to mention that if His Excellency the good doctor had been a little less confrontational, a little less dubious about the Holocaust, and a tad more diplomatic, perhaps the world leaders and businesspeople gathering in Switzerland wouldn't be so keen to avoid his company at any cost. Khatami told me he had been scheduled to be on a panel with Senator Kerry, which would constitute a rather high-level contact between Iran and the United States, and rather than be impolitic and ask Khatami directly if he had the approval of the Supreme Leader, I merely brought his name up, hoping to get my answer indirectly. And Khatami obliged, telling me that he saw the Supreme Leader regularly, a few times a month, and that they discussed all kinds of issues. Including, I suspect, whether he should accept the invitation to Davos and whether he should have a tête-à-tête with a former U.S. presidential candidate.

I saw Khatami again after his Davos trip and before I left Tehran; his appearance on the panel with Kerry had received scant attention in the Iranian media, either because Ahmadinejad didn't want anything to do with publicizing Khatami for fear of raising his popularity or because enemies who might ordinarily want to attack Khatami for engaging the "Great Satan" were held in check by the Supreme Leader, or a combination of the two. Ali Khatami, his brother who continued in his job as the unpaid chief of staff, sat in on my meeting with Khatami (quietly, as he has in almost all of Khatami's meetings over the years), and the former president and I had a frank discussion about his role in the future of Iran. Ali, the uncharacteristically low-profile former high-ranking official, has always been his older brother's closest adviser, but he continues to shun the spotlight and avoids the media to the best of his ability. Scrupulously honest (he refused a salary during Khatami's presidency to avoid charges of nepotistic advantage in a country where nepotism is rampant and, to many, a right, and in fact suffered financially while in the administration when he was unable to tend to his businesses), he is a witty, American-educated engineer who has as good a grasp on Iranian politics as anyone in Tehran but, unlike the youngest Khatami brother, Reza, a former M.P. who fiercely opposes the status quo and openly criticized President Khatami for not doing enough for the cause of reform, maneuvers stealthily through the Machiavellian maze that is the Persian political system, fiercely defending his brother's interests and legacy.

Mohammad Khatami is a keen conversationalist, and although he is, as a true politician, careful with his words, he is not shy in setting out his philosophy. "Iran," he told me, "deserves a much higher status than it occupies today. Democracy is ultimately the only hope for Iran. Democracy in the West is shaped by their culture, by their history, and in Iran we have our own culture and history, and our democracy will be shaped in accordance with our culture." Was he trying to say that that meant it had to be an *Islamic* democracy? I wondered. "I don't mean 'liberal democracy,' " he answered. "Democracy means the government is chosen by the people and they have the power to change it if they are unhappy, but Islam is one of the foundations of our culture, and it will influence our democracy. Of course Islam must adjust to democracy as well," he added, a sentiment that puts him greatly at odds with influential conservative clerics who in some cases believe democracy to be incompatible with Islam, or, more precisely, with their God-given mandate to rule.

We talked at length about his ability to influence events in Iran as a private citizen, but I really wanted to know if he would, given that Ahmadinejad had proven to be vulnerable at the polls, run again for president in 2009. (The Iranian constitution forbids more than two consecutive four-year presidential terms, as does ours, but does not disqualify an ex-president who has served two terms from running for the office again.) Khatami insisted that it was not what he desired, telling me that Iranian politics has to move away from being so strongly personality based (parties are notoriously weak in Iran, and individual politicians are prone to creating cults of personality) and that he only wished to have some influence in the future. I knew, however, that more and more people were advising him to think about running, including his close adviser Sadeq Kharrazi, the fiercely loyal former ambassador, and I pressed him on the issue. "Of course," he said, *"che farda shavad."* He smiled knowingly. "As Ferdowsi [the great tenth- and eleventh-century Persian poet and author of Iran's epic masterpiece the *Shahnameh*, or *Book of Kings*] said," he continued, in the typically Persian way of making a point obliquely, *" 'Che farda shavad, fekr'e farda konim.' "* (When [if] tomorrow comes, let's think about tomorrow.)

FEAR OF A BLACK TURBAN

I could have sworn that the dogs went first. Those Islamic-ly unclean creatures, strays, wild, and pets, howling in the dark mountains and valleys of Shemshak, a ski resort an hour or so north of Tehran. It was the ninth day of the Ten-Day Dawn in February 2007—almost a fortnight of celebrations commemorating the Islamic Revolution of 1979—and in anticipation of the national holiday on the tenth day, the day the revolution succeeded, many Tehran residents, or those who could afford a cabin in the mountains, had fled the city much as many New Yorkers do the week of the Labor Day or Memorial Day holidays. I had driven with a friend up the narrow, winding, and often treacherous roads to the resort for a party, and we were to drive back the same night so that I could attend the rallies and marches in the city the next day.

Shemshak, and some of the other ski resorts in the Alborz Mountains, would seem to a visitor out of place in the Islamic Republic, and not just because of the deep, powdery snow on the slopes or the chic men and women in Chanel sunglasses and the latest ski fashions on lifts at ten and twelve thousand feet above sea level, but also in the resemblance of the villages and the valleys they occupy to

European resorts in Switzerland, France, and Austria. The chalet where the party was being held was on the edge of a steep cliff, and the views from the curtainless panoramic windows were breathtaking, but the windows also afforded a clear view *into* the house, where I was standing by the bar, liquor bottles arrayed on shelves behind me for the world to see, chatting with a French couple who had also driven up from Tehran. An oil executive and his wife, they had chosen to remain in Iran after his retirement, and he had become a consultant, a particularly lucrative occupation in Iran, even if it remains unclear what one actually consults on, as long as one knows the right people. They spoke no Farsi, and neither did the hostess, also European but married to an Iranian and a longtime resident of Tehran, and they found it strange that I would wonder if they were interested in learning.

As dusk turned to night, other guests arrived, some still in ski gear, and the party went into full swing. It was right before dinner was served, which included illicit appetizers such as pork salami and Parisian ham, and which the French couple took great delight in devouring, that I heard the dogs howling and I stepped to the windows. Then I heard the cries reverberating from the hills and amplified in the valleys: *"Allah-hu-Akbar! Allah-hu-Akbar!"* They were punctuated by the barking of the dogs, which politely waited until the cries died down before vigorously providing a chorus. And then, *"Allah-hu-Akbar!"* again. And again. No other guest, nor the host and hostess, seemed at all curious or disturbed by the sounds coming from the mountains. They had undoubtedly heard them in years past and on the same February evening—cries of *"Allah-hu-Akbar!"*—in remembrance of Ayatollah Khomeini's request on the eve of the revolution that all Iranians take to their roofs and proclaim, "God is Great!" Which they did by the millions, sealing the fate of the monarchy and its unsure military apparatus, which the very next day withdrew to barracks and publicly proclaimed that it would abide by the wishes of the people. Khomeini's request to the people had been a brilliant tactical move: he knew that the army, made up mostly of conscripts from the religious working class, would not only be deeply moved by the cry but also find it impossible to counter with any violent reaction. It had already been proven so: in the weeks leading up to that night, many soldiers had been unable to bring themselves to fire on crowds of demonstrators, crowds shouting the one slogan they could all agree upon—"God is Great!" I have often wondered why protesters in modern-day Iran who are set upon by the police and sometimes government-allied vigilantes do not employ the same tactic, for they have even more reason now to believe that the truncheon-wielding authorities might balk at harming those who proclaim the greatness of Allah, but perhaps the expression, even if they believe in it, leaves too bitter a taste of the regime to utter.

The sounds in the hills and valleys of the ski resort on this evening, twenty-eight years after the revolution, may have become white noise to these Iranians and foreign residents of Tehran, but it seemed remarkable that they didn't see the irony of their discussing, as is common at middle- and upper-class parties, what they believed to be the singular unpopularity of the Islamic regime while supporters of that regime, in their very own upscale backyard, were proclaiming their allegiance to the revolution and to the Islamic state, piercing the silent mountain night with their defiant cries that even the loud stereo emitting Western pop couldn't drown out. One could be forgiven for wondering why wealthy Westernized and indeed even Western-passport-holding Iranians, some of whom have sizable assets overseas, choose to continue to live in the Islamic Republic and raise their children under a less-than-liberal government. The answer, as one friend put it a few years ago, is that anyone who stayed during the worst of times early in the revolution—when not only could a glass of beer bring you thirty lashes or a trace of lipstick a trip in a paddy wagon, but Saddam's missiles also rained down nightly on Tehran—hardly has a reason to leave *now*.

––––––––––––

The next morning I was up early and only slightly hung over from the high-altitude drinking the night before, ready to head for the culmination of the Ten-Day Dawn, or Dah-e-Fajr, with an enormous rally at Azadi Square in Tehran. February 11, the actual anniversary of the Islamic Revolution, followed in 2007 hot on the heels of Shia Islam's holiest days of mourning, Tasua and Ashura, and preceded the very solemn Arbaein, the fortieth-day commemoration of Imam Hossein's death on the plains of Mesopotamia all those years ago. (Forty days of mourning for any death is prescribed by Islam.) Iran had been, for all intents and purposes, in a somewhat surreal state of deep mourning and ecstatic celebration for almost a month (as it is every year), all the while nervously peering into the Gulf, watching a massive U.S. naval buildup clearly intended by the Bush administration to make Iranians at the very least, well, nervous.

Tehran had been rife with speculation in the days immediately preceding February 11 on just how nervous the Iranian leaders actually were, and there were conflicting reports on whether President Ahmadinejad's promised nuclear announcement or even publicly promoted "nuclear symphony," to be played by an orchestra on a stage in the massive square, would actually take place. Ali Akbar Velayati, a former foreign minister and current foreign policy adviser to the Supreme Leader but not in the president's cabinet, had made an unusually high-profile trip to Moscow, prompting questions about the level of confidence the Supreme Leader had in Ahmadinejad and his foreign minister, Mottaki, who would normally have been entrusted with diplomatic overtures to West and East. Ali Larijani, head of the

Supreme National Security Council and Iran's chief nuclear negotiator, had first announced, then canceled, then finally confirmed that he would attend a global security conference in Munich on the weekend, providing much fodder for political gossip in the capital, gossip that included everything from the Supreme Leader's estrangement from the president to the continued rumors about the state of his health. Was a last-minute flurry of diplomatic activity outside of Ahmadinejad's purview intended to signal the West that Iran was ready to back down on the issue of uranium enrichment? Or had the president been indeed effectively sidelined, as some had come to believe, in the foreign policy and nuclear arenas?

His dismissal in late January of Javad Zarif, Iran's UN ambassador, had been a signal to some that he still held some sway, for that highly sensitive post is always filled at the exclusive pleasure of the Supreme Leader, but the fact that the Leader had subsequently personally chosen the moderate Mohammad Khazaee—someone far closer to Khatami than to the president—to replace him raised new questions. The Supreme Leader himself of course had already addressed the rumors of his illness and even impending death in an appearance on state television, but former Hojjatoleslam and now Ayatollah Rafsanjani,[1] on a visit to Qom, had recently reassured senior clerics and the nation that there were qualified individuals to assume the mantle of Supreme Leader—to some a gaffe that confirmed Ayatollah Khamenei's illness and to others a clumsy attempt to emphasize the continuity of the Islamic Republic in the face of external and internal threats, but at the very least an assertion of Rafsanjani's own power. It had been reported in the early days of the Ten-Day Dawn that President Ahmadinejad was also due to visit Qom and the various marja-e-taghlid ("sources of emulation," or Grand Ayatollahs) imminently, just as Ali Larijani had done in a much-photographed and symbolic visit with Grand Ayatollah Fazel Lankarani, but as the days passed and he remained in Tehran, it became obvious to most Iranians that his attempt to ingratiate himself with the center of clerical power had been rebuffed. February 2007 marked some lonely days indeed for the proud and defiant president of Iran, but it couldn't matter to the Ten-Day Dawn. For Iran's national day, once the birthday of the Shah (and thus more a celebration of a man's vanity and conceit than of a nation), was now, like the Fourth of July for Americans, a day of nationalistic pride and a celebration of an independent nation. It could certainly not be about Ahmadinejad, or any other president for that matter, regardless of his popularity or accomplishments, and although the president would take center stage and make a speech, February 11 is for Iran, not for a person.

On Friday, February 9, a text message joke made the rounds of Iran's upwardly mobile cell phones, a now-standard practice in distributing licentious and antigovernment material. The Saudis, it read, had announced that the 22nd of Bahman (February 11), Iran's national holiday, would fall on Saturday, February 10. Both a dig at Iran's ruling clergy class, who regularly and obstinately announce major Islamic holidays a day or two later than the Saudis (who are, after all, the guardians of Islam's holiest sites and theoretically the defenders of the faith), and a dig at Iran's contrarian foreign policy, it was wildly popular and the source of much hilarity among those Iranians who would most certainly not be attending the festivities and rallies on that Sunday, the national holiday. But Iran's ruling class cares little for the wealthy and secular elite, those whom foreign reporters come into contact with most, and those who are quickest to tell anyone who cares to listen that the Islamic Republic's days are numbered. Like proverbial ostriches with heads buried in the sand, and like my fellow guests at the party the night before, they spent the holiday skiing in resorts like Shemshak, on shopping trips to Dubai, or at home with friends watching illegal satellite broadcasts, rather than observing millions of their fellow citizens taking to the streets to proclaim their devotion and loyalty to their country and velayat-e-faqih, the very political concept that some of them insist is gasping its last breath.

And millions they were, at the mother of all rallies in a nation that has grown accustomed to the distraction of all too many government-sanctioned public gatherings. From early in the morning one could see men, women, and children marching along the streets of Tehran, miles from their destination, waving Iranian flags, and some holding banners, thoughtfully provided by the government, proclaiming their right to enjoy nuclear energy (in English, for the benefit of the foreign press and television cameras).

Ali Khatami, the former president's brother, picked me up from my house in downtown Tehran early, and driving through alleys and streets not yet closed, past cars double- and triple-parked, we made our way to an area filled with buses about four or five kilometers from Azadi Square—Tehran's Arc de Triomphe or Trafalgar Square—where the huge rally was to be held at midday. Ali himself triple-parked, careful to leave an exit route, and we walked the few blocks to Azadi Street, the main thoroughfare that had been lined with loudspeakers and was already filled with marchers who moved slowly toward the monument where President Ahmadinejad was to speak. The crowd on the sidewalk seemed to thicken rapidly, and walking soon slowed to a crawl. It was at a complete standstill by the time we reached the spot where former president Khatami stood outside a white SUV, surrounded by machine-gun-toting Revolutionary Guards, to say a few words to the crowd and the cameras. (By tradition, the Islamic Republic's senior clerics and dignitaries do not join the president on the podium or even enter the main square, but make short appearances on the sidelines of the mass rally to show their support for the revolution without upstaging the administration in power. The Supreme Leader himself never makes an appearance at the rally, which is, after all, in some ways a celebration of his and his clerics' authority.) And both Rafsanjani, who was elsewhere along the route, and Khatami could well have upstaged the beleaguered Ahmadinejad in 2007, whose very few posters were far outnumbered by those of the Ayatollahs Khomeini and Khamenei, who, more than any sitting president, represent the continuity of the Islamic Republic. As the crowd pressed in toward the beaming Khatami, he got into his car before his brother and I could say hello, and the crowd then rushed the vehicle, forcing it, with men standing on its roof, to maneuver with great difficulty onto a side street, crushing a few bodies, including mine, along the way. It disappeared to cries of "Khatami, Kahatami, we love you!" sung with both emotion and conviction, and if anyone had imagined that this was the national day for hard-liners and conservative supporters of the government only, the scene surrounding Khatami, a person some hard-liners had accused of wanting to dismantle the Islamic state, proved otherwise.

We caught our breath and continued along the sidewalk at a snail's pace, hearing the by-now-standard chants of "Nuclear energy is our obvious right," "Death to America," "Death to Israel," and "Death to the hypocrites" (MEK) every few minutes, and we were surrounded by many halfheartedly waving preprinted signs, in English, with a bright red check mark by "yes" for nuclear energy. The chants were shouted with some vigor and emotion but without anger, and lacked the conviction required of a literal interpretation. "Death to," in a society where an exclamation of surprise is *"Khak-bar-saram"*—"May I be covered with dirt" (struck dead)—is rarely truly meant. We were still stuck on the sidewalk when the president started his speech, which was being broadcast along the route, and we were still a kilometer or so away from the square. The crowd could no longer move forward, even at a shuffle. Caught in a sea of people, I could do nothing but stand and listen to the president make his speech, moderate by his standards and evidence of sorts that the rumors that he'd been instructed to tone down the rhetoric were true. On the nuclear issue, he reiterated the long-standing Iranian position that the government desired negotiations and talks, but that uranium enrichment would not be suspended as a precondition. But he chose, rather than his belligerent and confrontational tone of the past, a more rational argument that questioned the logic of the U.S. position, which demanded Iran first do as it said before it would entertain any negotiations on the issue. "If we suspend enrichment," Ahmadinejad asked softly and to great applause, "then what is there to talk about?"

The crowd where I was standing, far less interested in his speech than in the spectacle of celebration, suddenly started moving backward, then forward, as if we were a human battering ram trying to break down the gates to the city. Women started screaming for the men to stop shoving, some of them trying to protect crying children they held tightly from being trampled, but the crush went on. Forward at a pace that would have meant falling headfirst were it not for the sea of bodies, and then backward, sideways, and forward again, with no crowd control or any police presence to ensure a modicum of safety, we were being slowly crushed, but when the crowd decided to make an escape along a side street, I became truly worried. I could barely see Ali, a former president's chief of staff who himself was bobbing up and down, struggling to break free, and I wondered if he now regretted his modesty in keeping a low profile while in office, a profile that meant he was unrecognizable, despite his resemblance to his brother, to the people in the crowd who were shoving him with as much verve as they were shoving everyone else.

The street the crowd had decided upon for escape was as packed with people as Azadi Street was, and that crowd was trying just as hard to get to where we were as *we* were trying to escape. The slightest panic, I thought, would have resulted in tragedy, but somehow the crowd on my side overwhelmed the side-street crowd, and like a great wave we crashed into them, scattering whoever was in our way. At this point there was no hope of making it onto the square, so I let myself be pushed and shoved down the street, and then, after I found a somewhat-battered Ali, we slowly made our way back to where he had parked, passing people who were heading to the square and still shouting revolutionary slogans. I was sorry that I had been unable to enter the main square, but less sorry than I would have been had I missed hearing the "nuclear symphony," which unhappily never materialized.

———————

For ten days the Islamic Revolution of 1979 had been replayed over and over on television, reminding Iranians who watched that for all their post-revolution worries the revolution itself, the once popular concept of a religious democracy, was alive and well. The claim by secular and uninterested Iranians, and echoed by ABC's Diane Sawyer, who was in the crowd the day I was, that thousands of people had been bused in by the government from other cities to bolster the numbers for the festivities was belied by the fact that in every other city in Iran, even smaller towns, huge numbers also showed up to celebrate their revolution—the evidence clear from nonstop television reports throughout the day.

I asked people gathered by a group of old, rusty municipal buses parked at a roundabout, well away from Azadi Street, where they had come from to join the rally, and all said that they had been picked up at various points in the city. Ali Khatami, a former top official himself, explained that buses were indeed provided by the government, but more as a traffic-control issue, to ferry marchers to the square from predesignated points across the city, than anything else. At any rate, no one present had been forced to attend, not even schoolchildren or government employees, as evidenced by the full restaurants and cafés and busy sidewalks far away from the rally in the northern parts of the city that I retreated to after my bruising encounter with fervent supporters of the Islamic Revolution. But every year the 22nd of Bahman, the tenth day of the Ten-Day Dawn, affirms for many Iranians their faith in their nation and their revolution, if not in their president, and in their own peculiar form of democracy, a form of democracy that celebrates majority rule but increasingly, and despite occasional setbacks, allows the minority to quietly ignore the masses. By skiing, by drinking, or by partying, as I did that very night at a high-rise apartment building in a duplex penthouse, where on one level an opium den had been set up in the library for the older men and a poker table and bar in the dining room for the younger men and women, who played, drank, and never once mentioned the Ten-Day Dawn or the Ayatollahs whose revolution it celebrates, a revolution that (with apologies to Gil Scott-Heron) will *always* be televised.

Perhaps the booze-soaked furloughed political prisoner from Evin, the man who insisted to me that 80 percent of those born after the revolution had to be killed if there were to be another revolution, had a point, perverse as the way he made it might have been. For many of those in the majority of the population with no memory of a pre–Islamic Republic Iran, perhaps even 80 percent, those for whom patriotism means allegiance to the only republic they've ever known, the revolution wasn't just a revolution: it was the birth of their *nation*. The rally at Azadi Square is never an ordinary rally, yet another tedious propaganda affair in a country where the government is given to propaganda; and if we fear the black turbans who rule Iran, then surely we must fear those who rally too.

If patriotism, and perhaps only the false patriotism that Samuel Johnson may have been referring to, is indeed the last refuge of a scoundrel, then Iran is not bereft of scoundrels at the highest levels of government. They have their followers, sometimes many, but they are hardly as fearsome as they would like to think they are. A few months after the Ten-Day Dawn, on Friday, May 25, 2007, an interim prayer leader of Tehran, the archconservative cleric Hojjatoleslam Ahmad Khatami (no relation to former president Mohammad Khatami), gave a speech to the thousands gathered at the University of Tehran for Friday prayers. On Fridays, the Tehran prayers are where Iran's clerical leaders, in the social and political section of the sermon, outline their views. "Interim prayer leader," and there are a few of them, denotes that the official prayer leader, Supreme Leader Ayatollah Ali Khamenei, is not present that day, and of course he rarely is. Ahmad Khatami was giving an official response to continued statements in the spring of 2007 by U.S. officials regarding the possibility of the United States using force to stop Iran's nuclear program, and in particular a response to Vice President Dick Cheney, who had recently made an aggressive anti-Iran speech aboard an aircraft carrier in the Persian Gulf, right on Iran's doorstep. Khatami's speech was translated and covered, as it always is, by IRNA (the official state-run Islamic Republic News Agency) exactly as follows (and I've left the English uncorrected, reflecting the government's persistently defiant use of incorrect English):

> Khatami reminded the worshipers of US Vice President Dick Cheney's comment aboard a US warship in Persian Gulf, where he said that the presence of US warships in the Persian Gulf convey a clear message to United States friends and foes, adding, "We would not permit Iran to get access to nuclear arms, and in order to achieve that goal, all options are on the table."
>
> According to Political Desk reporter of IRNA, Hojjatoleslam Khatami added, "We tell this notorious and extremely corrupt individual you have repeated such words so often that one feels like vomiting when one hears them uttered anew, so why don't you try to say something new now?"
>
> The interim Friday prayer leader of Tehran, addressing the US officials, added, "Just as you bully, uttering such nonsense, you should be aware that the Iranian nation, too, has all options on the table for punching the United States on the mouth."
>
> He reiterated, "It is truly befitting to tell these narrow minded wretched figures, 'O little fly! The high peaks where eagles build nests are far above your flight altitude. You are just ruining your own reputation, yet, not really troubling us, either.'"
>
> Friday preacher of Tehran this week added, "Thanks Allah, this nation is a weathered one, and you (Americans), too, are not

competent for committing such mischief, because you have not forgotten having received severe blows on the mouth from this nation continually for eight straight years."

Ta'arouf? Certainly not, and really more along the lines of "Who's your daddy?" sentiments, albeit without the implied sexual-dominance innuendo. The less-than-comely Ahmad (who is probably fearsome only in the disquieting context of a sexual encounter with him) was in fact engaging in the opposite of ta'arouf, but a companion to it in Persian public discourse: fiery rhetoric and flowery, often poetic, insults that lie to the other extreme of politesse are packed with gholov, and may be intended to be fearsome but rarely are. Shias have long been taught to not provoke their enemies, who in olden days were the Sunni majority surrounding them, and, as discussed before, taghiyeh, the permitted dissimulation or even outward lying to protect the person and the faith, is an example of Shia concerns with avoiding conflict that could mean the annihilation of the minority sect.

Although anonymity excuses the Persian from ta'arouf, and public speaking is the antithesis of anonymous behavior, Ahmad Khatami and others who make such speeches are speaking on behalf of the nation (or the clerical establishment) and against another nation, and the collective "we" makes them impersonal outbursts that some Iranian politicians today, with a sense of power that Shias haven't felt in centuries, believe appeal to the masses of their supporters who are more accustomed to being the downtrodden and oppressed majority of society than a people that can strike back against any injustice. Punching or smacking the mouth, *tou-dahany*, is a Persian threat (really more insult) extraordinaire, one that IRNA seemed uninterested in giving an English equivalent for, as the speech was intended for a domestic audience exclusively, but it is not usually a literal expression of a desire to physically harm; it is more a form of braggadocio suggesting that there are ways of shutting a mouth that has uttered an insult or threat itself. Although the cleric's pronouncement that the United States has "received severe blows on the mouth from this nation continually for eight [a mistranslation: it should have read twenty-eight] straight years" could be viewed by the more sinister-minded as an admission that Iran has physically harmed the United States, perhaps through terrorist proxies in Lebanon, for example, or in Africa and Saudi Arabia and more recently in Iraq, and a veiled threat that it can do so again, it in reality harks back to the days of the U.S. Embassy hostage crisis and Ayatollah Khomeini's famous statement, met with incredulity by many at the time, that the United States "cannot do a damn thing."

What Ahmad Khatami was saying, in effect, was that Iran has weathered years of threats from and hostile behavior by the United States and, despite a stated desire on America's part to see the Islamic Republic fall, has been, and, more important, will continue to be, able to withstand any pressure from the world's greatest superpower. *Who's your daddy?*

The turbaned elite have, of course, if not punched America in the mouth, then certainly thumbed their noses at the country ever since the first days of the hostage crisis of 1979, and seemingly with impunity. Short of an all-out war, which the experience of Iraq seems to have told us *and* the Iranians by no means guarantees victory to a vastly superior military force, it appears that the almost-thirty-year hostile attitude and lack of meaningful relations between Iran and the United States (which have brought little advantage to either nation) are destined to continue for some time unless there are fundamental shifts in both American and Iranian foreign policy.

Why, many Americans wonder, do the black turbans and the many Iranians who support them hate the United States so much? Analysts point to the 1953 CIA-engineered coup that replaced the democratically elected prime minister, Mossadeq, under a constitutional and weak monarch, Shah Mohammad Reza Pahlavi, who had fled the country for Rome, with an absolute dictatorship under that very same monarch. True, the Iranian people have long resented American interference in their affairs and the Ayatollahs have played on that sentiment, and every Iranian can tell you the story of the infamous CIA coup (that the British were only able to convince President Eisenhower was necessary because of a communist threat), but the United States has conspired in coups d'état and supported tyrants elsewhere to the eventual forgiveness of the people and the patching up of relations. Why are Iranians different in that regard, say, from Chileans? Iranians are often adroitly reminded by their leaders that when their soon-to-be-deposed prime minister Mossadeq nationalized the Iranian oil industry, in effect demanding their right to the profits from their own oil, the British responded publicly, and at the UN no less, that Iran's exercise of its right was a "threat to the security of the world," words that have been repeated by the United States in response to Iran exercising its right, haq, as far as Iranians are concerned, to produce nuclear fuel.

To Iranians, since the eighteenth century, Western empires (and Russia) have simply refused to stop considering Iran theirs to play with as they like, rewarding it for supplication and punishing it for disobedience. And the United States, which has long taken over from Britain as the world's greatest power, is by definition the one power that is most likely to dictate to Iran and exploit its resources to the detriment of its people. Their country having never been a colony, Iranians have had to constantly wonder about the intentions of greater powers with respect to their affairs, and, having had to slowly assert their rights as a sovereign nation in the face of resistance from the West, they are notoriously conspiracy-minded when it comes to international relations. Iranians never made the black-and-white choices between "colonized" and "independent" that other Third World countries have had to, and as such they live in a constant state of worry that their nation can, almost without their knowing it, revert to its long and shameful role as vassal to a greater power in all but name. And the clerics take every opportunity to remind their people that without them, patriotic Iranians guarding Shia, and therefore *Iranian*, Islam *and* their haq, their fear is likely to come true. Great Britain long figured as the power that most worried Iranians, and in fact today many Iranians still believe that the

English are behind everything, good or bad, in Iran, but the United States looms large, even more so since the demise of the Soviet Union, as the world power that most covets the "Persian prize." The Ayatollahs and Hojjatoleslams, some of whose turbaned forefathers the British knew well and used to great advantage in their manipulation of Persian politics in the nineteenth and twentieth centuries, may cleverly stoke the inherent paranoia of their citizens, but they have received some (perhaps unintended) assistance from various U.S. administrations, particularly that of George W. Bush.

If in the American popular imagination it is believed, as it usually is, that politicians will sometimes lie to their own people, then one has to try to imagine how Iranians generally view American political discourse on Iran. *Lies*, the Ayatollahs, and often other politicians, will tell them, all lies. And a perfect recent example of those lies, at least to Iranians, was the announcements in late 2006 and early 2007 by the U.S. military in Iraq that roadside bombs and other munitions used to kill Americans were manufactured in Iran. Little proof was offered, except for at one press conference where unexploded bombs and shells were displayed with markings, in a perfect English lacking even on unfortunate Iranian road signs, that allegedly showed they were made in Iran.[2] Except the dates of manufacture stenciled onto the bombs were not only in English but in the American form—that is, month, day, year—rather than in the Iranian (and rest of the world's) standard format of day, month, year. That the Iranians would be sending weapons into Iraq conveniently and obligingly labeled not only with their country of origin in English but also with the date of manufacture designed so as not to confuse the Americans (who, one supposes, the Iranians know are short on Farsi interpreters) beggars belief, as Javad Zarif, the Iranian ambassador to the UN at the time, told me he had complained in one of his speeches. But few American analysts, and even fewer reporters, including those with experience in the Middle East, questioned out loud this apparently clumsily manufactured evidence, leaving many Iranians to wonder yet again about real U.S. intentions with respect to their country.

Democracy, or the lack of it, is in Iran inextricably intertwined with Iran's external relations. Suspicion of foreigners is nothing new, but the mullahs have exploited that suspicion better than any of their predecessor Shahs, who were, by contrast, seen as mere tools of the great powers. In Iran, the turn to Islam as a political system stemmed partly from the notion that Western political systems, liberal democracies and communism, were less than desirable within the country's own culture, a culture that is, it's true, proud beyond the comprehension of most Westerners. Most Persians at the time, and with encouragement from their Ayatollahs, desired a political and social life that was dominated neither by an imported Judeo-Christian tradition (America and Europe) nor by an atheistic tradition (Marxism), and many Iranians, particularly the religious, had long felt that the socialism that was viewed as a significantly better and fairer form of communism was in fact the Islamic political tradition, at least in its Shia form, abandoned by the rulers of Muslim nations.

The Iranian revolution of 1979 was a clear rejection of non-Iranian political concepts, and although rage and animosity toward the United States in its aftermath were consequences of this, it was hardly understood that the real fear of Iranians at the time was that the United States, the most powerful country in the world, would simply not allow a political system to develop that didn't mirror its own. What the Iranians were saying, in effect, was: "Leave us alone, and if you don't, we'll find ways to make your life miserable." Almost thirty years later, the Iranians, although seemingly far more "moderate" in the eyes of the West, are still saying the same thing. When Shirin Ebadi, the Nobel Prize winner, rejects foreign interference in the affairs of her country and refuses to denounce Islam, some in the West are alarmed or believe that she is afraid of being jailed. Ms. Ebadi is hardly afraid of jail, having spent time there, but she probably understands that what the West wants Muslim so-called moderates to say and to promote is merely a vision of a secular culture imported from the West, a vision that doesn't carry much weight with a people that is moving, albeit very slowly, toward a democracy that is self-defined and that may not be recognizable to Westerners, accustomed to defining democracy as either liberal or not a democracy at all. But given that Iran has, even within its power structure, many who are working toward the goal of a more democratic political system, those who push for sudden, drastic change or change encouraged by foreign powers have little chance of garnering much support from ordinary Iranians. The last Shah of Iran tried everything to discredit Ayatollah Khomeini, whom he had exiled way back in 1963, and the other mullahs who resisted his autocratic rule. The one accusation that he could *not* make with any credibility, and the one that would have had the most effect in discrediting the Ayatollahs, was that they were tools or agents of foreigners looking to gain influence over Persia.

───────────

When Akbar Ganji, perhaps the most famous Iranian dissident, traveled to Europe and America on an extended trip upon his release from prison, he refused, on more than one occasion, an invitation to the White House. It was not, as some might think, a personal snub of George Bush; had even Dennis Kucinich been improbably in residence, Ganji would have refused him too. And his refusal to meet with any American officials was not because he feared being imprisoned by the state when he returned home; rather, he feared that the people, whom every dissident claims to speak for, would forever brand him as an illegitimate tool of the foreigners.

When I arrived in Tehran in the summer of 2005, the hunger-striking Ganji had been moved from his cell in Evin prison to a hospital, and his condition appeared to be critical. As a journalist who had dared reveal the government's hand in the murders of five writers and intellectuals in 1998, he had been arrested in 2000 after he attended a conference in Berlin on political and social reform in Iran, and in 2001 he was sentenced to six years for writing about matters of "national security" and spreading propaganda against the Islamic system. The political murders of 1998 had always been assumed by the public to be the work of government agents, but when Ganji first publicly exposed the connection, at a time when Khatami and his reform government had enabled press freedoms unknown in Iran under the Shahs or the mullahs, the Intelligence Ministry claimed that the murderers were "rogue agents." Ganji's exposé, however, detailed more than a few "rogue agents" acting on their own, and his finger pointed all the way up to the extremely powerful former president, Ali Akbar Hashemi Rafsanjani, a pillar of the Islamic regime. Embarrassing as Ganji's writings were to Rafsanjani personally, the conservatives were far more concerned with the stability of Islamic rule, and they moved quickly to curtail press freedoms over the objections of Khatami and other reformists (whose weakness in the face of the hard-liners' pressures contributed to the eventual public dissatisfaction with the reform camp).

In 2005, Ganji, who refused to renounce his writings and apologize to the Supreme Leader in exchange for leniency, had begun a hunger strike to protest his detention and bring attention to political prisoners in Iran, and the government of President Khatami had implored him (as Ali Khatami had assured me) to quit, especially since he was already very close to his release date. But I was taken aback, once in Iran, by the almost complete lack of concern, even among intellectuals who are quick to decry the lack of press freedoms, for the defiant dissident. Although much had been made of his plight and his struggle in the West (he was made an honorary member of PEN), in Tehran his cause was less than célèbre. His bravery in calling in July, during the presidential elections, for the Supreme Leader to "go" in a letter widely read on the Internet (intentionally evocative of Khomeini's simple call for the Shah to "go") was the talk of many a party in middle-class Tehran, but Iranians by and large ignored the Ganji issue. Some Iranians even questioned his bravery—all the attention from the West, including from George Bush, they said, guaranteed him immunity from harm—and others, even while admiring his stand, thought his hunger strike to be hopeless and therefore pointless, particularly since he had served most of his sentence anyway and would have soon been released from prison. Even when Massoud Moqadasi, the judge who had presided over his trial and conviction, was assassinated a week after I arrived in Tehran in a rare instance of political violence, there seemed to be no expressions of delight among reform-minded Iranians.

Why? Certainly some viewed Ganji suspiciously because he had been a part of the system himself, a former Revolutionary Guard who had served the Islamic Revolution at its most terrifyingly intolerant early stage, a personal history that for those, openly dissident or not, with a deep hatred of the mullahs could not be redeemed. Others felt that he was grandstanding, and of course there were always those conspiracy-minded Iranians who believed that he had to be an agent of the West, witting or unwitting, since he seemed to receive all the attention outside the country while others just as deserving were suffering as much (or had suffered worse) without even a peep by any foreigner.

But the reality is that ordinary Iranians, despite what we're told about how much they dislike their government, do not seem to desire a revolution; rather, there are those who are politically minded who want democratic change, even if it is gradual, and there are those for whom the only real changes that are important are economic. Revolution, for a people that remembers the last one all too well, entails too much uncertainty, and Ganji was for many simply too revolutionary. Though he has been keen to emphasize that he is for democratic change from within Iran, his headline-grabbing hunger strike and his radical words challenged the very legitimacy of the Islamic Republic and have given him a revolutionary aura. Perhaps if he had died in prison, or had been executed, Ganji could have become a dangerous rallying force for opponents to the Islamic regime, but the government was far too shrewd to allow that to happen. With the knowledge that a generation earlier the executions of Khosro Golsorkhi and Keramat Daneshian, two poets who had been improbably accused of plotting to kidnap the crown prince by the Shah's government, had been one of the sparks that ignited the populist revolution of 1979, the Islamic government had no intention of creating a martyr who could most influence the youths, as Golsorkhi, a Che Guevara–like figure for young Iranians in 1974, had done. At the time the Shah, eager to both intimidate his rivals and show the world that his rule was based on law, chose to allow televised broadcasts of Golsorkhi's military tribunal, a colossal mistake that accomplished neither goal. Golsorkhi recited poetry, what Persians consider their highest art, throughout his trial; he made a mockery of the military judges; and his bravery, including his refusal to beg the Shah for clemency (or to wear a blindfold at his execution), only served to make him a hero and a symbol of the Shah's merciless dictatorship. (A documentary film on the trial of Golsorkhi has been shown in art house theaters throughout the world since the revolution, and is still riveting to watch.[3]) Ganji, intentionally or not, evoked Golsorkhi in his steadfast refusal to admit any crime, his calls for democratic rule, and his defiance in not begging for forgiveness, but the government's releasing him from prison and allowing him to travel abroad freely, as it well knew, deflated any chance, however remote, of his someday becoming a martyr for a new revolution.

A slightly different attitude prevailed in Iran two years later (when Ganji had long been released from prison and was still busy touring the United States and Europe), when Iranian-American academics, a reporter for the U.S.-run Radio Farda, and NGO representatives were arrested in Iran on charges of espionage. Foreign journalists remarked on how little coverage or sympathy the Iranian-American cases received inside Iran while making headlines in the rest of the world (which may be one reason why Haleh Esfandiari, who had access to the local news, remarked upon her release and return to the United States that one of her greatest fears while in prison was that the world had forgotten her). Iranians, even reformists and intellectuals, indeed seemed to show very little sympathy for the plight of the detainees, certainly less than for Ganji, but it was not out of any fear. Many Iranians simply felt less than sympathetic because they viewed the Iranian-Americans as a privileged lot—Iranians who lived abroad in luxury (with foreign passports no less!) and who suffered none of the travails of living and struggling day to day under a difficult system, as domestic dissidents and political activists do, but who nonetheless felt that they had a right to opinions on the future of Iran. These were not Iranians who had chosen to stay through the worst of times, as my Iranian friend, no fan of the Islamic government, who *had* stayed so fittingly put it, revealing the value Iranians place on what they believe to be *true* patriotism. Shirin Ebadi, for example, the Nobel laureate lawyer who often represents the most high-profile political cases (and whom I have heard referred to as a "political ambulance chaser" by precisely the reformist and anti-authoritarian intellectuals who ought to be her biggest fans), garners far more public support when she represents ordinary women activists, or other often-ignored domestic dissidents, than when she takes on the cases of those who are the least likely to suffer prison sentences in anonymity.

On a few occasions in Tehran, when I have expressed political opinions not to the liking of those who truly loathe the mullahs, I have been admonished with the expression *"Nafas-et az jay-eh garm meeyad"*—"Your breath emanates from a warm place," meaning that someone who lives in that "warm place," the free West, really has no right to an opinion on Iran at all. It is perhaps for this reason that Iranian dissidents abroad, or exile groups intent on regime change, have had so little success in gaining any measure of popularity inside Iran. Their satellite television broadcasts are watched often enough, sometimes disdainfully and with intent to mock, but the very idea that Iranians in the diaspora might hold the solution to Iran's political problems is laughable to most. Of course the level of support they receive even in their own countries of residence, their bases of operations if you will, might be indicative of the hopelessness of their ambitions.

When President Ahmadinejad made his first trip to the United States in the immediate aftermath of his election, an election that exiled Iranians had encouraged their compatriots to boycott via television and the Internet, he said at a breakfast meeting with journalists (where I was present) that he had intended to stop by the massive protests he had been told were to occur at Dag Hammarskjöld Plaza across from the UN in New York, and to even speak to the Iranians assembled there and hear what they had to say. He said he drove by in his limousine, but when he saw the pitifully small handful of protesters, he decided they weren't worth talking to. Ahmadinejad may have been dishonest, or more accurately using ta'arouf, in expressing a desire to speak to Iranians who were against the Islamic regime, but he clearly savored the moment when he could, in the presence of American journalists, point out how preposterous the idea was that exiled Iranians, some with influence in Washington, might be the catalysts for a change in the Iranian regime.

I had gone to the demonstration myself and had been surprised not only at the lethargic turnout of two groups, one pro-Shah and the other pro-MEK, but also at the incongruous attendance of many obviously out-of-place and even indigent Americans in the MEK contingent, some wearing brand-new anti–Islamic Republic T-shirts, contrasting sharply with their otherwise cast-off Salvation Army attire. (I asked a few why they were there, and one man, missing most of his teeth and the laces on his well-worn boots, and badly in need of a shower, admitted that he had been lured there in a bus from near the Bowery Mission with the promise of fifteen dollars and the T-shirt.) Reza Pahlavi, the man who would be Shah, was not present himself when I visited, but his face was on the placards his supporters held high for motorists passing by to see. The fifty or so royalists, Shah-philes if you will, in keeping with their aristocratic sense of themselves, were enthusiastic but did not shout or yell, vulgar as that might be seen to be, and Ahmadinejad, if he did drive by, must have given a scornful snigger.

———————

It is perhaps ordinary Iranians' views on democracy and political issues that reflect their ambivalence toward the people we in the West believe to be working to make the country a democracy more along the lines of a Western model. Iran is not a totalitarian state; Iranians have a good measure of political freedom, at least compared with many Third World countries, and there is often lively public debate on what we might presume would be sensitive political issues. There may be tens or even hundreds of political prisoners in the notorious Evin prison, but there are also plenty of public figures opposed to the ruling clergy who state their views with relative freedom. But what many Iranians want most, if they are young, are social freedoms and, if they are older, a better economy. Politics, and an idealized political system, are simply not the overwhelming concerns of most ordinary Iranians who are struggling to better their lives, and those for whom they are, the intellectual elite who love nothing more than discussing politics at every opportunity, are, despite their inflated sense of relevance or influence, better at talking among themselves than at galvanizing the people into a real opposition. And nothing demonstrated this fact better than the reformists' dismal showing in the elections that brought President Ahmadinejad to power.

An ambivalence toward political activism we might think appropriate to the young is in evidence in Elahieh, one of the most fashionable districts of Tehran, where there's a busy hamburger stand called, without irony (a word that in any event has no good translation in Farsi),

Bobby Sands Hamburger. Bobby Sands, the IRA political prisoner who starved himself to death in a British prison in 1981, also has a street named for him in Tehran: formerly Winston Churchill Boulevard, it runs conveniently beside the British Embassy and is the automobile access to the compound but, in true uncaring government fashion, is misspelled on signs and on maps variously as "Babi Sandez" or "Boby Sendz," somewhat defeating its purpose in tweaking the noses of British diplomats as they enter and leave their offices. In 2005, while Shirin Ebadi was representing Akbar Ganji, she had been told by the government that her client's hunger strike was illegal, and Ebadi, who *does* understand irony, had asked for a clarification. A nation that names a street after a hunger striker, she had famously argued and been quoted in the papers, could hardly be in a position to outlaw the practice. Needless to say, the judiciary did not issue the clarification she requested.

The Bobby Sands burger joint was crowded with young boys and girls on the night I visited, in the midst of Ganji's hunger strike and as he was wasting away, but none of them seemed to care very much about him. I asked a few people about their concerns that the new government of Ahmadinejad may crack down on many of the liberties granted them in the Khatami years. "Granted?" one young man snorted as he munched on a Bobby Sands special. "Nothing was given to us, not by Khatami or any one else. We fought for our freedoms. Beaten, imprisoned, and harassed by the police, we took them back. Do you think we'll ever let them take them away?" Spoken like a true revolutionary indeed, but he wasn't talking about political freedom, freedom of the press, or being able to criticize the government—freedoms that to one degree or another were ushered in under Khatami. He certainly wasn't talking about the freedom to go on a hunger strike; what he was talking about was being able to chat with a girl, exchange a phone number, and maybe dress as he pleases (all of which he was doing). Being able to watch satellite TV and bootleg DVDs. Or being able to drink and party at home, or hang out with girls at coffee shops like the

Doors, an inviting place downtown with a large photo of Jim Morrison on what would be the bar if there were any booze, and typical of the many coffee shops that Iranian youths hang out in. And sex? Many young Iranians manage to have girlfriends or boyfriends, many have sex quietly and discreetly, and for those men who are single for whatever reason, there are always the prostitutes. In recent years prostitution has become so widespread in Iran that even the state-controlled press mentions it regularly and politicians rail against its spread. On the night after Ahmadinejad's swearing in, prostitutes were out in full force in Vanak Square, near the hotel I was staying in on that trip. How, I wondered, can one tell them apart from the girls who have merely pushed back their headscarves a few inches and applied a little too much makeup? "Twenty-six years in an Islamic Republic," my Iranian companion who was giving me a ride home told me, "and you can tell."

———————

The dynamics of Iranian politics, which make the Islamic Republic a difficult target for regime-change proponents, can be witnessed a few miles farther north of Vanak Square at the Center for Strategic Research, a quasi-governmental organization, which occupies a striking blue glass modern high-rise in Niavaran, one of the northernmost and wealthiest districts of Tehran. The center, a think-tank-like arm of the Expediency Council (whose chairman is Ayatollah Rafsanjani), employs a legion of former government employees, allies of Rafsanjani and Khatami, who have found themselves unemployable in President Ahmadinejad's administration. The Expediency Council is one of those governmental bodies that mystifies Westerners; it was set up originally to settle disputes between the elected parliament, the Majles, and the Guardian Council (the body that ensures the principles of Islam are adhered to by the Majles and also vets candidates running for election, theoretically on their Islamic qualifications), but its true power lies more in its advisory role to the Supreme Leader, who in 2005 delegated some of his own authority to the council—granting it supervisory powers over all branches of the government of President Ahmadinejad—some think as a consolation prize demanded by Rafsanjani after suffering his humiliating defeat at Ahmadinejad's hands.

A former ambassador under the previous administration invited me to a lunch there one day in early 2007, a political salon of sorts where former government officials who now presumably do strategic research for the benefit of one or another branch of the government (though certainly not the president, who couldn't be less interested in the views, strategic or not, of any of his rivals) gather in a capacious conference room every Thursday to exchange ideas and, of course, discuss politics. Hassan Rowhani, the center's highest-profile strategist, former chief nuclear negotiator in Khatami's regime, a close confidant of the Supreme Leader *and* Rafsanjani, a member of the Assembly of Experts, and a potential rival to Ahmadinejad in the next presidential elections, does not participate in the salon; perhaps he knows that if he did, it would take on an uncomfortable hue of intrigue against an already paranoid presidency.

The conference room where we gathered was on the first floor (or "1th," as was indicated by signs on the pillars, perhaps a *strategic* goof) of the building. A stream of attendants laid out steaming platters and plates of rice, kebabs, stews, and salads on the huge table around which we sat. The conversation was interrupted every few minutes by someone's cell phone ring, usually an unlikely tone such as the "William Tell Overture" or a Muzak version of the theme from *Titanic* (also evidently the most popular song in elevators throughout the Islamic Republic), and at one point it seemed that half the room was talking on phones between mouthfuls rather than listening to any of the conversations that started and stopped in fits. But as the plates were cleared of the last morsels, talk turned to Ahmadinejad and his hated government, which had put these men out of work. "Do you realize," one man said, "that he's even tightened the customs office? I used to be able to just call the customs depot and have personal stuff I'm importing cleared through, but just last week I was forced to actually drive down there!" Others shook their heads in dismay that Ahmadinejad's anticorruption drive had inconvenienced one of their own. "He's serious about this business," the man continued, shaking his head.

"That's not all," piped in a round and balding man, finishing a phone conversation by shutting his flip phone with a decisive snap while still noisily chewing on a piece of chicken. "Do you know any-one who wants an almost-new Mercedes S?"

"Why?" a chorus of voices responded.

"Ten million *tomans!*" he said incredulously (about eleven thou-sand dollars, and one-tenth the going market rate). "But you can't get plates." Sounds of "tsk, tsk" echoed in the room. "Maybe you can just wait this thing out," he continued, shrugging his shoulders and reach-ing for another kebab. Ahmadinejad's anticorruption drive had, seem-ingly, driven the price of stolen cars, usually from Dubai or other Gulf states, way down, because there was no longer a way to register the ve-hicles, not even with once-common bribes and influence. The conver-sation continued with indignant stories of how difficult life had become under a new administration, and I wondered if Ahmadinejad, if he could hear these men, would be slapping his thighs with delight at how he had not only shut them out of government but deprived them of what they thought was their right to a privileged life. But de-spite their loss of real political power, these men were still very much part of the ruling class of Iran, and they all believed that their situa-tions could only be temporary. They were very much against men such as Ahmadinejad, either for rational reasons of opposition to hard-line policies or for less virtuous reasons of self-interest, but they could never be recruited to a cause against the Islamic Republic.

As I left the building that day, I couldn't help but think of my father's friend Mr. N., a former diplomat in the Shah's regime who had taken me to a very different lunch at the Diplomatic Club a week before. Mr. N. is, like everyone associated with the Shah's regime, most definitely not part of the ruling class, and never will be, but unlike so many members of the ancien régime, he continues to live in Iran and even take lunch at the Diplomatic Club, an outpost of a Foreign Ministry that one would suspect prefers to have nothing to do with him. Mr. N. has few contemporaries in Tehran to lunch with, unlike the men at the Center for Strategic Research, let alone the opportunity to regularly complain with friends about their loss of privilege. Mr. N. was recalled to Tehran from a foreign posting after the revolution of 1979, and he continued to show up for work every day at the Foreign Ministry, in a suit and tie, until he was finally forced into early retirement less than a year later.

He recalled for me his worst days at work, which had nothing to do with being harassed by revolutionaries who had taken over the ministry. No, it was during the U.S. hostage crisis, when Bruce Laingen, the U.S. chargé d'affaires (who had been visiting the Foreign Ministry when students overran the embassy), was being held captive, for his own safety, the Iranians argued, at the ministry building. Mr. N. had to cross a courtyard and quadrant every day to get to his office, and Laingen would often be at a window looking straight out in his direction, but Mr. N. would hold a cup of coffee and a newspaper and walk on, pretending to be juggling the two as he passed Laingen, just so that he could avoid waving at him and acknowledging a fellow diplomat. "The poor man," he said to me. "I felt absolutely awful every single morning. He didn't even have the comfort of receiving a dignified wave!" Mr. N. still wears a suit and tie every single day, sometimes a hat too, making him highly conspicuous in a society where ties are frowned upon as symbols of Western decadence. The suits are probably the same suits he had at the time of the revolution, for they are all cut in the late-1970s style, but perhaps Mr. N.'s fashion sense, for someone who has rarely gone abroad since his permanent return to Iran almost thirty years ago, is simply frozen in 1979.

Mr. N., who drives around Tehran in an old Peugeot but probably shouldn't be driving at all, and certainly not in a city like Tehran, picked me up one Friday morning and with much difficulty—including stopping in the middle of a busy freeway, getting out of the car, and asking directions of surprised and honking drivers—drove me to the far northern reaches of the city, where the Foreign Ministry's Diplomatic Club is located. Built at the urging of the former ambassador Sadeq Kharrazi, the ardent bespoke-suit-wearing reformist who tried to infuse the ministry with some of the elegance of its past, the club is shunned by the most conservative allies of Ahmadinejad but attracts diplomats, their families, and the odd mullah to its beautiful grounds and sumptuous buffet lunches.

We sat alone at a table in the expansive dining room, overlooking the vast city of Tehran through floor-to-ceiling windows, Mr. N. the only one in the room wearing a tie, and we comfortably talked politics without lowering our voices to a whisper. Other tables were filled with stubble-faced men in ill-fitting jackets, women in scarves and hijab, and unruly children who banged into the glass windows as they played noisily while their parents dined. If Mr. N. was aware of the stares we received, he didn't show it, and the maître d' was uncommonly courteous to him, but as others in the dining room table-hopped to say hello to one another, we were conspicuously left alone. But Mr. N., the least privileged but by far the most elegant man in the room, was unperturbed, and as he finished his meal, he fell silent. He stared out the windows at his beloved city, and I wondered what this dignified man, someone who had refused the opportunity to leave his country and start a new life elsewhere like many of his contemporaries, someone who continued to live his life exactly as he thought he should without fear of the black turbans, someone who might have at one time been recruited to a strong democratic movement, was thinking. I didn't ask, but then again, I didn't need to.

———————

"Yeki-bood; yeki-nabood." Other than God, there was no One. Islam was never supposed to have a clergy; in fact there is no "church" in mainstream Islam, and part of the appeal of the Koran for believers is that it is the word of God Himself, and therefore not subject to interpreta-

tion by man. Except, for Shias, by the Ayatollahs. Shia Islam, the over-whelming majority sect in Iran, a less-overwhelming majority in Iraq and Bahrain, and a large segment of the fractured religious makeup of Lebanon, has both a church *and* a clergy. Ayatollahs, those "signs of God," are in some ways the Shia equivalent of Catholic cardinals. There is no pope-like figure in Shia Islam, however, although the most senior Ayatollahs, the Grand Ayatollahs, hold positions of respect and authority not dissimilar to the authority of a living pope, the Patriarch of the Orthodox Church, or, say, the Archbishop of Canterbury. They are men and not considered divinely appointed (and certainly not divine— not even the Prophet was divine, according to Islam), but they are men who instruct others to behave according to how they believe God wishes. Ayatollah Khomeini, the founder of the Islamic Republic and the one man responsible for making his title a household word, wasn't Iran's first political cleric; he was merely its most successful.

Much has been written about the Shia split from mainstream Sunni Islam over thirteen hundred years ago, and the narrative often centers on the seminal event of the Battle of Karbala and Hossein's martyrdom— what is dramatically commemorated at Ashura every year. It may be the simple story of what Shias believe to be Hossein's just cause against the unjust Yazid, but it is really a sort of David and Goliath tale where Goliath wins, and it is what forms the Shia worldview—a worldview particularly suited to Persian sensibilities, formed as they have been by centuries of perceived injustices to their nation and to themselves. The modern Shia world had in Ayatollah Khomeini its first David who defeated a Goliath (the Shah), and a David who stood up to another, far more powerful Goliath: the United States. In 2006, *shi'at Ali* ("followers of Ali," as "Shia" means) had Seyyed Hassan Nasrallah of Lebanese Hezbollah as their victorious David against the Goliath of Israel, a Goliath that still stands, and must do, as a constant threat to the ever-believing David. For Shias are always Davids, always the underdogs fighting for a just cause in an unjust world, except it matters not that they actually slay their enemy, but merely that they hold their ground and chalk it up as a victory of justice over tyranny. To them, there is no Goliath today greater than the United States. The Ayatollahs and all their little Davids are determined to stand up to it whenever necessary, whenever the cause is just, and to never lose, even if, or maybe *because*, they can't win outright.

Iranians, whether religious or not, and with or without the Ayatollahs, have always had a *Shia* sensibility. Akbar Ganji, the onetime Islamic revolutionary, did not lose his Shia sensibility when he turned against the regime he helped bring to power, and Shirin Ebadi, who fights injustice with the law but, like Ganji, refuses help from any Goliath, maintains a Shia sensibility whether she even believes in God or not. Golsorkhi, the Marxist poet executed by the Shah's firing squad, had a Shia sensibility, and his death, he knew, would at least keep his ideas alive. Iranian opposition groups in exile, some of whose members have not walked the streets of Tehran for almost thirty years, believe that they are the Davids that justly fight the Goliath that (to them) is the Islamic regime, and they have a Shia sensibility too. Iran may evolve or even change politically, and its constitution may become as fastened with amendments as ours is one day, but the character and sensibilities of the people will not change. The Ayatollahs may from time to time silence dissent at home, they may rule autocratically, and with their infuriating manners they may annoy and even repulse many in the West. But they rule for now with the confidence that they do not face a population that seeks to overthrow them. As long, that is, as they don't lose their Persian sensibilities.

Notes

Iran is widely covered in the Western media, and almost all the major newspapers, news organizations, and wire services have offices or correspondents based in Tehran. There is no paucity of information on current events in Iran, and for every news item referred to in the book that I have not directly witnessed, the sources are either my contacts inside Iran or, in the case of widely reported news, the various media outlets, including Iranian state-owned and private media. A few specific references are given in the notes below.

INTRODUCTION

1. From a quatrain by the twelfth-century poet Sanai. Translated by Coleman Barks. In *Persian Poets*, selected and edited by Peter Washington (New York: Knopf, 2000).

PERSIAN CATS

1. Mujahedin-e-Khalq, the largest political and military group in opposition to the Islamic regime, was initially formed in opposition to the Shah, who referred to its philosophy as "Marxist-Islamic." The group allied itself with the Islamic Revolution of 1979 but broke with the regime soon after, taking refuge in Saddam Hussein's Iraq. It has claimed responsibility for some of the most spectacular terror operations against the Islamic Re-

public, and is on the U.S. and European lists of terrorist organizations. In the 1970s, the group was responsible for the assassination of U.S. military personnel in Iran.

2. Iran's Jewish community, numbering twenty-five to thirty thousand individuals according to estimates quoted by news organizations, is the largest in the Middle East outside of Israel. Under Iran's constitution, Jews, along with the other recognized minority religions of Christianity and Zoroastrianism, have a representative in parliament, the Majles. Although many Iranian Jews left during and after the revolution of 1979, Jewish families are still active in trades they've been traditionally engaged in for centuries, namely, antiques, jewelry, carpets, and import-export.

3. Saddam Hussein invaded Iran in 1980, igniting the Iran-Iraq war that lasted eight years and resulted in nearly a million deaths. The Iranian Basij, volunteers sometimes as young as ten years old, were famously known to have thrown themselves under Iraqi tanks with live grenades strapped to their waists, and to have cleared minefields by running onto them. Many Basij wore plastic keys around their necks as they went into battle, keys to the gates of paradise.

4. Velayat-e-faqih, or "rule of the jurisprudent," was the basis of Ayatollah Khomeini's political philosophy, one he formed and wrote about while in exile in Najaf, Iraq. His argument was that a Shia Islamic nation should be guided by a supreme religious authority, and, in Iran's case, him. A collection of Khomeini's writings is available in English: *Islam and Revolution 1: Writings and Declarations of Imam Khomeini*, translated by Hamid Algar (Berkeley, Calif.: Mizan Press, 1981).

5. Agence France-Presse, Tehran, April 23, 2007.

6. It has been rumored that Ahmadinejad was at one time a member of the Revolutionary Guards' foreign expeditionary force, the Qods Force, and as such may have served in Lebanon in the 1980s, when Iran helped set up Hezbollah. Neither he nor the government has addressed the question, nor, curiously, have they been asked, even by Western reporters.

THE AYATOLLAH HAS A COLD

1. There are many books on the CIA-sponsored coup of 1953, and one particularly well-researched one is Stephen Kinzer, *All the Shah's Men* (Hoboken, N.J.: Wiley, 2000).

2. www.pajamasmedia.com/xpress/michaelledeen/.

3. Hired cars in Iran range from dilapidated old Paykans, 1960s-technology Iranian-made cars (no longer manufactured), to more comfortable Peugeots, to plush new Samands, also Iranian made, but with somewhat more recent technology. For long trips, one must always specify a "comfortable" and "reliable" car.

IF IT'S TUESDAY, THIS MUST BE QOM

1. All satellite dishes are illegal in Iran, although many households, religious and supportive of the government or not, have them. In a country where entertainment outside the home is extremely limited, and where inside the home most people find state-owned television lacking in entertainment value, dishes that pull in signals from Europe and the Gulf are viewed not as a luxury but as a necessity.

2. Qom's famous shrine and pilgrimage site, the tomb of Fatima (sister of Reza, the eighth Shia Imam, himself buried in Mashhad, in northeast Iran).

PRIDE AND HUMILITY

1. Reza Shah Pahlavi, the last Shah's father and the founder of the short-lived Pahlavi dynasty, was a great admirer of Germany and all things German, including the fascism of the Third Reich. A modernizer intent on bringing Iran into the twentieth century, he looked to Germany for technology, architecture, and infrastructure, and his coziness with Hitler's regime (although Iran officially remained neutral in the early stages of World War II) led to his removal and exile by the Allies and his son's ascendancy to the throne.

2. Political nonfiction books are very popular in Iran and not subjected to censorship as often as one might think, or as often as many novels are. Although I didn't see a copy in the windows of the Foreign Ministry bookstore, I did see Hillary Clinton's autobiography (translated into Farsi) prominently displayed, its cover art intact, in almost every other bookstore in Tehran.

3. Photos of the Holocaust conference were published by the wire services, including AP and Reuters. Mohammadi is shown in a Reuters photo smil-

ing as Ahmadinejad warmly greets Rabbi Yisroel Dovid Weiss of the Brooklyn-based ultraorthodox and anti-Zionist group Neturei Karta.

4. The series was called *Zero Degree Turn* and can be viewed on www.youtube.com.

5. See Tom Holland, *Persian Fire* (New York: Doubleday, 2006).

6. See Mojdeh Bayat and Mohammad Ali Jamnia, *Tales from the Land of the Sufis* (Boston: Shambhala, 2001).

7. Inter Press Service News Agency, Sept. 5, 2007, and *Guardian*, Sept. 30, 2007.

8. Twelver Islam is the predominant branch of Shia Islam and Iran's state religion. Twelvers believe in twelve Imams, descendants of the Prophet Mohammad, whom they consider the legitimate rulers of Muslims.

9. *Offside*, written and directed by Jafar Panahi (best known for *The White Balloon*), released in the United States by Sony Pictures, 2006.

10. Agence France-Presse, April 22, 2007.

11. In my regular telephone conversations with individuals in Tehran, even those opposed to the hard-liners told me that in most neighborhoods the effect of the crackdown was not visible in the way that men and women dressed. The chances of being stopped or arrested, in a city of some fourteen million people, were still slim.

VICTORY OF BLOOD OVER THE SWORD

1. The Grand Ayatollahs of Shia Islam all operate their own Web sites, and their opinions on important matters (such as self-flagellation and self-injury) are available online. A Shia Web site has thoughtfully addressed the issue with answers by Ayatollahs Khamenei and Sistani (of Iraq) at www.ezsoftech.com/mazloom/zanjeer.asp.

2. My grandfather was a renowned scholar of the Sohravardi (more commonly "Suhrawardi" in the Latin alphabet) "School of Illumination." Shihab al-Din al-Suhrawardi, one of Iran's greatest philosophers, lived in the twelfth century, and *Hikmat al-ishraq* is his best-known work. (A translated version, *The Philosophy of Illumination*, by John Walbridge and Hossein Ziai, was published by Brigham Young University Press in 1999.) A physical School of Illumination, where my grandfather taught, still stands in Tehran, and educates clergy and laymen alike on the philosophy, but none of my grandfather's own books have been translated into English.

3. Ardakan, my father's hometown, is the site of an important uranium mine, and on a list of suspect nuclear sites in the ongoing Iranian nuclear dispute with the West.

4. Under its constitution, Iran can have numerous vice presidents, appointed by the president. Some have great influence because of their mandate (such as the vice president and head of the Atomic Energy Organization), while others have far less (such as the vice president and head of the National Sports Organization).

PAIRIDAEZA: THE PERSIAN GARDEN

1. The Persian princess was Shahrbanu, daughter of Yazdegerd III, the last Sassanid (and last Zoroastrian) king of Persia before Muslim rule. Yazdegerd was assassinated in Merv, an ancient city near Mary in present-day Turkmenistan (and once part of the Persian Empire). See *Encyclopaedia Brittanica*, 11th ed.

2. The Muslim prayer, or *namaz*, is always recited in its original Arabic. Although few Iranians, even the pious, speak or know the language, they learn the prayer by rote at an early age.

3. There have been occasional raids on homes that host underground raves of sorts (which make the local news), although it is impossible to know whether they have been identified by government informers or by neighbors' complaints.

4. *Shepesh'oo* is a common derogatory term for mullahs, reflecting upper-class disdain for the less-sophisticated classes. "Flea-ridden" implies a lower class who do not (or cannot) bathe properly. (Iranian homes generally lacked bathing facilities until the second half of the twentieth century, and the local bathhouse was visited with a frequency dependent upon one's status and purse.)

5. Many Iranians of a certain age continue to believe that the British somehow control, or at least influence, everything to their favor in Iran. The fact that, despite U.K. involvement in the 1953 coup (or their effectively having instigated it) and a long history of interference in Iranian affairs (including notorious oil and tobacco concessions), the British continue to maintain a large embassy in Tehran (while the United States suffered the indignity of the hostage crisis) is often pointed to (by conspiracy theorists at every so-

cial gathering) as evidence that British influence has not diminished with the creation of the Islamic Republic. In the 1970s, Iranian obsession with British intrigue was satirized in one of Iran's best-selling novels of all time, *My Uncle Napoleon*, by Iraj Pezeshkzad (a friend and contemporary of my father's at the Foreign Ministry who moved to France after the revolution), which was also turned into a hit TV series of the same name. (See *My Uncle Napoleon*, translated by Dick Davis [New York: Modern Library, 2006].)

6. Kharrazi has admitted his role in the proposal (a role that has been made public in the U.S. media) but will no longer speak about it with reporters. While I was in Tehran in 2007, he told me that he was inundated by requests from U.S. media to go on record about the proposal but that he would not do so.

7. See the official Web site: www.wechange.info/english/.

8. See "A Quiet Battle for Rights in Iran," *Washington Post*, Aug. 26, 2007.

THE AYATOLLAH BEGS TO DIFFER

1. Iran does not recognize dual citizenship (and did not under the Shahs' regimes). Under Iranian law, an Iranian citizen can only become a national of another country if he or she first renounces Iranian nationality, which has to be done officially. If an Iranian renounces citizenship, however, he or she is no longer permitted to enter Iran, which means that for years most Iranians hid their U.S. or European citizenship from Iranian consulates. Under Khatami (although the law was never changed), Iranians could openly admit to their foreign citizenship, although they had to continue to travel to Iran only on an Iranian passport.

2. According to a statement from his office and reported by the newspaper *Ham-Mihan*, picked up by Agence France-Presse, June 21, 2007.

FEAR OF A BLACK TURBAN

1. A cleric becomes an Ayatollah by consensus of other Ayatollahs, and there are no official rules for acquiring the title. He is expected, of course, to have been a Hojjatoleslam, to have published works on Islamic theory and law, and to have followers, but in Iran is generally elevated to the position when he is referred to as "Ayatollah" by one or more other established Ayatollahs. Rafsanjani began to be referred to as "Ayatollah" in Iranian me-

dia in late 2006. See "So You Want to Become an Ayatollah," *Slate*, April 6, 2004, www.slate.com/id/2098364/.

2. Press conference in Baghdad, Feb. 11, 2007, conducted by anonymous Pentagon officials. See news.bbc.co.uk/2/hi/middle_east/6351257.stm.

3. *The Trial of Khosro Golsorkhi* was also broadcast on Iranian state television immediately after the revolution, but has since been banned in Iran. Poor-quality bootleg DVDs are, however, available.

Index